'As an educator working at the intersection of schools, teac
Government Organisations, I find this book timely and hig
with an interest in global learning. It encourages proper ex
and the challenges and complexities within this work, whils
useful and – most of all – hopeful ideas for teachers and educators to take forward
in practice.'

– Andrea Bullivant, Lecturer in Teacher Education and
Global Learning Adviser, Liverpool Hope University/
Liverpool World Centre, UK

'Peterson and Warwick's immensely comprehensive book promotes understanding and
critical analysis of many of the most pressing issues of our times. The book presents
a compelling case for Global Learning across the curriculum, introducing nuanced
arguments and diverse perspectives illustrating why it is essential, and how it is possible,
to incorporate Global Learning into all areas of education.

I recommend this book as compulsory reading for anyone interested in how
education can encourage active and optimistic engagement with the wonders and
challenges of the world as it really is: unique, diverse and interconnected, but currently
also unequal and unsustainable. This valuable book certainly facilitates this crucial
and timely discussion.'

– Mary Young, Senior Lecturer in Citizenship and
Global Issues, University of Chichester, UK

'This is a wonderfully impressive book that will be of great value to all those involved
in global learning. Peterson and Warwick provide refreshingly clear, insightful com-
ments about the nature of globalisation, global citizenship and global education.
They suggest ways in which professional development can occur and illustrate how
valuable work can take place with learners. The first chapter provides penetrating
insights into the concepts to be understood and the processes that are to be experienced
and engaged with. The second chapter discusses the nature of teaching and learning
as something that is integrated across knowledge, skills and disposition, imbues all
aspects of education, and is developed in relation to particular contexts. Prior to a
valuable conclusion that emphasises the key ideas, issues and messages of the book
there are four additional chapters (interconnections, cultural diversity, social justice
and sustainable development) that allow for precise elaborations of key ideas and the
further evelopment of professional abilities. Throughout there is a wealth of practical
activities that will engage, inspire and educate. I strongly recommend this book.'

– Ian Davies, Professor, University of York, UK

Global Learning and Education

What is globalisation?

How are its effects felt by different people across the world?

How can educators help young people flourish in a world characterised by globalisation?

Conflict, poverty, breaches of human rights, and environmental sustainability are everyday issues for global citizens today, old and young. *Global Learning and Education* presents a detailed and challenging introduction to a central concern facing education systems and curricula around the world: how young people understand and experience globalisation and how meaningful global learning can be developed.

Encouraging a critical and reflective approach in order to advance understanding of a range of theoretical and practical factors, *Global Learning and Education* considers the meaning and definitions of globalisation, global citizenship and global education. It explores key issues including interconnectedness and interdependency, cultural diversity, social justice and sustainable development. It considers how global learning should and can imbue all aspects of education, within curriculum subjects, through project-based learning, and through extra-curricular activities that help students participate and engage in global issues. It argues the importance of the mission and ethos of a school itself, of shaping global learning for different educational contexts, and of ensuring teaching and learning meets the needs of individual learners.

Global Learning and Education is a comprehensive, thought-provoking, sometimes contentious introduction for educationalists concerned with what globalisation means for our young people. Illustrated throughout with case studies that seek to inspire creativity and hope, and including questions and suggested reading for further investigation, it is essential reading for all those involved in the teaching and learning of young people, as well as those studying this vital topic on Education Studies and Masters level courses.

Andrew Peterson is Senior Lecturer in History and Civic Education at the University of South Australia, Australia.

Paul Warwick is a Research Fellow at the Centre for Sustainable Futures, Plymouth University, UK.

Global Learning and Education

Key concepts and effective practice

Andrew Peterson and
Paul Warwick

Routledge
Taylor & Francis Group

LONDON AND NEW YORK

First published 2015
by Routledge
2 Park Square, Milton Park, Abingdon, Oxon OX14 4RN

and by Routledge
711 Third Avenue, New York, NY 10017

Routledge is an imprint of the Taylor & Francis Group, an informa business

British Library Cataloguing in Publication Data
A catalogue record for this book is available from the British Library

Library of Congress Cataloging in Publication Data
Peterson, Andrew, 1976–.
  Global learning and education: key concepts and effective practice/
  Andrew Peterson, Paul Warwick.
  pages cm
  Includes bibliographical references.
  1. Education and globalization. 2. Multicultural education.
  I. Warwick, Paul, 1968–. II. Title.
  LC191.P425 2014
  370.116–dc23
  2014020522

ISBN: 978-0-415-71724-3 (hbk)
ISBN: 978-0-415-71726-7 (pbk)
ISBN: 978-1-315-74524-4 (ebk)

Typeset in Sabon and Gill Sans
by Florence Production Ltd, Stoodleigh, Devon, UK

Printed and bound in Great Britain by
TJ International Ltd, Padstow, Cornwall

For Jessica, Oliver and George
                    A. P.

For Alice, Ella, Betsie and Danny
                    P. W.

Contents

Abbreviations

ACARA	Australian Curriculum and Assessment Reporting Authority
AFFLIP	Australian Foundation for Fostering Learning in the Philippines
ASEAN	The Association of South East Asian Nations
AU	African Union
BBC	British Broadcasting Corporation
BME	black and minority ethnic
BTS	Bigger Than Self
CAFOD	Catholic Agency for Overseas Development
CPD	continuing professional development
CRC	United Nations Convention on the Rights of the Child
DCSF	Department for Children, Schools and Families
DEA	Development Education Association
DESD	Decade of Education for Sustainable Development
DfE	Department for Education
DFID	Department for International Development
EC	European Community
EEC	European Economic Community
ECHR	European Convention on Human Rights
ESD	Education for Sustainable Development
EU	European Union
FAPSA	Federation of Australasian Philosophy in Schools Associations
GFC	global financial crisis
HE	higher education
HRA	Human Rights Act 1998
HRE	Human Rights Education
HREA	Human Rights Education Association
ICCPR	International Covenant on Civil and Political Rights
ICESCR	International Covenant on Economic, Social and Cultural Rights
IEA	International Association for the Evaluation of Educational Achievement
IGS	Internet Growth Statistics
IMF	International Monetary Fund
IPCC	Intergovernmental Panel on Climate Change
ISAF	International Security Assistance Force
IUCN	International Union for the Conservation of Nature and Natural Resources

LTV	'Learning Through Values'
MDG	Millennium Development Goals
MNC	multinational corporation
MUN	Model United Nations
NATO	North Atlantic Treaty Organization
NGO	non-governmental organisation
OAS	Organization of American States
OECD	Organisation for Economic Co-operation and Development
OSDE	'Open Space for Dialogue and Enquiry'
P4C	Philosophy for Children
PIRLS	Progress in International Reading Literacy Study
PISA	Programme for International Student Assessment
QCA	Qualifications and Curriculum Authority
RRSA	Rights Respecting School Award
TIMSS	Trends in International Mathematics and Science Study
UDHR	United Nations Universal Declaration of Human Rights
UKOWLA	UK One World Linking Association
UN	United Nations
UNA-UK	United Nations Association of the UK
UNCED	United Nations Conference on Environment and Development
UN-DESA	United Nations Department of Economic and Social Affairs
UNDP	United Nations Development Programme
UNECE	The United Nations Economic Commission for Europe
UNESCO	United Nations Education, Scientific and Cultural Organization
UNHCR	United Nations High Commissioner for Refugees
UNICEF	United Nations Children's Fund
WCED	World Commission on Environment and Development
WHO	World Health Organisation
WSSD	World Summit on Sustainable Development
WTO	World Trade Organization

Acknowledgements

We have a number of people to thank for their help in writing this book. First, we would both like to thank our families for their inspiration, support and patience. Without them we could not have written this book. Second, we would like to thank all of the colleagues, schools and organisations who have inspired the contents of this book as well as helped to provide the case studies and activities contained within it. These are too numerous to name individually, but we thank them wholeheartedly. Finally, we would like to express our gratitude to colleagues at Routledge – in particular Helen Pritt, Sarah Tuckwell and Rhiannon Findlay – for their advice, guidance and patience in supporting this book from its original conception through to publication.

Introduction

The following is an extract from a speech given to the Earth Summit in Rio de Janeiro by twelve-year-old Severn Suzuki in 1992 on behalf of the Environmental Children's Organization:

> Here, you may be delegates of your governments, business people, organizers, reporters or politicians – but really you are mothers and fathers, brothers and sisters, aunts and uncles – and all of you are somebody's child. I'm only a child yet I know we are all part of a family, 5 billion strong, in fact, 30 million species strong and we all share the same air, water and soil – borders and governments will never change that. I'm only a child yet I know we are all in this together and should act as one single world towards one single goal. In my anger, I am not blind, and in my fear, I am not afraid to tell the world how I feel . . .
>
> At school, even in kindergarten, you teach us how to behave in the world. You teach us:
> not to fight with others,
> to work things out,
> to respect others,
> to clean up our mess,
> not to hurt other creatures,
> to share – not be greedy.
> Then why do you go out and do the things you tell us not to do?
>
> Do not forget why you're attending these conferences, who you're doing this for – we are your own children.
>
> My father always says 'You are what you do, not what you say.' Well, what you do makes me cry at night. You grown ups say you love us. I challenge you, please make your actions reflect your words.
>
> (Suzuki, 1992)

A central feature of recent globalising processes has been their fast-paced, dynamic and fluid nature, meaning that the world today is very different to the world in the early 1990s. Suzuki's speech was given shortly after the fall of the Berlin Wall and in the aftermath of the Gulf War. The speech also came at a time when claims that climate change was of human cause were relatively new to the global political agenda, several years before the Internet was widely available, and around a decade before the invention of leading social and digital online media such as Facebook, YouTube and Twitter.

Yet, and as we return to in our conclusion, the words spoken by Severn Suzuki still hold relevance today. Conflict, poverty, breaches of human rights and a range of issues concerning sustainable development and the environment remain part of the everyday lived experiences of global citizens today, old and *young*. Indeed, how young people understand and experience globalisation and what global learning should consist of are central questions facing education systems and curricula around the world.

Most educationalists accept that education should play some part in preparing young people to live and participate in today's globalised world. People differ, however, as to what this education should consist of. Consider the following questions: What is globalisation and how are its effects felt by different people and in different political, economic, social and cultural contexts across the world? How should young people be educated to help them live and flourish in a world characterised by globalisation? What form should such global learning take, and what should be its main themes? Should it focus on young people's knowledge and understanding of globalisation, or should it also seek to develop the skills and dispositions through which young people can become active participants in globalised communities and networks? The answers to these questions are rather difficult to arrive at, and even if we do have a strong sense of how we would answer them, our answers may be different to the responses of others.

About this book

The aim of this book is for you to explore and engage critically and creatively with key elements of global learning in the early twenty-first century. Following this introduction, the book comprises six chapters and a conclusion. Chapters 1 ('Globalisation, global citizenship and global education') and 2 ('Global learning for global citizenship') establish the scope and key frameworks for considering global learning and education. These chapters inform Chapters 3 ('Interconnectedness and interdependency'), 4 ('Cultural diversity'), 5 ('Social justice') and 6 ('Sustainable development'), which each focus on a core element of global learning. In the conclusion, we draw together the main themes of the book in the context of *futures learning*. In addition to the core content, each chapter includes:

- chapter objectives;
- an introduction;
- activities;
- case studies;
- a conclusion;
- questions for further investigation;
- further readings.

As you work through the book we ask that you bear the following, inter-related considerations in mind, as these underpin the analysis and activities contained within:

- As we make clear in Chapters 1 and 2, global learning comprises a complex inter-relationship between knowledge, understanding, skills and dispositions. For this reason, it is important that as educators we consider how our curricula and pedagogies support students' global learning in ways that develop this range of capacities.

- In line with education curricula around the world, we do not envisage global learning as a separate subject. Rather, global learning is a theme that should imbue all aspects of education. This is likely to involve a range of educational processes that are all necessary, none sufficient alone, to further students' global learning. Such processes start with the development of a global perspective within curriculum subjects. While some subjects, such as geography and science, naturally lend themselves to a global perspective, there is potential for *all* subjects to contribute to global learning. Increasingly, it is being recognised that interdisciplinary approaches where global issues and topics are explored through project-based learning across a range of subject areas provide for vibrant and engaging learning opportunities. Supplementing global learning within curriculum is the range of extra-curricular activities through which students can participate and engage in global issues. Overarching both curricular and extra-curricular learning is the place of global learning within the mission and ethos of the school itself. If schools are not committed to global learning at an institutional level, approaches across and extra to the curriculum will become isolated and compartmentalised. It is only when schools adopt a holistic approach that transformative global learning can truly take place.
- While we would argue strongly that global learning is a universal concern for educational jurisdictions (whether national, regional or local) around the world, we would also contend that its form and nature should be informed and shaped by the needs of particular contexts. What makes for effective global learning in one country may be differentiated from what makes for effective global learning in another. In fact, there will also be different needs for global learning within different schools in the same city. This means that as educators when we are exploring globalisation and global learning we must be mindful of how these can be formatted to best suit the needs of learners within our own particular context. Indeed, a considerable number of the activities contained within the chapters have been designed in order to support you in doing just that.

As you work your way through the book we ask that you engage critically and reflexively with the ideas, issues and questions raised. Many of the areas considered are highly contested, and you should think carefully about where you stand on the respective issues, as well as the basis of your points of view. Indeed, having explored the various positions on hand there may be issues about which you are undecided. The key is to know why you are undecided and what the implications of this are for your work with learners in your context. While we consider a wide range of issues relating to globalisation and global learning, we are aware that the book is not exhaustive in its coverage – no book of this kind could claim to be so. We do, however, hope that you enjoy your engagement with its contents and that these stimulate your interest in teaching for global learning.

Chapter 1

Globalisation, global citizenship and global education

Chapter objectives

By the end of this chapter you should have:

- considered what 'globalisation' and 'global citizenship' are, including debates and issues about their meaning;
- explored what is meant by 'global education';
- analysed a number of contemporary issues of global education.

Introduction

Think about an eleven-year-old student in a school in a large city anywhere in the world today. Their life will undoubtedly be affected by the processes of globalisation in a multitude of ways. To name but a few, these could include: the languages spoken within the school; the technology they use to further their learning; the focus of the school curriculum; the origin of the clothes they wear; the cultural mix of students within the school; and the origin of the food they eat during their lunch break. In short, processes of globalisation are increasingly affecting the lives of most (if not all) people in the world, but they do so in different, complex, unequal and contested ways. But what are these processes of globalisation and how do they inform notions of global citizenship? What part can education play in preparing students for their current and future role as global citizens? How, as educators, can we support students' global learning? These are the questions that you will be asked to engage with throughout this book.

The purpose of this first chapter is to introduce the main concepts of globalisation, global citizenship and global education. It will require you to think critically about these terms, understanding them as open to a range of interpretations and lived experiences. This last point is crucial – globalisation and global citizenship are not simply theoretical concepts to be analysed. Rather they are processes that are experienced, and engaged with, by people as part of their daily lives, at times positively and at other times negatively. Recognising the dynamic and fluid nature of globalisation and global citizenship has important implications for education, and reminds us that any holistic approach to global education must incorporate an idea not only of living in a globalised world today but also, and crucially, *in the future*. Such a focus is central to global learning.

Globalisation and global citizenship

In this section you will be introduced to the main concepts of globalisation and global citizenship, including some significant disagreements about their meaning and importance. As we progress through the discussion, it will be useful for you to start thinking about how these concepts might relate to your understanding of the aims of education, how they relate to your own educational experiences, as well as the sorts of educational questions they raise. We will look into each of these areas in more detail in the chapters that follow.

Globalisation

Generally speaking, globalisation refers to a set of processes, which in some way (their origin, their scope, their affects) transcend individual nation-states. Central to the concept is the idea that the world and its people continue to be increasingly interconnected. Across the literature, globalisation is frequently seen to involve four main, inter-related elements. These can be summarised as follows:

- *Economic globalisation* includes the increasing prevalence of multinational corporations (such as McDonalds, Nike and Ford), the spread of trade across borders, and the interconnectedness of global finance. A key feature of economic globalisation is the breaking down of traditional market and trade boundaries across nation-states. Of particular importance is the operation of tax, tariff and trade agreements (for example the free trade areas of the European Union and the Association of South East Asian Nations), which support greater access to markets and flows of trade and finance, as well as international financial organisations such as the International Monetary Fund and the World Bank.
- *Political globalisation* refers to the growth of supra-national and inter-governmental organisations that play an important role in political and legal governance throughout the world. Political globalisation is exemplified by the roles of the United Nations, the International Court of Justice, and the G8 and G20 organisations. A notable feature of global politics is the growth of non-governmental organisations that campaign around particular issues or interests within the space that has been termed 'global civil society'. The Occupy movement, which seeks to challenge and redress the unequal distribution of wealth and power, provides an interesting illustration of a contemporary global political organisation.
- *Cultural globalisation* is a wide-ranging element of globalisation that includes the international spread of music, art, literature and sporting events. It also refers to the spread and diversification of religions, cultures and ideas brought about by international migration and the growth of technology and media, including recent developments in digital and social media. For some commentators, cultural globalisation has also involved forms of 'cultural imperialism' in which certain cultural values and expression become dominant and imposed.

- *Environmental globalisation* refers to ways that the environment is impacted upon by globalisation and also to the ways in which changes to the environment have global effects. Issues such as climate change, air pollution, water availability, natural resource depletion, agriculture and fishing are increasingly global concerns.

Activity

Living in a global world?

Consider a day in the life of a student from a school that you know. List the ways that globalisation affects their daily life. Now consider the items on your list.

1 How many of these effects do you consider to be positive, how many do you consider to be negative, and how many are both positive and negative? Justify your responses.
2 How different is this list to the ways in which globalisation affected your life when you were the same age?

Globalisation, then, is a multifaceted phenomenon that is both empirical (it is actually happening and can in some senses be observed) and normative (it raises ethical questions about its aims, nature and effects). Given this, globalisation can be viewed as 'a radical transformation of the world' (Peim, 2012: 292). For example, let's consider the following statements all made about globalisation:

> Throughout much of the developing world, the awakening to globalization's down side has been one of resistance and resignation, a feeling that globalization is a false God foisted on weaker states by the capitalist centres of the West. Globalization is seen, not as a term describing objective reality, but as an ideology of predatory capitalism.
>
> (Kofi Annan, then Secretary-General of the United Nations, 2000: 127)

> There's no question that we have an increasingly integrated world economy, and that this has very serious implications, socially and politically. We also have a cultural phenomenon: the emergence of a global culture, or of a cultural globalization.
>
> (Peter Berger, Sociologist, 1997)

> Globalization is getting more complex, and this change is getting more rapid. The future will be more unpredictable . . . The last 40 years have been extraordinary times. Life expectancy has gone up by 25 years. It took from the Stone Age to achieve that. Income has gone up for a majority of the world's population . . . and illiteracy has gone down, from half to about a quarter of people on Earth . . . But there is an underbelly. There are two Achilles' heels of globalization. There

is the Achilles' heel of growing inequality – those that are left out, those that feel angry, those that are not participating . . . The second Achilles' heel is complexity – a growing fragility, a growing brittleness. What happens in one place very quickly affects everything else. This is a systematic risk, systematic shock. We've seen it in the financial crisis. We've seen it in the pandemic flu. It will become virulent and it is something we have to build resilience against.

(Ian Goldin, Director of the 21st Century School,
Oxford, UK: 2009)

These quotations attest to globalisation as a dynamic and powerful force. However, they also highlight that globalisation is far from unproblematic, and is a process that gives rise to a range of issues and tensions. According to Peim (2012: 298) most conceptualisations of globalisation 'emphasize the "new global order" as a process to be resisted, demanding a critical stance towards "neo-liberal" reorganization of global capital and power'. Given this, it is important that we consider some of the criticisms made of globalisation as well as thinking about how these might feature in our work with students.

Globalisation's critics

It is important that we remember when working with students that globalisation is a process which is both celebrated and critiqued. As teachers, we should be mindful not to polarise debates on globalisation and its effects – that is, we should not try to portray globalisation as being either a 100 per cent positive or a 100 per cent negative phenomenon. Because of its pervasiveness, very few people are either fully supportive of every aspect of globalisation or, conversely, are opposed to each and every aspect of globalisation. Trying to attain a balanced approach within global learning is not always easy, and the appropriateness of doing so depends on the particular element of globalisation being focused on. Adopted as a general rule, however, providing a balanced approach enables students to identify, consider and investigate the benefits and drawbacks of globalisation – and indeed the contested nature of these.

One way to start trying to arrive at some sort of balanced, critical approach of globalisation is to explore the main criticisms levelled at it. So what are the main criticisms of globalisation and, indeed, who are its main critics? In the last fifteen years a number of texts – often with evocative titles – have raised important issues with the processes of globalisation. Titles include *The New Rulers of the World* (Pilger, 2003); *Profit Over People: Neoliberalism and Global Order* (Chomsky, 2004); *The Bottom Billion: Why the Poorest Countries are Failing and What Can be Done About It* (Collier, 2007); *The Shock Doctrine: The Rise of Disaster Capitalism* (Klein, 2007); *How Rich Countries Got Rich and Why Poor Countries Stay Poor* (Reinhert, 2008); and *The Global Development Crisis* (Selwyn, 2014). Each of these texts takes issue with the economic and political inequalities and deficiencies that they identify as inherent within, or as resulting from, globalising processes. Aside from the analysis they provide, a notable feature of many of these texts is that they have sold in large quantities outside of traditional academic markets and into mainstream popular audiences. This is evidence of great interest in globalisation, including its discontents.

For the purpose of clarity it may be useful for us to break these into two broad categories of inter-related criticisms: (1) economic criticisms and (2) political criticisms. Here, we consider each in turn.

Economic criticisms of globalisation have focused primarily on its inequitable impact on the world's poorer nations and the world's poorest people. Such criticisms are aimed at inequalities in wealth distribution, including the perceived exploitation and oppression of some producers and workers resulting from international capitalism, the operation of free-trade markets and the pervasive influence of neoliberal economic policies. According to the most recent figures, for example, 39 per cent of the world's wealth is controlled by 1 per cent of its population (CNBC, 2013). In other words, economic criticisms of globalisation tend to focus on the sorts of market failure that result from global, free market economics. A lucid and thoughtful evaluation of globalisation is provided by Joseph Stiglitz, former Chief Economist at the World Bank, Chairman of President Clinton's Council of Economic Advisors, and Nobel Prize winner for Economics. Stiglitz' book – *Globalization and its Discontents* – has sold well over a million copies worldwide. In it, Stiglitz (2002: 5) cites the World Bank's motto, 'Our dream is a world without poverty', and explores a number of 'broken promises' that have resulted from globalisation. Stiglitz (2002: 5; emphasis in original) argues that:

> Those who vilify globalization too often overlook its benefits. But the proponents of globalization have been, if anything, even more unbalanced. To them, globalization . . . *is* progress; developing countries must accept it if they are to grow and to fight poverty effectively. But to many in the developing world, globalization has not brought the promised economic benefits.

In his follow-up book – *Making Globalization Work* – Stiglitz addresses a number of ways for changing how globalisation operates that could overcome its ills. We will return to many of these as we progress through this book (in particular in relation to development and development education in Chapter 5).

An interesting recent rejoinder to the economic criticisms of globalisation is provided by Bill and Melinda Gates in their 2014 Annual Letter for their Foundation. The letter commences with the following claim:

> By almost any measure, the world is better than it has ever been. People are living longer, healthier lives. Extreme poverty rates have been cut in half in the past 25 years. Child mortality is plunging. Many nations that were aid recipients are now self-sufficient. You might think that such striking progress would be widely celebrated . . . But they're not, at least not in proportion to the progress. In fact, I'm struck by how few people think the world is improving, and by how many actually think the opposite – that it is getting worse.
>
> (Gates and Gates, 2014: 1)

According to the Gates and Gates (2014: 1) this view is not only mistaken, but is 'harmful'. They argue that three commonly accepted 'myths' are particularly detrimental. The myths they identify are:

1   Poor countries are doomed to stay poor.
2   Foreign aid is a big waste.
3   Saving lives leads to over-population.

The Gates challenge the prevailing viewpoints often found in popular literature on globalisation and its impacts. Perhaps most stark is their prediction that, rather than 'staying poor', by '2035 there will be almost no poor countries left in the world'. This means that 'every nation in South America, Asia, and central America [with the possible exception of Haiti] and most in coastal Africa will have joined the ranks of today's middle-income nations' (2014: 7). Throughout the letter, the Gates directly address what they view as the misconceptions frequently made in relation to each of the myths (again, we will return to these in more detail later in the book).

Activity

Challenging the myths?

Download and read the 2014 Gates Annual Letter from the Bill & Melinda Gates Foundation website: http://annualletter.gatesfoundation.org/~/media/Annual%20Letter%202014/PDFs/2014_GatesAnnualLetter_ENGLISH_1.pdf.

How do their identified myths confirm or challenge your perceptions of global poverty, foreign aid and health?

How do their identified myths confirm or challenge the perceptions of global poverty, foreign aid and health you can find within the teaching resources used by yourself and the educational institutions in which you work or study?

In addition to, and often inter-related with, the economic criticisms of globalisation are a number of *political* criticisms that typically centre on the perceived or actual democratic deficit that has resulted from globalisation. Two particular examples illustrate this democratic deficit, both of which raise questions about the role and power of individual nation-states in the twenty-first century. The first example is the increasing role played by supra-national institutions and bodies in shaping and leading political and economic policies. Global financial institutions such as the World Bank and the International Monetary Fund play a significant part in influencing the domestic policies of nations in receipt of financial support. An important distinction to make here is that between supra-national institutions that are constituted by directly elected representatives (such as the European Parliament) and those whose accountability is not subjected to periodic and regular elections (such as the International Monetary Fund). Without a clear system of democratic accountability, critics of globalisation point to a lack of legitimacy in such institutions themselves, as well the impact they have on undermining democracy within individual nation-states (Elliott *et al.*, 2004: 18).

Over the last twenty years, a defining image played out in the popular media of globalisation's critics has been the series of large-scale protests, which have accompanied meetings of the leading international financial and economic institutions. These have included the World Trade Organisation, the International Monetary Fund, the World Bank, the Free Trade Area of the Americas, as well as summits of G8 and G20 leaders (Elliott *et al.*, 2004: 18). Perhaps the highest-profile protest association in recent years has been the Occupy movement. Originating in the United States, and now a global phenomenon, Occupy presents itself as a bottom-up, community-led movement based on the work and interests of individual activists who come together around a shared commitment to challenging global financial and economic inequalities. The movement's slogan – 'We are the 99%' – directly highlights the disproportionate concentration of financial wealth in the hands of the top 1 per cent of the world's population. Its methods are based on three principles: 'resist', 'restructure', and 'remix' (www.occupytogether.org).

In their analysis of what they term the 'alternative globalisation movement', Elliott *et al.* (2004: 25–26) identify three dimensions around which similarities and differences between groups critical of globalisation could be explored. The three dimensions are:

1   *Key issues*: Different groups focus on issues related to specific areas – such as 'development, human rights, and the environment' (2004: 25) – while others focus on issues related to a mix of areas.
2   *Role in the movement*: Different organisations play different types of roles within the alternative globalisation movement. According to Elliott *et al.* (2004: 25–6) some 'tilt more toward activism and others more toward research; some also provide not-for-profit services, such as emergency relief in crises, monitoring and verification of corporate compliance with codes of conduct'.
3   *Advocacy style*: Different organisations adopt different methods for making their interests known. Elliott *et al.* (2004: 26) distinguish between 'confronters' and 'engagers'. The former have 'explicitly rejected any cooperation with or called for the abolition of existing economic institutions', while the latter have 'joined in multi-stakeholder initiatives that include representatives of all parties interested in an issue, such as the UN Global Compact'.

We pick up on the work of global protest movements and organisations in the following activity, and return to them in more detail in Chapter 3, where we consider 'global civil society'.

Activity

Global protest movements

Global protest movements are increasingly prevalent and receive extensive media attention. They also provide a useful case study of opponents of globalisation. Research the Occupy movement, using the www.occupytogether.org website as well as other information sites about the movement. Now consider the following questions:

continued . . .

1   How useful is the Occupy movement as a case study for teaching students about globalisation's critics? In what ways might employing Elliott *et al.*'s (2004) three dimensions of the alternative globalisation movement – 'key issues', 'roles in the movement' and 'advocacy style' – be helpful in structuring students' inquiry?

2   Would you have to be selective about what elements of the Occupy movement you teach students about? If so, why?

3   Can you find any critics of the Occupy movement and its methods? What are these and where do they come from?

Before ending our overview of globalisation's critics it is worth pausing briefly to raise a further clarification. This is whether the criticism being made is of globalisation *per se* or the particular process that globalisation has taken. As Elliott *et al.* (2004: 17) explain, the broad term 'anti-globalists' is misleading because 'some are, but others are not. Many of these critics are strongly internationalist and want to see globalisation proceed, but under different rules'. Bennett (2003: 162) cites a range of people and organisations that have sought to criticise globalisation from within. For example, for the American labour leader, John Sweeney, it is 'clear that globalization is here to stay. We have to accept that and work on having a seat at the table when the rules are written about how globalization works'. Bennett goes on to take issue with the broad use of 'anti-globalization' as a catch-all term to refer to groups opposed to various forms and/or effects of globalisation. In citing the work of George (2001), Bennett (2003: 163) raises the importance of fluid and diverse understandings of the movement that is 'multi-focus and inclusive', and which moreover is 'concerned with the world: omnipresence of corporate rule, the rampages of financial markets, ecological destruction, misdistribution of wealth and power, international institutions constantly overstepping their mandates and lack of international democracy'.

Given the diversity within groups critical of globalisation, a term such as 'globalisation's critics' – which following Elliott *et al.* we have adopted here – is perhaps an apt description. This raises questions regarding the best pathways for dealing with the world's economic problems, such as poverty. There are no easy answers to these questions. Writing at the turn of the millennium, Crook (2001) suggested that debates are often polarised between three positions: (1) national governments in affluent countries which 'present [global] economic integration to voters as an unfortunate but inescapable fact of life'; (2) multinational businesses that present a picture of social responsibility as a goal alongside maximising profits, something that people do not always believe; and (3) activists and protestors that at times adopt confrontational methods and do not always offer clear alternatives. According to Crook, a somewhat confused environment has been created:

With advocates like these on either side of the globalisation debate – dissembling governments and businesses in favour, angry and uncompromising protestors against – it is natural that the general public stands firmly in support of neither. It has no deep commitment to international capitalism, but it can see no plausible alternative . . . So people are mostly puzzled, anxious and suspicious. This climate of opinion is bad for democracy and bad for economic development.

For Crook, there is also a sense that processes of globalisation are so entrenched that somewhat paradoxically it is only through greater globalisation that ills such as poverty can be remedied. He argues that 'globalisation, far from being the greatest cause of poverty, is its only feasible cure' (2001). The argument Crook is making is similar to that made by Joseph Stiglitz – the cure to the problems of globalisation is not its removal, but rather its continuation in different forms.

As educators we need to consider critically a range of questions regarding criticisms of globalisation. These include: the role they can and should play within our lessons; how to ensure that our students are aware of the positive and negative influences of globalisation and how these affect and are understood differently in different contexts; and how we ensure that a range of perspectives on globalisation are integrated within global learning. The answers to these questions will depend on a range of factors, not least the context of our teaching, the prior understanding and engagement of our students in global learning, and the age of the students with whom we are working.

Global citizenship

The empirical fact of globalisation, as well as the normative issues to which it leads, raises serious and important questions regarding the status, role, power and agency of humans at a global level; in other words, about 'global citizenship'. As with many of the concepts that we will explore throughout this book, the term 'global citizenship' is ambiguous and contested. This means that different people have different ideas and interpretations of what global citizenship does and should mean. Indeed, to some extent the term could be seen as an oxymoron – to be a citizen is to be a member of a given state, deriving rights and carrying obligations because of that membership, something which is not necessarily available at a global level. Others would reject this claim, suggesting that globalisation has brought about the possibility and need for people to view themselves (or at least part of their identity) as citizens of a global community or as citizens of the world. Thinking about global citizenship in this way challenges nation-based notions of citizenship by conceiving its possibility in terms of action, participation and membership in a community that exists beyond national borders.

What it means in practice to be a global citizen, then, is far from straightforward, but commonly referred to dimensions include:

- having an awareness and understanding of global issues, events and institutions;
- recognising a shared, common humanity, including a commitment to human rights;
- taking action (locally, nationally and globally) in an informed, appropriate and responsible way, including when not to act;
- adopting a global perspective or orientation;
- recognising, listening and hearing different perspectives and understandings;
- being committed to a shared future, including the importance of sustainability; and
- possessing a global consciousness, including caring about events, issues and others living around the world, and seeing oneself as a participating member of a global community of shared humanity.

The last point on this list – that global citizenship may include seeing oneself as a participating member of a global community of shared humanity – is an idea central to 'cosmopolitanism'. The idea that individuals have a sense of world, or global, citizenship is not new. In the fourth century BC, the Cynic Diogenes of Sinope, when asked from where he came, responded 'I am a citizen of the world'. This sentiment has been embraced by proponents of cosmopolitanism to suggest that humans share a common sense of humanity, which crosses and transcends the boundaries of nation-states. The educational implication of this is that students should learn a compassionate concern for all human beings in a global world, and should be taught about ways in which they can act to help reduce breaches of human rights whether locally or globally. This reminds us that being a global citizen is not just about a legal status or about our actions, but also about our mind-set.

A key part of global citizenship is the ability to recognise, hear and listen to the viewpoints and perspectives of others; in other words, to adopt a 'cosmopolitan' outlook. This is what Audrey Osler (2008: 22) is referring to when she writes:

> [E]ducation for cosmopolitan citizenship . . . requires us to re-imagine the nation . . . as cosmopolitan and to recognise local communities and the national community as cosmopolitan. It implies a sense of solidarity with strangers in distant places but it also requires solidarity, a sense of shared humanity and dialogue with those in the local community and the national community whose perspectives may be very different from our own.

One of the world's foremost writers on cosmopolitanism, the American political and legal theorist Martha Nussbaum, has written of the need for education to cultivate a cosmopolitan outlook in students in a context in which 'all modern democracies are inescapably plural' (2002: 291). In her work, Nussbaum (1997, 2002, 2006) identifies three capacities needed for preparing students for democratic citizenship in today's plural and globalised world: (1) the capacity for critical self-examination of one's own beliefs, values and traditions and the ability to see one's own views as revisable in the light of new evidence and/or different perspectives; (2) the capacity to see oneself as part of a common, shared humanity bound together by 'ties of recognition and concern' (2002: 295); and (3) the capacity to develop what Nussbaum terms as 'the narrative imagination' (2006: 390). Developing a narrative imagination requires students to place themselves in the shoes of another and to consider their perspectives and emotions – in others words, to be empathetic.

Drawing on the historical basis of cosmopolitan thought, Nussbaum (1994) also reminds us that being a global citizen does not mean forgetting our other commitments and relationships altogether. Rather – as the Stoics did – we should envisage ourselves as living within a number of concentric circles: 'the first one is drawn around the self; the next takes in one's immediate family; then follows the extended family; then, in order, one's neighbours or local group, one's fellow city-dwellers, one's fellow countrymen' and so on. The task of the global citizen – as a citizen of the world – is to pull the circles inward to widen and deepen our affections for those on the outer circles. For Nussbaum (1994) 'we should work to make all human beings part of our community of dialogue and concern'. Writing in the context of the United States, Nussbaum suggests that the student:

may continue to regard herself as in part defined by her particular loves—her family, her religious, ethnic, or racial communities, or even for her country. But she must also, and centrally, learn to recognize humanity wherever she encounters it, undeterred by traits that are strange to her, and be eager to understand humanity . . . She must learn enough about the different to recognize common aims, aspirations, and values, and enough about these common ends to see how variously they are instantiated in the many cultures and many histories.

Activity

Spheres of citizenship

If we accept that global citizenship is both possible and important, two further important questions are raised. The first of these is how our commitment to global citizenship relates to other forms of citizenship as well as to other elements of our identity. Clearly for Diogenes, his commitment to world citizenship and a shared, common humanity outweighed his membership of a particular city-state. But is this the same for you and for your students?

Do you see yourself first and foremost as citizens of a particular locality (a village or a city, for example), of a particular a nation-state, or of the world?

Do you feel an attachment to a locality, a nation-state and the world simultaneously and, if so, are these attachments harmonious or do they conflict?

How you respond to these questions will be influenced by a range of factors, including your particular life experiences, and may also change over time or according to particular circumstances.

If we think about global education as being, at least in part, about students developing a global perspective then we need to ask which, or more precisely, whose global perspective is being developed. There does not exist just one global perspective, but rather a range of perspectives that are affected by a number of factors. In charting the recent history in the UK of what has become known as 'Development Education', Bourn (2012: 256) highlights the role that the media played in giving young people a certain perspective on what life was like in developing countries in Africa. Citing the work of Adamson (1993), Bourn suggests that 'the dominant views of children were of poverty and starvation' and that these 'perceptions of Africa, for example, as a continent of helplessness and "starving babies" were still evident in the school classroom in the first decade of the 21st Century'.

An insightful further position about the importance of perspective/s in relation to globalisation is provided by the author Chimamanda Ngozi Adichie in a TED Talk entitled *The Danger of a Single Story* (2009). In the talk, Adichie explores her writing in relation to her experiences growing up in Nigeria and being exposed to predominantly British and American children's literature. Reading such books heavily influenced the characters and features in the stories she wrote as a child – who were 'white and blue-eyed . . . played in the snow . . . ate apples . . . and talked a lot about the weather'. Reflecting on the influence of reading British books, Adichie (2009) suggests that:

What this demonstrates . . . is how impressionable and vulnerable we are in the face of a story, particularly as children. Because all I read were books in which characters were foreign, I had become convinced that books by their very nature had to have foreigners in them and had to be about things with which I could not personally identify. Things changed when I discovered African books. There weren't many of them available, and they weren't quite as easy to find as the foreign books . . . what the discovery of African writers did for me was this: It saved me from having a single story of what books are.

In her talk, Adichie goes on to depict a range of similar instances in her life in which different people had single stories, leading to stereotypical and limited apprehensions either of individuals, groups, nations and continents. At the heart of each of these instances of a singular story is power, which Adichie conceptualises in the following way:

There is a word, an Igbo word, that I think about whenever I think about the power structures of the world, and it is 'nkali'. It's a noun that loosely translates 'to be greater than another'. Like our economic and political worlds, stories too are defined by the principle of nkali: How they are told, who tells them, when they are told, how many stories are told, are really dependent on power. Power is the ability not just to tell the story of another person, but to make it the definitive story of that person.

The forging of the integral connection between what it is to be a global citizen and how one might learn to become a global citizen central to cosmopolitanism, along with recognition of the need to consider a range of perspectives, leads us nicely to the second question that an acceptance of global citizenship raises. This relates firmly to education and is concerned with the content and processes through which the knowledge, skills and attributes needed for global learning to be a global citizenship are developed. It is this second question which is the focus not only of the rest of this chapter, but also the remainder of this book.

Global education

The term 'global education' has been part of educational discourse since at least the 1960s and has grown significantly since the 1980s (for example, in the work of Boulding, 1988). The importance of preparing young people for their lived experiences in the globalised twenty-first century has been widely stated. For example, drawing on a large-scale, international research project into Civic Education conducted by the International Association for the Evaluation of Educational Achievement (IEA), Torney-Purta *et al.* (1999: 172) contend that 'new global realities call for a major reconsideration by educators and policy makers of how young people are being prepared to participate in democratic societies in the early twenty-first century'.

However, there is no uniform sense in which the term 'global education' is used. Part of the complexity is that a number of different terms have been used under the umbrella of global education. These include: 'global citizenship education', 'global learning', 'the global dimension', 'global perspectives', 'development education', 'human rights education', 'cosmopolitan education' and 'peace education'. Some of these terms (such as 'global citizenship education' and 'global perspectives') have been used interchangeably with 'global education', while others (such as 'peace education' and 'human rights education') might be seen better as components of global education.

Even if we settle on the term 'global education' there still remains a number of definitional problems. According to Graham Pike (2008: 468), 'the wide range of ideological and pedagogical assumptions to be found in the host of educational initiatives that shelter under the umbrella of "global education" renders an agreed and succinct definition unlikely', while Harriet Marshall (2007: 356) has suggested that '[G]lobal education could be characterised as a rather woolly and ill-defined term'. In a similar way, Davies *et al.* (2005: 74) have argued that 'although we have a massive literature associated with exploring forms of education relevant to global or international contexts there is little coherent understanding'. This conceptual uncertainty regarding what global education does and could mean is problematic for teachers. Indeed, as Pike (2000: 64) has pointed out, for many teachers 'just defining global education or explaining what it encompasses constitutes a major conceptual challenge'.

Case study

Global Education Project: teacher resources to encourage a global perspective across the curriculum

www.globaleducation.edu.au

Global Education is a national project in Australia, which is funded by the Australian Government's Department of Foreign Affairs and Trade. Through its website, the project publishes a range of curricular materials on issues relating to globalization and aid, as well as providing case studies, teacher notes, student activities, videos and posters. In addition to the *Global Perspectives Framework*, some examples of the online resources provided by the project are:

- a range of professional learning modules that allow teachers to expand their knowledge and skills in teaching with a global perspective at their own pace;
- country profiles;
- case studies on a range of global projects;
- information about a range of global issues;
- teaching activities;
- images; and
- videos.

Contracted representative organisations in each state work with teachers in schools and student teachers to support their professional development in teaching about global dimensions within and across the curriculum (www. globaleducation.edu.au).

So how can we start to make sense of what 'global education' might mean and how it can connect to ideas on global citizenship? This is something you will explore in more detail in the next chapter, so here we will consider some initial conceptions to start our thinking about what global education might comprise. One useful way is to think about how the term is used by various governmental and non-governmental organisations around the world. The Global Education Project in Australia (2008: 2) employs the following definition in response to the question 'What is global education?':

> Twenty-first century Australians are members of a global community, connected to the whole world by ties of culture, economics and politics, enhanced communication and travel and a shared environment.
>
> Enabling young people to participate in shaping a better shared future for the world is at the heart of global education. It emphasises the unity and interdependence of human society, developing a sense of self and appreciation of cultural diversity, affirmation of social justice and human rights, building peace and actions for a sustainable future in different times and places. It places particular emphasis on developing relationships with our neighbours in the Asia-Pacific and Indian Ocean regions.
>
> Global education promotes open-mindedness leading to new thinking about the world and a predisposition to take action for change. Students learn to take responsibility for their actions, respect and value diversity and see themselves as global citizens who can contribute to a more peaceful, just and sustainable world.
>
> With its emphasis not only on developing knowledge and skills but also on promoting positive values and participation, global education is relevant across all learning areas.

In England, the *Developing a Global Dimension in the School Curriculum* resource published jointly by the Development Education Association (DEA) and Department for International Development (DFID) presents eight key concepts, which underlie the global dimension to the curriculum:

- Global Citizenship: *Gaining the knowledge, skills and understanding of concepts and institutions necessary to become informed, active, responsible citizens;*
- Diversity: *Understanding and respecting differences and relating these to our common humanity;*
- Human Rights: *Knowing about human rights including the UN Convention on the Rights of the Child;*
- Interdependence: *Understanding how people, places, economies and environments are all inextricably interrelated, and that choices and events have repercussions on a global scale;*
- Sustainable Development: *Understanding the need to maintain and improve the quality of life now without damaging the planet for future generations;*
- Values and perceptions: *Developing a critical evaluation of representations of global issues and an appreciation of the effect these have on people's attitudes and values;*

- Social Justice: *Understanding the importance of social justice as an element in both sustainable development and the improved welfare of all people;*
- Conflict Resolution: *Understanding the nature of conflicts, their impact on development and why there is a need for their resolution and the promotion of harmony.*

(2005: 13; emphasis in the original)

These concepts are central to the work of Think Global (formerly known as the DEA), which is also underpinned by an understanding that:

global learning . . . puts learning in a global context, fostering:

- critical and creative thinking;
- self-awareness and open-mindedness towards difference;
- understanding of global issues and power relationships; and,
- optimism and action for a better world.

(www.think-global.org.uk)

The resource also reminds educators that these elements have to be considered and interpreted in relation to particular contexts given that the needs of students will differ across these. As you progress through and engage with the elements of global learning within this book, we ask you to pay particular attention to how the ideas and issues relate to your own context/s.

By considering these two definitions we can see that global education refers both to knowledge and skills, but also involves certain forms of learning. This is most clearly and usefully explained by referencing the influential work of Graham Pike and David Selby (1998), who understand global education as combining *world-mindedness* and *child-centredness*. World-mindedness is the development of an understanding and attitude about the world, globalization and the inter-dependency that defines the conditions of the late twentieth and early twenty-first centuries. The recognition of the importance of child-centredness highlights the significance of pedagogical approaches which start from students' experiences and understandings and that seek to help the development of attitudes and dispositions; this will form the focus of our next chapter.

Globalising education

Throughout this book we will consider ways in which schools and teachers do, and can, develop a global awareness. As such our concern will be with the content of students' global learning and the pedagogical processes, which might successfully bring about this global awareness. However, we should also be mindful of some of the impacts of globalisation upon education itself. These include:

- *The question of whether education is a generalized human right* as declared with the 1948 United Nations Universal Declaration of Human Rights, the United Nations' 1959 Convention on the Rights of the Child, and the 1976 UN International Covenant on Economic, Social, and Cultural Rights. However, there remains 'no universal agreement on what amounts to an education to meet the minimum requirements to fulfil that right' (Peim, 2012: 294) (for an interesting discussion of education as a human right see McCowan, 2013).

- *The practice and experience of differential access to education* between nations and within nations on the basis of particular characteristics. For example, the 1990 (Jomtein) and 2000 (Dakar) UNESCO Education for All conferences, as well as the Millennium Declaration (United Nations, 2000), each provided a commitment to the goal of 'universalising primary education and to achieve gender equality in school enrolments by 2015' (Sundaram, 2012: 284).
- *The increasing commonalities in the form and curriculum of the school* across Westernised nations (including the four nations of the United Kingdom, the United States, Canada, Australia, New Zealand, Japan, Hong Kong, South Korea and Singapore) and, to a lesser extent, across all nations. According to Peim (2012: 295) the school 'has been adopted, and adapted, as the key instrument for development in virtually all global contexts'. But critics such as Pasi Sahlberg (2011) raise important points of concern as to the overall direction this global reform movement in education is taking, with the centralisation of prescribed curricula and market-driven standardisation of testing dominating at the expense of collective responsibility and creative innovation at the local level.
- *The role and importance of international tests and measures of educational attainment*, most prominently the Programme for International Student Assessment (PISA) conducted by the Organisation for Economic Co-operation and Development (OECD) (but also the Trends in International Mathematics and Science Study (TIMSS) and the Progress in International Reading Literacy Study (PIRLS) both conducted by the International Association for the Evaluation of Educational Achievement (IEA)). Reflecting the OECD's (2012: 10) claim that 'skills have become the global currency of twenty-first century economies', such tests are central to government education policies that are commonly aimed at raising achievement in them, with the results of the periodic PISA tests receiving a great deal of media attention. The tests and their use within policy rhetoric have however received a good deal of criticism (see for example Sellar and Lingard, 2013).
- *The increasing internationalisation of higher education and movement of higher education students*, which has occurred throughout the world over the last two decades. In his analysis of internationalisation and global citizenship education, Haigh (2014) usefully sets out a number of layers involved in this process: universities recruiting international students; universities teaching international learners; universities becoming institutions of international enterprise; recognising international standards; embracing, respecting and preparing students for multicultural and diverse employment and communities; education for global citizenship; e-learning and digitisation; and 'education for planetary consciousness' (16).

Activity

The importance of context

Pike's suggestion regarding the conceptual challenge of defining and explaining global education cited earlier raises an issue for teachers who are looking to develop a global dimension within their schools. A key approach to which we are seeking to contribute through this book is to support your own inspiration and sense of ownership in developing global learning through creative and contextualised innovation. Towards this aim begin to consider for a moment by yourself and in the light of your unique and particular context:

1   Why is it important for a global dimension to education to be developed here?
2   What does the nature and content of this global dimension need to be?
3   What sorts of global actor am I aspiring to nurture my learners to be and become?

Drawing from your reflections on reading this first chapter, write a one paragraph response to each of these three questions in an attempt to begin to capture your own vision for global learning in the twenty-first century.

Conclusion

In this chapter we have introduced some of the key definitions and issues concerning global learning, all of which we investigate in more detail in the remaining chapters. For now, we would like to summarise three main points:

- First, that globalisation, global citizenship and global education are all contested terms which can mean different things, to different people, in different places and at different times.
- Second, that a range of normative issues are raised by globalisation about which there is clear disagreement; these impact on and inform approaches to global education.
- Third, that global citizenship education involves both the content of teaching (knowledge, skills and attributes) as well as the process of learning (the pedagogical and environmental methods which make learning possible).

The content of this chapter informs and underpins the remainder of the book, and as such we would ask that you bear in mind the issues, ideas and principles it has introduced as you progress through each of the remaining chapters. This will require you to be both *critical* and *creative* as you get to grips with the various ideas and issues of globalisation and education.

Questions for further investigation

1 What does 'global citizenship' mean and is it possible for someone to be a 'global citizen'? If so, how?
2 How have global technologies affected the flow of information across national boundaries and what are the effects of these flows?
3 What do commentators imagine the global world could be like in five, ten and twenty years' time and how might we start to think about how to prepare young people for this?

Further reading

globaldimension.org.uk
The companion site to think-global, global dimension provides a wide range of resources for teachers and schools to support global learning.

Reid, A., Gill, J. and Sears, A. (2010) *Globalization, the Nation-State and the Citizen: Dilemmas and Directions for Civics and Citizenship Education.* London: Routledge.
An insightful and wide-ranging academic text that explores the relationships between globalisation and education for citizenship across a number of different nations.

Stiglitz, J. (2002) *Globalization and its Discontents.* London: Penguin.
A fascinating and insightful examination of globalisation and its problematic effects, written by one of the world's leading economists.

www.think-global.org.uk
An extensive and wide-ranging website with a number of resources, think-pieces and links that provide an excellent introduction to global learning. A national education charity in the UK.

Chapter 2

Global learning for global citizenship

Chapter objectives

By the end of this chapter you should have:

- considered what are the core dimensions of global learning, and how these relate to global citizenship;
- explored key pedagogies for global learning;
- analysed a number of contemporary issues in developing pedagogies for global learning.

Introduction

In the first chapter we introduced a central theme of this book, namely that the reality of growing up in an increasingly globalised world requires a new kind of education in and for the twenty-first century. Students in their present and future capacity as global citizens require a dimension to their education that draws out their global consciousness and global competence. As Merryfield and Kasai (2010: 165) suggest:

> The primary goal of global education is to prepare students to be effective and responsible citizens in a global society. Toward this end, students need to practice real-life skills, gain knowledge of the world, and develop expertise in viewing events and issues from diverse global perspectives.

In this chapter we move on to consider the educational approaches that are most apt to bring about global learning for global citizenship. In doing so we are particularly interested in 'pedagogies', and by this we mean the bringing together of teaching methods, learning activities and the curriculum to develop knowledge, understandings, skills, capacities and dispositions. As Lingard (2007: 247) makes clear 'it is through pedagogies that education gets done'. In particular, in this chapter we consider student-centred pedagogies that enable effective global learning. These approaches start from students' own experiences and understanding, and seek to engage with a wide range of active and participatory learning methods (Pike and Selby, 1998; McInerney, 2010; Dill, 2013; Wierenga and Guevara, 2013).

Approaches to global learning for global citizenship

Before we explore a range of pedagogies for global learning, it is worth us spending some time thinking about the aims and foci of global citizenship education. In Chapter 1 we highlighted that in its contested and unfolding nature global learning can hold a wide range of holistic learning intentions relating to knowledge, skills, attributes and dispositions. When we consider the literature, we can see that while a range of intentions can be found, these relate to different interpretations of 'world-mindedness', as described by Pike and Selby (1998), and the competencies that are required by global citizens in the twenty-first century. Based on their extensive analysis of literature in the field, Oxley and Morris (2013) have constructed a helpful typology – set out in Table 2.1 – to identify and distinguish between different approaches *within* global citizenship education, each of which relates to specific learning intentions (or as they use, different 'foci and key concepts').

While they acknowledge that the categories are not 'fixed or absolute', Oxley and Morris (2013: 316) suggest that they 'provide a powerful tool for analysing the curriculum'. This is necessary given that there may be a mis-match between the global citizenship education intentions of policy makers and the experiences of students in schools. This is because there are a number of different factors and processes involved in translating policy into learning experiences. As Reid, Gill and Sears (2010: 5) assert in regard to global citizenship education:

> No matter how tightly the state seeks to prescribe educational practice to conform with the educational settlement, there is always 'wriggle room' for educators . . . That is, there is never a one-to-one correspondence between the state's agenda and its realisation in the classroom.

Categories such as those developed by Oxley and Morris can help teachers to be mindful of the specific forms of global citizenship that they are – intentionally or unintentionally – exploring with students in the classroom.

A further piece of research that illustrates the *actual* intentions of global learning in classrooms across jurisdictions has been provided by Jeffrey Dill (2013). Dill's work is one of a few studies to adopt an in-depth, multination and multisite focus in studying schools' intentions and practices for global citizenship education. In his ethnographic study of schools in the United States and Asia, Dill (2013: 4) identifies two elements of global citizenship education: 'global consciousness' and 'global competencies'. The former refers to a 'particular way of understanding one's self and world', and includes being aware of the perspectives and interests of others, seeing oneself as being a member of a global human community, and having a moral conscience to act in support of others. The latter refers to the skills and knowledge needed to be a global citizen. In recognising the importance not only of knowledge and skills, but also of attributes and feelings, Dill (2013: 3) makes clear that 'global citizenship represents an ideal, and therefore, like all pedagogical ideals, global citizenship represents a vision of the good'.

Oxfam's approach to developing students' global consciousness and global competence can be summarised as a 'learn–think–act' process. This holistic approach recognises the need to engage students intellectually with new insights into the global dimensions of life as and when they are discovered and revealed by research. The knowledge base upon which global citizens must navigate their worlds is constantly unfolding.

Table 2.1 Categories of global citizenship identified from the prevailing literature (taken from Oxley and Morris, 2013: 306).

Conception	Key theorists (contemporary proponents)	Focus, key concepts
Cosmopolitan types		
Political global citizenship	Kant; Rawls (Held; McGrew; Linklater; Carter; Archibugi; Wendt)	A focus on the relationships of the individual to the state and other polities, particularly in the form of *cosmopolitan democracy*
Moral global citizenship	Stoics; Kant; Sen; Nussbaum (Osler and Starkey; Veugelers; Cabrera)	A focus on the ethical positioning of individuals and groups to each other, most often featuring ideas of *human rights*
Economic global citizenship	Hayek; Freidman; Smith; Quesney; Bowan (Carroll and Shabna; Waddock and Smith; Logsdon and Wood)	A focus on the interplay between power, forms of capital, labour, resources and the human condition, often presented as *international development*
Cultural global citizenship	J. S. Mill; Nietzche (*übermensch*); (He; Brimm; de Ruyter and Speicker)	A focus on the symbols that unite and divide members of societies, with particular emphasis on *globalisation of arts, media, languages, sciences and technologies*
Advocacy types		
Social global citizenship	Habermas (communicative rationality) (Falk; Cogan and Derricott)	A focus on the interconnections between individuals and groups and their advocacy of the 'people's' voice, often referred to as *global civil society*
Critical global citizenship	Escobar; Said; Gramsci; Marx; critical pedagogy (for example, Freire) (Andreotti; Tully; Shultz)	A focus on the challenges arising from inequalities and oppression, using critique of social norms to advocate action to improve the lives of dispossessed/subaltern populations, particularly through a *post-colonial agenda*
Environmental global citizenship	Enviro-scientific research (Dobson; Richardson; Jelin)	A focus on advocating changes in the actions of humans in relation to the natural environment, generally called the *sustainable development agenda*
Spiritual global citizenship	Danesh; religious texts (Noddings; Golmohamad; Lindner)	A focus on the non-scientific and immeasurable aspects of human relations, advocating commitment to axioms relating to *caring, loving, spiritual and emotional connections*

Activity

Oxfam's model of Education for Global Citizenship

The international non-governmental organisation Oxfam (2006: 1) defines Education for Global Citizenship as enabling students to secure 'a just and sustainable world in which all may fulfil their potential'. They conceptualise a tripartite approach to global citizenship education with the three key elements of engagement being: knowledge and understanding; skills; and values and attitudes. More specifically they consider the following to be key elements in each dimension:

KNOWLEDGE AND UNDERSTANDING

- Social justice and equity
- Diversity
- Globalisation and interdependence
- Sustainable development
- Peace and conflict

SKILLS

- Critical thinking
- Ability to argue effectively
- Ability to challenge injustice and inequalities
- Respect for people and things
- Co-operation and conflict resolution

VALUES AND ATTITUDES

- Sense of identity and self-esteem
- Empathy
- Commitment to social justice and equity
- Value and respect for diversity
- Concern for the environment and commitment to sustainable development
- Belief that people can make a difference

(Oxfam 2006: 4)

Oxfam considers this conceptualisation of global citizenship education to be relevant for constructing curriculum throughout primary, secondary and post-16 educational institutions. More information about these intentions and their application is available from www.oxfam.org.uk/education/global-citizenship. Consider the vision of global citizenship education provided by Oxfam.

1   Based upon Oxley and Morris' typology, how many conceptions of global citizenship education do you think the approach potentially touches upon or overlooks?

2   With a particular age group with which you are familiar in mind, how many of these key elements in each dimension do you consider to be appropriate, and how many are you aware of being practised within your own setting?

3   Which of these areas of global citizenship education do you feel the least prepared for facilitating yourself, based upon your own professional training and prior learning experiences? Where might accessible sources of support and training exist?

Oxfam's holistic approach also highlights the need to engage students with *critical*, *creative* and *collaborative* aspects of learning.

- *Criticality* is a fundamental and necessary dimension to global citizenship education if we are to avoid de-politicised engagement that merely seeks to address symptoms and not the root causes of contemporary global issues. The critical dimension of global learning involves learners in considering a range of different, and sometimes conflicting, perspectives on global issues and encourages processes of reflexivity that support the learner in considering the implication of self with regard to these issues (Whitney and Clayton, 2011). This deliberative and questioning approach towards learning to live together in a diverse and unequal context is one that researchers have increasingly been identifying as propitious to the education of informed and active citizens in the twenty-first century (Peterson, 2009; Jerome, 2012; Leighton, 2012).

- *Creativity* is central to global learning processes that seek to prepare young people to face the future challenge of moving towards a more just and sustainable world. The uncertainty and complexity of global challenges, Robinson (2011) argues, requires global citizens who have been equipped with the resilience and creative adaptability to be able to take action that is underpinned by original ideas of value and worth within their personal and community contexts.

- *Collaboration* recognises the importance of interdependence within global learning, as well as the importance of developing effective and meaningful relationships. Collaborative global citizenship education gives greater recognition to the principle of solidarity and co-operative approaches to tackling global challenges. Such a co-operative approach also supports the principle of inclusion; where all participants are listened to and involved in the process of praxis, critically and creatively reflecting together on how to act wisely in given situations.

So as we progress through this chapter, and indeed through this book, we ask you to bear in mind the need to develop students' knowledge and understanding, alongside cultivating criticality, creativity and collaboration, as we explore pedagogical approaches to global learning that have been embraced as being apt for twenty-first-century schooling.

Pedagogies for global learning and global citizenship

There are, of course, a number of ways in which schools can include intentions related to global learning within their work. These include recognising global citizenship within the school's mission and ethos, making explicit connections to global learning within *all* curriculum subjects, building a range of extra-curricular activities related to global citizenship, and developing a range of community-related opportunities for students to develop their understanding and engagement with global issues. It is important to remember that an integrated approach is essential, with no single way being sufficient alone for effective and deep global learning.

A major challenge for educators and educational institutions is to develop pedagogies that are congruent with the holistic aims of global learning for global citizenship. The global learning movement has not shied away from the fact that key aspects of the global citizenship agenda are complex and contested, as we have highlighted in Chapter 1. Differences of perspective are possible, are continually present and are valid within the field, and therefore it is vital that the pedagogy of global citizenship education is congruent with living in a cosmopolitan world. In addition, due to the scale and potentially devastating implications of many points of crisis that global learning touches upon, there is also the real risk that engagement in this area can actually contribute to an individual's sense of despair about the future. This can foster in students a sense of powerlessness and apathy about the role they themselves can play in bringing about positive change. Consequently, global citizenship education is a field characterised by pedagogies that are student-centred (or to use Pike and Selby's term identified in Chapter 1, child-centred) and that are dialogic, interactive and participatory in their methodology. Attention is given to acknowledging the students' different contexts and prior knowledge, and to the personalising of learning in order to allow for a variety of engagement styles and educative experiences. Indeed, global citizenship education is a field that requires that as educators we remain particularly wary of overly didactic pedagogical approaches that seek to transmit to learners what to think, how to feel and how to act. In the remainder of this chapter we consider three broad pedagogical approaches to global citizenship education that can be applied along these student-centred lines. These are issue-based learning, problem-based learning and service-learning.

Issue-based learning

Global citizenship education can be characterised as commonly engaging students in issue-based learning. Research conducted by Holden (2007) and Warwick (2008) reveals the extent to which young people today can hold an interest in a broad range of global issues and consequently an enthusiasm for issue-based learning. Such global issues lie across the social, economic, political and environmental spectrum as exemplified in the following list of commonly referred to topic areas. While this list of nine areas is by no means exhaustive, it does illustrate the range of global issues that young people are growing up in the midst of:

1   *Climate change* – climate change refers to the long term warming of the earth's climate system and is described by Kagawa and Selby (2010: xv) as 'the greatest

human-induced crisis facing the world today'. In its most recent summary for policy makers, the United Nations Intergovernmental Panel on Climate Change (IPCC) re-asserted that the evidence of climate change is unequivocal and also confirmed the anthropogenic nature of this warming of the climate system (IPCC, 2014). These changes in temperature and precipitation as well as rising sea levels are affecting natural habitats as well as agriculture and food supplies.

2   *Environmental degradation* – significant problems remain with regard to ocean acidification and terrestrial ecosystem weakening specifically through deforestation, desertification and negative impacts upon soil quality through agricultural over-use. The Millennium Ecosystem Assessment reports that 'over the last 50 years human activity has altered ecosystems at a faster rate and on a larger scale than at any other time in human history' (cited in Oxford Martin School, 2013: 27).

3   *Biodiversity loss* – the International Union for the Conservation of Nature (IUCN) claim that we are currently witnessing the greatest species extinction rates ever recorded in human history. The IUCN red list for threatened species had by 2013 evaluated over 71,000 different species and identified 29 per cent of these to be threatened with extinction (IUCN, 2013).

4   *Pollution and waste* – industrial processes of production, which strive to meet increased per capita consumption of resources, continue to produce unprecedented levels of waste and pollution. This is despite considerable efforts in recent years to increase the recycling of waste. The prevalence of toxic, chemical and biological wastes continue to be particularly problematic (Gore, 2013). The World Health Organisation (WHO) identifies air pollutants of major public health concern to include particulate matter, carbon monoxide, ozone, nitrogen dioxide and sulphur dioxide. These are contributing to a range of chronic and acute respiratory diseases with indoor and outdoor air pollution being estimated to cause over 3 million deaths per year (WHO, 2011).

5   *Fresh water scarcity* – population growth and demographic changes, including a rapid rise in urbanisation and increased demands from agricultural and industrial processes, continue to place considerable stresses on fresh water supplies. A recent study by the Joint Program on the Science and Policy of Global Change at MIT projected that by 2050, 5 billion (52 per cent) of the world's projected 9.7 billion people will be living in water-stressed areas, most notably in India, Northern Africa and the Middle East (Schlosser *et al.*, 2014).

6   *Extreme poverty* – the United Nations estimate that there are still over 1 billion people living in extreme poverty in the world today (United Nations, 2013b). This is despite considerable progress in recent years in pursuit of the Millennium Development Goals with regard to reducing poverty levels worldwide (about 700 million fewer people lived in conditions of extreme poverty in 2010 compared with 1990).

7   *Inequality* – the gap between the economically rich and poor continues to widen, with income inequality rising both within and between many countries. In 2014 an Oxfam briefing paper calculated that the world's 85 wealthiest people hold as much wealth as the poorest 3.5 billion (Fuentes-Nieva and Galasso, 2014). Their report also claims that 7 out of 10 people live in countries where economic inequality has increased in the last 30 years.

8   *Food and nutrition insecurity* – sustainable access to food and nutrition remains a pressing problem within many parts of the world, with 1 billion people still suffering from food insecurity. The United Nations (2013b: xi) estimate that 'food production will have to increase 70 per cent globally to feed an additional 2.3 billion people by 2050'.

9   *Disease and health risks* – while radical improvements have been made in treatments (for example, for HIV/Aids, TB and Malaria), access to these treatments remains unequal, with the most socio-economically disadvantaged suffering disproportionately (Oxford Martin School, 2013). This is resulting in the continued global presence of disease epidemics. In recent years increased attention is also being given to the emerging global problem of non-communicable diseases, largely caused by lifestyle choices. One emerging global problem in this area is obesity, now affecting more than 10 per cent of the world's population. The World Health Organization recently identified obesity and being overweight to be a major global public health concern and estimated that it is a cause of death of nearly 3 million adults per year (cited in United Nations, 2013b: 91).

Global issues, such as those listed above, can form important stimuli for engaging students in global learning that is centred on pursuing the well-being of all, and on exploring concepts such as interconnectedness, diversity, social justice and sustainability (Hicks, 2014). Cowan and Maitles (2012) show engagement with issue-based learning to be an effective means for students to practise active democratic participation skills, to develop more respectful and trusting relationships and to critically consider the humanity of their own values and attitudes. Drawing from a variety of international scholars and practitioners they present a compelling case for issue-based learning to even be included within the primary classroom. This is in recognition of the fact that children of all ages are being exposed to and expressing concern about a wide range of global issues. In so doing Cowan and Maitles (2012) point towards a new vision of schooling where space is made for this kind of issue-based learning opportunity to be provided for all.

However, the intellectual, moral and social aims behind the teaching of global issues place considerable challenge upon teachers and students. This raises the importance of appropriate professional development for teachers in supporting students' learning about and through global issues.

Working with controversy

A key area of challenge for educators seeking to use this issue-based approach is that global issues by their very nature are often interpreted as being *controversial*. This recognition of controversy is important, requiring us as educators to think carefully about the ways in which a given global issue is contested, and how this needs to inform a sensitive and personalised approach. Controversial issues are commonly defined as 'those issues on which our society is clearly divided and significant groups within society advocate conflicting explanations or solutions based on alternative values' (Stradling, 1985; see also Hicks and Holden, 2007). For Deardon (1981: 38) issues are only validly controversial when different 'views can be held . . . without those views being contrary to reason', but we can add to this that controversial issues are often sensitive, drawing different emotive responses from individual people. In their research, Oulton *et al.* (2004: 415) advise that students need to explore controversial issues, but also 'how it is that individuals can apparently hold different perspectives on an issue'. They continue: 'introducing them to multiple perspectives is therefore an essential part of the methods of teaching about controversial issues'.

There is a wide variety of approaches that educators can take to engage students with controversial global issues. For example, Oxfam (2006) identify a range of different roles that a teacher can adopt with students, and these include:

- *Impartial chairperson* – teacher seeks to ensure that a wide variety of viewpoints are represented either through students' statements or stimulus material. In this role the teacher refrains from stating their own opinion.
- *Objective* – teacher seeks to offer a balanced approach where they present students with a wide range of alternative views without stating their own position.
- *Devil's advocate* – teacher adopts a provocative or oppositional position to the one expressed by students or the stimulus material. This helps to provide an atmosphere of challenge within the discussion and can prevent a sense of consensus quickly dominating the participants' exchanges.
- *Declared interest* – teacher makes their position known within the discussion but presents or engages in considering a variety of positions as objectively as possible.

A recurring question regarding teaching controversial global issues is the extent to which educators should remain neutral and should provide a balanced perspective regarding the issue at hand. The actual answer to this question is extremely difficult to arrive at, as it is clearly influenced by a range of contextual factors – such as any laws and regulations within the jurisdiction, the nature of the school, the needs and interests of the students, the specific nature of the given issue, and the character of the individual teacher – that all restrict the value of generalisable solutions. Given this, the following statement from Oulton *et al.* (2004: 416–17) strikes us as of particular resonance:

> While supporting the need to avoid indoctrination, our concern is that the requirement to maintain balance is unhelpful as perfect balance is probably impossible to achieve. Teachers have to make subjective views about what information to present . . . Even if the teacher thinks they have presented matters as fairly as possible, others with different worldviews may still judge the presentation to be biased. An alternative . . . is to be open about the fact that balance can never be fully achieved but counter this by developing in students a critical awareness of bias and make this one of the central learning objectives of the work.

With this in mind, a key task for educators is to be sensitive and wise in their approach to engaging students with controversial global issues, helping them to develop both their critical thinking and critical literacy skills. Critical thinking is essentially concerned with students making judgements over the reasoning underpinning the opinions on global issues that they encounter, and examining the logic and discerning the knowledge basis for different perspectives (Lewis and Chandley, 2012).

Critical literacy can be conceptualised as helping learners to question the social construction of the self, and to consider the sources, assumptions and implications of their own world views. Drawing in particular from the work of Paulo Freire, Ira Shor describes the process of critical literacy as learning to question 'power relations, discourses and identities in a world not yet finished, just, or humane' (Shor, 1999: 1).

Dialogic approaches to issue-based learning

Underpinning a student-centred approach to engaging students with controversial global issues is the use of dialogic learning in the classroom. A dialogic approach seeks to avoid practice that amounts to indoctrination where only one point of view is unproblematically presented as true. It also provides a mechanism through which the educator can attempt to manage their own opinion on a given issue when working with their students, remaining critically aware and mindful of where and how they might be communicating their own personal bias. There exists a broad range of dialogue-based methodologies and resources for educators seeking to develop students' critical enquiry skills through collaboration and deliberation (Hess, 2009). These all place student 'voice' at the heart of pedagogies, requiring students to share their own views and listen to those of others.

A leading example of a dialogical approach is provided by Philosophy in Schools, also sometimes known as Philosophy for Children (P4C). Growing out of the work of Matthew Lipman in the US during the 1970s, Philosophy in Schools has developed into a large and diverse field. Central to Matthew Lipman's work are two inter-related elements, namely *critical thinking* and *communities of inquiry* (Vansieleghem and Kennedy, 2011). By developing critical thinking through participation in discursive *communities of inquiry*, Philosophy in Schools is an approach that integrates individual cognition (critical thinking as the ability to govern oneself) with a property that is communal (critical thinking as the ability to participate within a community). According to Pardales and Girod (2006: 306), a community of inquiry can be understood as involving dialogue about 'topics of interest, in the service of constructing knowledge and common understanding, and internalising the discourse of the inquiring community'.

As Sharp (1997: 12) suggests, adopting a philosophical approach brings numerous benefits, and we can reflect on the ways in which the capacities she sets out are useful for global learning:

> The community of inquiry reflects democracy and initiates the children into the principles and values of this paradigm, it engages young generations in a process of individual and political growth . . . By exercising in school freedom of thought and action, democracy will become their way of living and being when they become active adults within their society.

A range of materials are available to support teachers in developing philosophical inquiry in their schools, in particular the work of Philip Cam (2006). In addition, there are a number of national and international organisations that promote the use of the philosophical, dialogical approach in schools. Leading examples include: the *Society for the Advancement of Philosophical Enquiry and Reflection in Education* (www.sapere.org.uk), *Philosophy for Children New Zealand* (www.p4c.org.nz), the *Federation of Australasian Philosophy in Schools Association* (FAPSA) (www.fapsa. org.au), the *Institute for the Advancement of Philosophy for Children* (www.montclair. edu/cehs/academics/centers-and-institutes/iapc) and the *International Council of Philosophical Inquiry with Children* (http://icpic.org).

Outlined below is an example of educational practice in this area, which used an alternative dialogic methodology specifically designed for introducing controversial global issues in order to develop students' critical literacy skills.

Case study

The Otherwise workshops – University of Leicester, UK

This series of dialogic workshops on controversial global issues is based on a methodology previously developed within an international curriculum development project led by Vanessa de Oliveira Andreotti and titled 'Open Space for Dialogue and Enquiry' (OSDE). The OSDE methodology was specifically referred to within the British Curriculum Review of Diversity and Citizenship led by Keith Ajegbo (DfES, 2007) as an example of effective pedagogy for developing students' critical literacy skills.

The Otherwise workshops aim to create a participatory and collaborative learning space where students encounter different perspectives on pressing global issues, including the points of view of their peers. In the light of these different perspectives, students critically examine their own points of view and receive support in identifying and questioning the assumptions, information sources and implications of their respective positions.

The rationale behind this approach is that learning to live together in a global, diverse and unequal context requires students to develop capacities to negotiate and cope with change, uncertainty and insecurity. Working with multicultural groups of students within higher education, further education and secondary school settings in the Midlands region of the UK, the Otherwise workshops seek in particular to develop intercultural understanding. Each workshop follows a procedure as outlined below:

Step 1 – establishing a set of shared values for participation

The educator first facilitates students identifying the shared values and core conditions required for every individual to feel safe to participate in the workshop. This is in an attempt to establish the trusting, respectful and open conditions conducive to a dialogic enquiry taking place. It requires participants constructing a set of common principles that they voluntarily agree to try and follow together. Here is an example of a model set of core principles:

1   Including everyone: The knowledge each person brings deserves to be actively listened to in order to be understood.

continued . . .

2   Lifelong learning: People can see the world from different points of view that can change and develop over time.
3   Recognising diversity: Our points of view are in part related to who we are and where we come from.
4   Critical engagement: All knowledge, including our own, can be questioned and re-considered through dialogue.

(Andreotti and Warwick, 2007)

With some classes of students, particularly where there has been little previous exchange across the diverse cultural groups, practical activities can be incorporated in order to enhance communication, such as active and empathic listening exercises, and trust building challenges.

Step 2 – critical engagement with different perspectives on a global issue

Students are introduced to a number of stimuli presenting different perspectives on their chosen global issues of interest. Issues covered within the Otherwise workshops have included: climate change; the root causes of poverty; inequality of access to clean drinking water; multiculturalism; and inner city gang culture. The different perspectives on each of these global issues serve to represent alternative worldviews, knowledge bases and values systems. They are presented using a range of web-based resources, television clips, newspaper articles, stories, photographs and external speakers. A key element within the Otherwise workshops to date has been the cultural diversity of participants, so as much room as possible has been made for the students themselves to identify stimuli that reflect this diversity.

Step 3 – personal reflection and first thoughts

Students are provided with the reflective space to contemplate on these different stimuli; considering what they themselves think about the global issue and their personal responses to the different perspectives. This can involve students working either by themselves or in pairs, and drawing, writing down or discussing their thoughts. When conducted within pairs this begins the process of students sharing their points of view and encountering the views of their peers within a deliberative setting; potentially beginning to identify aspects of commonality and difference in perspective.

Step 4 – group dialogue and reflexive questioning

Students raise questions for further deliberation as a community of inquiry. This step utilises participatory procedures such as students constructing in pairs a range of questions and then voting on which ones they commonly hold as being of most interest. During the subsequent dialogue the educator facilitates students in exploring diverse perspectives on the global issue and taking on the challenge of developing their critical literacy skills by analysing assumptions, implications and contradictions. Drawing from the OSDE (2006), methodology questions that the educator might use to facilitate both critical thinking and critical literacy include:

- Where is this perspective coming from? (How did you come to think like this?)
- Where is this perspective leading? (What are the consequences?)
- How could this issue be thought of otherwise? (What are other ways of thinking about this issue?)
- What are the dominant views on this particular issue and why are they dominant and how have they been constructed? (What groups shape this understanding of the issue?)
- Who benefits from this perspective and who does not? (What are the gains and losses for different groups of people, the environment, power relations etc.?)
- How does this global issue connect with other pressing issues (What is the interconnectivity and larger context of this issue?)

Step 5 – closing the dialogic space

The Otherwise workshops close with students reflecting on their participation, providing *feedback*, either written or verbal, on what has been learnt about the global issue, themselves, others, or the learning process. Students are also invited to *feed forward* and identify aspects of the global issue that they might be interested in conducting future enquiry into through free-choice learning, or within future Otherwise workshops.

Staff and student evaluations of the Otherwise workshops indicate a significant shift in intercultural exchanges and relationships being built, not only within, but also beyond the timeframe of the workshops themselves. Students speak of having a growing confidence in being able to sensitively share their views about global issues with peers who might not hold their particular perspective, as well as being more self-aware about their own points of view. They also comment on the high levels of enjoyment of being in a learning space where they are supported in actively listening to one another and talking openly about real world issues of concern.

Activity

Whose perspectives?

Consider creating your own dialogue-based workshop on a topical global issue. First, choose a global issue of concern and interest. Then, seek to identify three different stimuli that illustrate in some way a diversity of perspectives on this global issue.

1   In light of these different perspectives, what questions do you think would be interesting for a group of learners you are familiar with to explore dialogically?
2   What do you consider might be the major challenges of facilitating a dialogue between this group of learners around this particular global issue, and what training or resources do you think might help you in this role?

Problem-based learning

Building upon issue-based approaches within global learning, there are pedagogical methods that seek not only to raise students' consciousness but to more explicitly involve them in considering innovative local solutions to global issues and imagining new futures. Problem-based learning is a participatory student-centred approach, which commonly uses collaborative group work to engage learners with problem exploration (Bessant *et al.*, 2013). It represents a constructivist approach to global learning and draws, in particular, from social learning theory. This is where learning takes place in a group setting that is directed towards collectively solving a specific problem in context. It involves students in the creative social learning processes of action, reflection, communication and negotiation (Wildemeersch, 2009). In doing so, problem-based learning provides students with the opportunity to apply constructive conflict resolution strategies. To facilitate this, Johnson *et al.* (2000) argue that a key aim for educators is to set up constructive controversy in classrooms and to teach young people to deal effectively with conflict through a co-operative problem-solving approach.

Examples of problem-based learning in practice include the use of forum theatre as a method for engaging students in identifying new solutions to the problem of racism in their school, or the establishment of an eco-council with its own virtual learning environment within a secondary school to investigate ways in which the school could reduce its carbon footprint while also reducing its energy bills. These examples help to highlight that, within global citizenship education, blended approaches can be used that employ a range of creative learning strategies including role-play and simulations. They illustrate how online and digital technologies can help enhance student communication and negotiation as well as aid action and reflection as students rigorously investigate a specific problem area within a global issue of concern in order to develop alternative visions of potential solutions. They also facilitate students not only critically considering the validity and evidence base of different proposed solutions, but also reflexively considering their own values and behaviour choices. Outlined below is another example of practice in this area, which uses a values-based approach to engaging students with global problems.

Case study

'A Fairtrade World': Lifeworlds Learning, UK

Lifeworlds Learning is a community interest company in the UK that focuses on creating learning encounters (for students) and professional development opportunities (for teachers) that enable individuals to better connect their own lifeworlds with those of others and, beyond this, with the wider world. This pioneering approach interprets the 'lifeworld' as being the evolving total of individuals' lived experiences including their attitudes, opinions, actions and feelings – all of which are underpinned by values.

With values at the core, this organisation's engagement with global learning is primarily through a pedagogy called 'Learning Through Values' (LTV). Rob Bowden, the strategic director of Lifeworlds Learning, explains that while complex in application, the premise of LTV can be considered as a journey involving four key stages:

1   Exploration of self – discovering our own values: what we think and why.
2   Engagement with others – discovering other perspectives and challenging our own.
3   Seeing our agency – developing confidence, building language, finding our voice.
4   Shaping our lifeworlds – reorganisation of self: new ways of being and belonging.

As a pedagogy, LTV is about process and not content. It is not values, character, moral, or ethical education, whereby a predetermined set of values are taught. It is instead dialogic, philosophical, critical and personal in its approach.

The LTV approach uses Bigger Than Self (BTS) issues as stimuli for a learning journey to be built upon. One such global problem that is used in this way is fairness within world trade.

'A Fairtrade World' is a student workshop exploring the BTS issues of 'fairness', 'justice' and 'trade' using the LTV approach. The workshop evolves around a giant walk-on map of the world (5 × 4 m) that has the immediate effect of engaging students (and teachers) in the world beyond self and becomes the canvas through which they collectively paint more complex pictures. Fairness, for instance, is explored by students physically representing real data on the global distribution of people and wealth, or human indicators such as life expectancy and nutrition. The physical element brings data alive and the visual impact allows children to sense and feel the issue (developing empathy over sympathy, and justice over charity for example).

Trade-chains that physically represent the story of goods they may see at home, school or in the shops add meaning to the presence of a logo or brand, and children reference feelings (and values) of solidarity, rights, responsibility and interdependence, for example. Case studies give names and voices to data and products and provide the basis for drama and storytelling

continued . . .

that deepens students' experience of different perspectives and helps them to question their own.

Crucially, 'A Fairtrade World' does not aim to instruct or message, but instead aims to stimulate thinking, provides context and supports students to re-integrate their learning into their own lifeworlds. Its pedagogical approach seeks to empower learners as active global citizens: confident, willing and able to make informed choices. In turn this is intended to make a positive contribution towards building resilient learning communities, equipped to deal with the unfolding uncertainties that characterise twenty-first-century living, and learning, for students and teachers alike.

More information about the lifeworlds approach can be found at www. lifeworldslearning.co.uk.

Service-learning

An extended way of engaging students in global learning is for it to not only involve critical engagement with pressing issues, or to imagine solutions to global challenges, but for it to major on experiential engagement through direct action, as previously highlighted within problem-based learning. Building on experiential educational approaches to learning, another pedagogy for critical, creative and collaborative engagement of global citizens is service-learning. The goal of service-learning can be broadly summarised as integrating student personal development with community development agendas. The National Service Learning Clearing House (www.service learning.org), one of the largest resources in the field in the United States, describe service-learning as 'a teaching and learning strategy that integrates meaningful community service with instruction and reflection to enrich the learning experience, teach civic responsibility, and strengthen communities'. Within global citizenship education, service-learning can be used to actively engage learners in a range of global issues, within their schools and local communities. Examples include students creating a vegetable garden within their school grounds and in so doing reducing food miles and the carbon footprint of their school meals, or students running a city-centre homework cafe to specifically support peers who are learning to study in their second language. In some cases, service-learning can also be achieved through international exchanges and field trips, although great care needs to be taken to ensure mutual value for the host country and community rather than it being of benefit to the visiting students alone (Bringle et al., 2011).

Service-learning is an experiential learning process that is underpinned by notions of praxis, where experience is fused with critical reflection. Service-learning draws on a range of experiential pedagogical theories located across the work of John Dewey and David Kolb, among others (Annette, 2010). Speck and Hoppe (2004) help us to understand the diversity of approaches to service-learning, referencing three models: the philanthropic model; the civic engagement model; and the communitarian model. Common aspects of service-learning – regardless of its political context, educational rationale and philosophical underpinnings – are built around the development of core inter- and intra-personal skills and attributes. These resonate closely with the global citizenship skills framed by Oxfam discussed earlier in this chapter.

A growing body of research has pointed to the personal, educational and societal benefits of engagement in service-learning (Speck and Hoppe, 2004; Bernacki and Bernt, 2007; Hart, 2007). Hecht (2003: 28) illustrates the potential benefits of service-learning in the following way:

> Service-learning enriches a student's world, providing new experiences and challenges. Through planning, service and reflection, students are encouraged to examine the tasks at hand, to develop plans for dealing with the obvious and unexpected, to take action, and to consider how these actions are understandable given other academic and life knowledge. Service-learning is neither passive nor solitary. Rather, students deal with real-life activities in naturalistic settings. It is these features that make service-learning unique from most other types of learning.

Similarly, Bringle *et al.* (2011) hold international service-learning as a pedagogy that is ideally suited for preparing students as active global citizens in the twenty-first century, pointing in particular to its transformational potential for producing deep and lasting changes in present and future lives.

There remain, however, important areas of debate into the learning impact of service-learning approaches and the influence of key variables such as gender, ethnicity and the socio-economic background of participants. Within the UK, research has highlighted the lack of provision of structured and comprehensive and equitable opportunities for service-learning within formal schooling, despite the introduction of Citizenship Education in 2002 as a statutory subject area within secondary schooling (Cleaver *et al.*, 2007). Elsewhere, the provision of service-learning has been far more successfully integrated into formal education – in particular in the US with many schools and HE institutions incorporating service-learning components within their notions of graduate capabilities.

Key challenges for educators integrating this particular pedagogical approach within the schooling system include the complexity of teachers needing to move their learning spaces beyond the classroom and school, and out into community, including perhaps engagement with international settings. This requires educators to establish mutually beneficial connections and partnerships with community-based organisa- tions and service providers (Ellis, 2005). In particular, the importance of connections and partnership with informal youth organisations, that can have a rich heritage of engaging young people in participative and community-based activity, are being increasingly recognised. This partnership approach by educators helps to ensure that learners have the opportunity to engage in service within their communities, and that such service has an explicit pedagogical underpinning.

Another important consideration for educators is to recognise that the global citizenship engagement of young people within their communities may not always be experienced as positive. While we would want to emphasise the positive effects that service-learning can bring, it is essential that educators are wise to the fact that for some students, and for varying reasons, individual activities may sometimes become problematic. Engagement within communities is often a dynamic process, and at times complex, messy, challenging and not without tension (Gearon, 2004). The best forms of service-learning help young people by providing a mediating space that facilitates deliberative processes and reflective learning for those who might initially lack the confidence and interpersonal attributes to participate without structured support. Without effective pedagogical support the danger is that many students will be lost to the early experience of challenge, resistance and pragmatic setbacks in their enterprising efforts to make a difference through service-learning.

Leighton (2012) raises a further criticism from his own research with regard to the nature of active citizenship opportunities, such as service-learning, within schools. He cites incidents of students being *compelled* to volunteer in the community rather than participating in discussing, planning and evaluating community action of their own volition. This raises an important area of consideration for educators wishing to incorporate a service-learning aspect to global citizenship education, regarding the level of autonomy students are afforded, particularly where collaboration and team working are structural elements. There are also concerns over the nature and extent of relationships between students undertaking the service and community members who can be just recipients (rather than active participants) of the service, and this is particularly the case when it comes to international service-learning (Gelmon and Billig, 2007; Bringle *et al.*, 2011; Porfilio and Hickman, 2011).

The creativity mandate of service-learning involves working with students' enthusiasm and passion in order to provide the facilitating structure to enable them to envision, design and test their own ideas for transformative civic engagement. For this reason, service-learning places considerable professional development demands on educators to master its practices and to be sensitive to its tensions and complexities as well as it benefits and potential. To conclude, service-learning is a radical and transformative agenda within global citizenship education, the effective and equitable implementation of which will not be without difficulty. As such it is unlikely to be a panacea, but rather can provide a framework for supporting young people's learning through engagement with their communities as global citizens.

Activity

Developing service-learning for global citizens

Consider for a moment taking on the task of establishing a global citizen service-learning provision within your professional context and how you might approach the following question areas:

1   A common rationale for service-learning to be introduced into the UK context has been the notion of a civic deficit; that is, the framing of young people as being increasingly apathetic about public life (QCA, 1998). Many practitioners and scholars have challenged the basis of this negative stereotype of young people, but what is your view of young people within your local context? Do you think your students would be interested in participating in global citizenship service-learning opportunities? How might an invitation to engage with service-learning be most effectively pitched?

2   What organisations exist locally that could support you with the necessary network of resources and community action sites?

3   What do you consider to be your professional development and training needs in this particular area of pedagogy?

Spaces for global learning

With constructivist, student-centred notions of learning dominating within global citizenship education (rather than teacher-centred, transmissive approaches), interest is also developing in the role played by the physical learning environments in which learning is embedded. A number of studies have considered the characteristics of the physical learning environment and their potential impact upon student learning at school level (for example, Dudek, 2000; Taylor, 2009; Woolner, 2010). Boys (2011) highlights the need to consider the influence of learning spaces from a number of perspectives, including the social processes of learning that physical environments facilitate. This emerging area of pedagogical research supports a consideration of innovative and diverse designs for flexible learning contexts within global learning. It is therefore important to consider the range of different spaces that are possible to be utilised to engage students critically, creatively and collaboratively. What follows is a brief summary of commonly available learning space types, which draws from the work of Futurelab (Rudd *et al.*, 2009):

- *large group spaces* – areas that are used for presentations or performances or for large crowds of students to meet and engage in global learning activities together, such as summits and meetings;
- *small group spaces* – areas for deliberative engagement with a small group of peers working towards the same global learning goal through co-operative and collaborative processes;
- *personal solitude spaces* – areas that are designed specifically for independent study and quiet concentration, providing the space to consider for oneself, to take an interlude for new ideas to emerge or for solutions to encountered problems to be imagined;
- *relaxation spaces* – areas that are used by students to meet and socialise, perhaps to play or simply rest and sit down;
- *exercise spaces* – outdoor or indoor areas specifically designed and landscaped to encourage learning to be physically active through play and games;
- *specialist spaces* – these learning spaces may provide scientific equipment, digital technology or social media resources, for example, to engage students in global learning;
- *transition spaces* – thoroughfares, pathways and corridors that allow for easy movement between different learning areas that in themselves could be used for global learning purposes;
- *eating spaces* – areas used for preparing and eating food where students and educators share meals together – again can be viewed as an important learning space for potential global citizenship education purposes;

- *exhibition spaces* – a place for learners to authentically display and share their work and to see and hear about the inspiring work of others;
- *natural spaces* – outdoor environments, either within the campus or nearby, that can be used for immersive learning opportunities where learners can explore and discover.

Activity

Global learning beyond the classroom

As has been highlighted in this chapter, global learning for global citizenship supports the use of increasingly 'fluid' and integrated pedagogical models, exemplified by the application of blended learning across a variety of learning spaces. One commonly used vehicle for incorporating the global dimension within schools has been north–south school linking initiatives. With an integrated approach, these partnerships can be infused across the school curriculum as well as influence the school ethos and value structure. From the outset it is important to state that, as with all the pedagogical approaches discussed in this chapter, the school link initiative needs to be sensitively designed and carefully implemented. Relationships between the two schools need to be problematised in recognition that they are being established in often unequal contexts. As Martin (2007) warns, it is vital that the link does not endorse traditional stereotypes of dependency between north and south or repeat exploitative or patronising interaction.

Where two schools mutually and co-constructively form a partnership to create joint global learning experiences, possible benefits include:

- helping students gain new knowledge and understanding of other people and places, and in so doing;
- counteracting prejudice and stereotypical points of view about other people, and developing empathy towards other people and their ways of life;
- encouraging students to develop a knowledge and understanding of themselves, their local neighbourhood and country;
- enabling students to communicate to others this understanding of themselves, their community and environment, and their feelings and attitudes towards them;
- students developing a deeper sense of belonging and responsibility both locally and globally;
- engaging with different perspectives on key concepts such as inter-connection, justice, equality and sustainability.

Common school linking activities can include:

1   Classes exchanging creative work such as paintings, poetry, performances, stories and artefacts that they have written or collected. These can be then used as teaching aids in both schools.

2   Schools investigating and exchanging factual information about their area (e.g., what is made or grown locally).
3   Students exploring common global concerns (e.g., fair trade, climate change) from different perspectives and exchanging questions and information for deliberation, or organising joint service-learning ventures.
4   Staff sharing examples of global learning practice and innovation as a means of mutual professional development.

Drawing from the research of Young (2006), Martin (2007), Disney (2008) and Bourn and Cara (2013), as well as the experiences of linking organisations such as UK One World Linking Association (UKOWLA), a number of principles of good practice can be identified. School links need to be mutual, equal and partnership-based; with staff and students from both schools able to co-construct the nature of the link, agreeing its objectives, curriculum foci and timetabling. The link needs to engage staff and students in critically considering key concepts of mutual interest such as justice and sustainability. The profile and long-term security of the link is often helped by identifying cross-curricular themes rather than the link being housed within a single academic subject area. Finally developing the school link is a learning process in itself – coming into a deeper understanding of the agendas and needs of both partnering schools and their different challenges of context will undoubtedly require adjustments and learning from mistakes along the way.

As a final activity in this chapter, imagine that you have helped establish a school link and that a mutually agreed topic for the link to explore has been agreed as climate change. Seek to design a range of learning activities or resources that together offer a fluid and blended learning approach, using as many if not all of the ten learning spaces identified in the previous section.

Consider how you could integrate other learning spaces into your school linking project that our list above has overlooked.

Conclusion

By focusing on global learning for global citizenship, this chapter has begun to explore the ways in which educators can utilise a range of pedagogical approaches that are effective for helping students to learn to live together in a diverse and unequal context. We have presented the need for critical, creative and collaborative learning opportunities to support students with considering the different perspectives of others, while also reflexively considering their own sense of the world around them, its possibilities and choices. Reflection upon the nature of teaching and learning as framed by scholars such as Freire (1998), Fielding and Moss (2011) and Tasker (2008), with a particular focus on the aims of global citizenship education has led us to derive the following ten educational principles for a student centred approach to Global Learning:

1 *holistic* – each student's individual learning needs are met through attention being given to holistic aspects such as intellectual, moral, social and emotional development;

2 *personalised* – each student is personally known, with attention to their cultural contexts, unique personal experiences and global learning preferences;

3 *flexible* – a range of learning spaces provide for small-group, one-to-one and independent global learning;

4 *partnered* – all stakeholders are vital partners in the development and progress of global learning, including students themselves;

5 *equal* – each student's contribution to the group's learning process is vital and of worth;

6 *convivial* – learning is facilitated by an immersion in a friendly and lively atmosphere, where global learners listen in order to understand each other and are both encouraged and challenged;

7 *democratic* – all students are involved in decision-making processes within the global learning initiative;

8 *well-being based* – the educational action that forms the basis of global learning is underpinned by an active consideration of the well-being of others and the environment;

9 *rigorous* – the learning process is thorough, and is developed with close attention to being research informed and reflective;

10 *participative* – students are actively involved in core elements of the educational process.

While this list is by no means exhaustive, it represents one response to the concerns that continue to be raised over how global citizens can be better equipped to navigate the complexity of the world in which they live (Cowan and Maitles, 2012). Education is increasingly being seen as a key process through which students can develop the global awareness, skills and competencies that global citizenship requires. Global learning is essentially about students thinking, relating and living in a profoundly different way in the twenty-first century. It is a holistic cross-cutting theme within education, presenting reform implications for pedagogy and the culture of educational institutions; their organisational structures, aims and ethos. It represents a new paradigm of the educational mission in the twenty-first century rather than simply another educational objective that can easily be bolted onto existing subject-based patterns of schooling. In the chapters that follow, we turn our focus to considering some of the key substantive concerns and issues that comprise global learning – namely, interconnectedness and interdependency, cultural diversity, social justice and sustainability.

Questions for further investigation

1 How has your vision for global learning in the twenty-first century moved on in light of this chapter?

2 What are the pedagogies that you consider to be most apt for global learning and what are the key barriers for such pedagogies to be developed within your own practice and institutional/community settings?

3   Should engagement with controversial global issues be offered within primary schools as Cowan and Maitles (2012) argue, or should we not burden children with awareness of such 'tragedies', seeking to protect their childhood innocence for as long as possible?

Further reading

Cowan, P. and Maitles, H. (eds) (2012) *Teaching Controversial Issues in the Classroom*. London: Continuum.
This book draws upon a wide range of expert contributors to explore inclusive approaches to citizenship education and the teaching of controversial issues. In so doing, it not only grapples with a broad range of academic debates in this area, but also includes practical insights from numerous international case studies.

Hicks, D. (2014) *Educating for Hope in Troubled Times: Climate Change and the Transition to a Post-carbon Future*. Stoke on Trent: Trentham.
Provides an insightful exploration of how education can engage students with three of the most pressing global issues facing society today: climate change, peak oil and the limits to growth. It does this with particular attention to the affective as well as cognitive domains of learning and with a sensitivity towards how students can be engaged in hopeful and optimistic ways that inspire a sense that change is possible.

Scoffham, S. and Martin, F. (2013) *Frameworks for Intercultural Learning*. Free online resource at www.gpml.org.uk.
This website of resources, links and research vignettes for use by staff and students draws from the insights of a three-year research project on Global Partnerships for Mutual Learning funded by the Economic and Social Research Council in the UK. It provides some excellent food for thought across seven areas of relationships, development, culture, assumptions, identify, charity and footprints.

Wierenga, A. and Guevara, R. (eds) (2013) *Educating for Global Citizenship – A Youth-led Approach to Learning Through Partnerships*. Melbourne: Melbourne University Press.
This book explores educating for global citizenship through a youth-led approach. It draws from a case study of the Global Connections programme introduced into Australian schools and Indonesian communities by Plan International Australia. In so doing it provides a thought-provoking model of inter-agency and cross-sectoral education partnerships for global citizenship education.

Chapter 3

Interconnectedness and interdependency

Chapter objectives

By the end of this chapter you should have:

- considered the nature of global interconnectedness and interdependency;
- explored this nature in relation to governance, economics, global civil society and new technologies;
- reflected on different approaches to teaching and learning about and for diversity, giving particular thought to their applicability within your own contexts.

Introduction

In Chapters 1 and 2 we explored the meanings of globalisation, global citizenship and global education, and considered the importance of thinking carefully about our aims, intentions and pedagogies for supporting students' global learning. In this chapter we take a more detailed look at some of the various processes of globalisation, which have resulted in the world becoming increasingly interconnected *and* interdependent. In this chapter we view interconnectedness and interdependency as similar but importantly differentiated terms. To live in an interconnected world means that humans live in a world featuring multiple inter-related structures, organisations and attachments. An event in one corner of the world has implications for everyone, whether it is at an individual, local, national or global level. To live in an interdependent world refers to the sense that more than being connected, nations and humans need each other. Interdependency extends beyond familial, local and national boundaries, and can be seen in the relationships between nations as well as organisations that exist in the space beyond nations.

There are many ways to explore the nature of global interconnectedness and interdependence. In this chapter we structure the analysis by developing in more detail some of the main forms of globalisation identified in the first chapter – global governance, global economics, global civil society and global technology. As you read through the chapter you should also reflect on the inter-relationship between top-down and bottom-up understandings of globalisation. While the former focuses on the political, legal and economic organisations and structures that influence the world, the latter starts from the position of individuals and how they do (and could) envisage themselves as active agents locally, nationally and globally. As we have considered so far in this book, good educational provision for global learning *combines* a knowledge and understanding of the former with a recognition and appreciation of the latter. It also raises questions about the possibility of 'world citizenship' – a term that has received some attention within educational literature (see, for example, Golmohamad, 2009).

Global interconnectedness and interdependence: an illustration

The challenge with incorporating issue-based approaches within global learning is the complexity of the chains of interconnectedness and interdependence that exist and the diversity of perspectives that are held on these links. This is typified for example by the difficulty of efforts to engage students in the controversial issue of the implications and global coverage of the attacks that took place in the United States on 11 September in 2001. Consider for a moment the following chain of events:

- On 11 September 2001, nineteen members of al-Qaeda launched a series of suicide attacks on mainland United States of America, involving four hijacked passenger planes. Two planes were flown into the North and South Towers of the World Trade Center in New York, one of the planes was flown into the Pentagon, and the fourth crashed in Pennsylvania following attempts by passengers to combat the hijackers. In total, 2996 people died in the attacks.
- Shortly after the first plane hit the World Trade Center, news channels around the world started broadcasting events as they unfolded. Subsequent images of terror and human suffering were replayed and republished around the world through a range of media, including the attacks themselves, people fleeing from the scene, the response of emergency services, President Bush being informed while talking with a class of elementary age students, and the towers collapsing.
- Within approximately an hour of the first attack, flights within mainland United States were grounded, with many flights destined for the US redirected or cancelled leading to aviation disruption around the world.
- In a speech made on 20 September 2001 to a joint session of Congress and to the people of the United States, President George Bush (2001) referred to the attacks as 'an act of war' and made demands against the Taliban in Afghanistan under the threat of military action. In the speech, Bush pledged a 'war against terror' that would 'not end until every terrorist group of global reach has been found, stopped and defeated'. Part of the US' strategy was to investigate any connection between Iraq and the 9/11 attacks and to challenge their alleged possession of weapons of mass destruction.
- In October 2001, the United States and the United Kingdom commenced war against the Taliban rulers in Afghanistan. Later that year, the United Nations Security Council established the International Security Assistance Force (ISAF) to train the Afghan National Security Forces and to support the rebuilding of institutions. The ISAF were subsequently taken control of by NATO.

- In January 2002, the United States established a military prison within the Guantanamo Bay Naval Base. The prison has been used to hold 'prisoners of war' resulting from the 'war on terror', and has received international criticism from a range of organisations – including Amnesty International and the United Nations – for its operation and breach of the international rules of law. The closure of Guantanamo Bay formed an important element of President Obama's first presidential campaign in 2008, but at of the time of writing the prison remains open.
- In a 'Letter to America' published in 2002, al-Qaeda's leader Osama Bin Laden cited a number of reasons for the attacks. These focused predominantly on elements of US foreign policy in relation to Somalia, Chechnya and a number of states in the Middle East.
- In 2002, the United Nations Security Council issued Resolution 1441. This provided Iraq – and its leader Saddam Hussein – a final chance to ensure compliance with previous resolutions that had prohibited the production of weapons of mass destruction subsequent to the Gulf War in the 1990s. Iraq accepted the resolution and permitted entry to UN weapons inspectors. The subsequent interpretation of the UN weapons inspectors' findings led to a great deal of contestation within the UN Security Council. The United States and the United Kingdom claimed that Iraq was in material breach of Resolution 1441, and therefore war was a justifiable consequence. Other members of the Security Council, most notably France, Germany and Russia, disagreed, seeking a further resolution rather than immediate war. The United States, the United Kingdom and Spain presented a revised resolution to the Security Council, giving a deadline to disarm by 17 March 2003 that was rejected by France (King and Hamilos, 2006). Given the impasse, the United States, United Kingdom and Spain gave their own ultimatum to Iraq and subsequently commenced military action against Iraq at the end of March 2003.
- On 15 February 2003, millions of people in cities around the world marched against war. The march against the war in London was Britain's largest ever demonstration, while the march in Rome was attended by around 2 million people (Syalm, Alderson and Milner, 2003).
- On 2 May 2011, Osama Bin Laden was killed by US Navy Seals in Pakistan. According to many news reports, the operation was unknowingly covered by an IT consultant living close to Bin Laden's compound via Twitter (BBC, 2011), while the story was leaked by Keith Urbahn, a former Chief of Staff to the former Defence Secretary Donald Rumsfeld (Newman, 2011). The amount of tweets posted between 10:45pm and 2:20am Eastern Time set the record for the highest sustained rate of tweets ever, with an average of 3440 tweets per second during that period (Sutter, 2011).

Exposing students to this representation of a single chain of events fails to represent the complexity and contested nature of each incident and their relationships with one another. It is also somewhat selective, excluding other events and chains of interconnectivity from consideration before, during and after the timeline it depicts. But, as a stimulus, this chain of events highlights an important range of complex topic areas for consideration in global learning such as: international relations and diplomacy; the role of supra-national organisations such as the United Nations and NATO; global capitalism; news consumption; global civil society; and global digital technology.

In light of such complexity, as educators it is important that we consider what system frameworks we can provide to help students navigate connections between global issues and to help them consider the interconnectivity of their own lives in an interdependent world. In the rest of this chapter we will consider four frameworks of connection: (1) the main political organisations and institutions that oversee global governance, and how these relate to national political institutions; (2) global economic organisations, and how these relate to national political and economic institutions; (3) the nature and operation of global civil society; and (4) new forms of social and digital media. As we consider each of these in turn, and in line with the approach of the previous two chapters, we ask you to remember that meaningful global education does not focus solely on knowledge, but also requires the development of essential skills, including those of inquiry, critical thinking and reflection, advocacy and empathy.

Global governance

> We are caught in an inescapable network of mutuality, tied in a single garment of destiny. Whatever affects one directly, affects all indirectly.
>
> (Martin Luther King, 1963)

Is there, and if not will there ever be, a world government? If the answer to either of these questions is yes, then what form does/would this world government take, and what implications does/would this have for national governments? These are questions that have been asked for centuries, but which have taken on a renewed sense of importance and relevance over the last thirty years. The questions themselves are largely empirical – about what has happened, what is happening, and about what may or may not be possible in the future. In addition to these empirical questions, globalising processes also raise a number of normative questions about the desirability, form and scope of world government. For example, is world government desirable? If it is, why? If not, why not? Even if a world government is possible, what form should it take and what powers should it have?

Of course, in answering these questions we need to be careful and precise about the terms we are using. What, for example, is meant by 'world government' and how does this differ from associated terms such as global governance? For the purposes of simplicity we consider the term 'world government' to refer to an institution or set of institutions that have both the authority and legitimacy to govern the world independently of national governments. Such institutions would have executive, legislative and judicial powers, and may also have military power. At the time of writing, nothing close to world government exists in these terms, and so world government remains (depending on your point of view) as an ideal to be pursued, as something to be resisted, or as something that remains an impossibility. In some ways, the lack of anything close to approaching true world government does not reflect the course that globalisation has taken in other areas – including the economy and civil society (which we explore later in this chapter). According to Zürn (2004: 261), for example, the absence 'of a fully developed transnational political community is *incongruous* with the existence of transnational social spaces'. While as educators we should be mindful of the discussions around world government, our work with students in schools will predominantly focus on the existing institutions, organisations and networks through which global decisions and policies are constructed. For this reason, in this section we keep in the background speculative accounts of what world government could and should be, and instead focus predominantly on the *actual* institutions which symbolise governance at the global level.

When the term 'global governance' is used, it is generally employed in relation to forms of international co-operation embodied through a range of international organisations (Zürn, 2004). The period since the end of the Second World War has witnessed a proliferation in international organisations, institutions, and international agreements and treaties. These have particular features that it is important for us to note. First, the organisations themselves are for the most part *intergovernmental* and *transnational*. This means that they are brought about by and are dependent on national governments. As is made clear in *The United Nations Matters Teacher's Handbook* produced by the United Nations Association of the UK (UNA-UK, 2012: 2), the United Nations 'is not a "world government". Its activities are governed by its 193 member states and are the result of (often complex) political negotiations'. An important aspect of this intergovernmentality is the recognition that while nations remain the primary unit of political sovereignty across the world, national governments need to engage in the international political community. In this way, nation-states are interdependent as well as interconnected. This recognition is not new, and has been evident since at least the early part of the twentieth century. The nature of intergovernmentality is, however, fluid and dynamic and has been shaped in recent years by significant changes to international relations brought about by a number of processes – including de-colonisation, the ending of the cold war, and the democratising of formerly communist states.

Second, if we take the example of international agreements and treaties, these are frequently pronounced at an international level, but their ratification is dependent on national state-level governments. The United Nations Universal Declaration of Human Rights, the Kyoto Protocol to the United Nations Framework Convention on Climate Change, and the Millennium Development Goals each provide good examples of this process (Oxhorn, 2007). As Anthony Giddens (2000: 20) has suggested, the nation-state is not 'disappearing or losing its power in the world, but it is being reshaped, especially in the West and especially in Europe'.

To understand the nature of the reshaping of nations referred to by Giddens, we need to understand the main transnational, intergovernmental political bodies and organisations that operate today, many of which we set out below. We do not claim that the list provided below is exhaustive, but it does cover the central transnational bodies that students in schools are likely to encounter – both within their school education and also in their wider lives.

The United Nations (www.un.org): It makes sound sense to commence any exploration of transnational political bodies with the United Nations (UN), established in

1945 following the Second World War. The UN has three primary aims – to secure international peace, to eliminate poverty and to protect human rights (UNA-UK, 2012). The UN consists of 193 member states, and is structured around a number of organs (such as the General Assembly, the Security Council and the International Court of Justice). The UN also oversees a range of highly influential agencies, including the World Health Organisation, the World Bank Group, the United Nations Education, Scientific and Cultural Organization (UNESCO), and the United Nations Children's Fund (UNICEF). In this chapter we have already touched upon the central role of the UN and its Security Council in negotiating conflicts above, and we return to the work of its various agencies elsewhere in this book. The work of the UN is constructed through co-operation and negotiation between its 193 member states, as well as through the work of its key organs. A central element of the workings of the UN is the drafting of declarations and treaties that member states are able to ratify. Perhaps the leading example is the United Nations Universal Declaration of Human Rights that we explore in detail in Chapter 5.

Case study

Model United Nations (www.una.org.uk/globe)

As we explored in Chapter 2, active learning is a pedagogical strategy central to global learning. A profitable way of doing this is to develop and enact 'model' forums that demonstrate the ways key organisations work and that allow and enable students to engage in the sorts of issues on which the organisations are focused. A leading example is provided by Model United Nations (MUN). Help and advice on setting up a MUN can be found on the website of the United Nations Association UK – www.una.org.uk/mun.

Model UN programmes are structured around role-playing a meeting of one of the UN's committees or bodies. These typically include:

- Security Council committees
- General Assembly committees
- Conference on Trade and Development
- Human Rights Council
- Peacebuilding Commission
- Economic and Social Council (such as Sustainable Development or Social Development).

Children and young people from across the world participate in MUNs. Their flexibility provides possibilities for students of different ages and for inclusion in the curriculum in a range of ways. They can take place over a few hours or can be structured around a whole week's worth of activities, and can involve students from one school or across a number of schools.

There are four basic principles of Model UN programmes:

1   Participants are assigned a UN Member State. They assume the role of that country's diplomats at whichever UN body is being enacted. The delegations represent the views of 'their' country, reflecting that country's national interests, rather than their own personal opinions on an issue.
2   The delegates research their country's position on selected topics, paying particular attention to their country's perspective on the topics to be discussed at the Model UN. The topics are issues of global importance – such as provision of clean water, economic justice or the Israeli-Palestinian conflict.
3   The delegations come together and enact the UN meeting, based on agreed rules of procedure. The delegates present statements of their countries' positions and debate and negotiate with the other delegations, both through formal and informal debate.
4   A resolution is written, debated, negotiated and amended, in line with each country's interests and in response to the debate. Votes are held on the resolution and the amendments. A final resolution is produced, which is acceptable to a majority of delegations and represents the final product of the meeting.

(www.una.org.uk/mun)

As these principles highlight, through engaging in Model UN role-plays, students can build an understanding of the work and structure of the UN, gain a deeper awareness of the issue under discussion and develop a range of inter-personal and intra-personal skills and capacities (including adopting the perspectives of others, listening and responding to the views of others, working in a group, problem solving and critical thinking).

UNA-UK provide further teaching materials on the UN via their website: www.una.org.uk/content/united-nations-matters-teaching-pack.

The European Union (www.europa.eu): The European Union (EU), an economic and political entity with twenty-eight member states, is often cited as the leading example of transnational government. Developed within Europe over the last seventy years, the EU started as an economic organisation between six member states – the European Economic Community (EEC) of Belgium, France, Italy, Luxembourg, the Netherlands and West Germany – brought about by the Treaty of Rome in 1957. From the establishment of the EEC until the early 1990s, membership of the EEC grew and in 1979 the first elections to the European Parliament were held. The Maastricht Treaty signed in 1992 led to the renaming of the European Community (EC) as the European Union, and made preparations for a single currency (the euro) which was introduced across many EU nations in 2002. The EU is governed by seven main institutions:

1   the European Parliament (directly elected by universal suffrage every five years with legislative power, but not legislative initiative);
2   the Council of the European Union (comprised of ministers from each of the individual member states);
3   the European Commission (the body responsible for the daily running of the EU, made up of twenty-eight commissioners – one for each member state);
4   the European Council (the body that shapes the general direction of the EU, comprised of the President of the European Council, the President of the European Commission and the head of government or state of each member nation);
5   the European Central Bank (the central financial institution of the EU that oversees the euro and monetary policy);
6   the Court of Justice of the European Union (the central judicial body within the EU comprising both the European Court of Justice and the General Court); and
7   the European Court of Auditors (the body that oversees the accounts of EU institutions).

While the EU is perhaps the clearest international example of a transnational economic union, the extent to which it represents a full political union is contested. Certainly, some elements of the EU conform to supra-national governance, but these sit alongside, and are dependent on, intergovernmental agreements. A range of options – including opt-outs on certain matters – are available to different member states to retain sovereignty on particular issues and, of course, each member state holds the ultimate sovereignty to withdraw their participation in the union altogether. An integral aspect of the EU has been its commitment to education, and democratic education more specifically. This is exemplified by the 2010 *Council of Europe Charter on Education for Democratic Citizenship and Human Rights Education* (Council of Europe, 2010), as well as the 2005 *European Year of Citizenship Through Education*.

The African Union (www.au.int): The African Union (AU) consists of fifty-four African states and was established in 2001 as a successor to the Organisation of African Unity. The AU works to develop greater unity between African states and their people, to defend the interests of member states, and operates for peace and co-operation. The main decision-making body of the AU is its Assembly, constituted of the heads of state or government from each member nation, while the Pan African Parliament is the AU's representative body and is elected by the national parliaments of member states. Plans have been in place for an African Court of Justice to act as the main judicial body of the AU, but these have recently been replaced with plans for an African Court of Justice and Human Rights.

The Commonwealth (thecommonwealth.org): The Commonwealth comprises fifty-three member nations, and its policies are based on cooperation between these members. The Charter of the Commonwealth signed by members in 2013 sets out its commitment to a number of 'core values and principles', including democracy, human rights, international peace and security, sustainable development, access to health, education, food and shelter, and the role of civil society (The Commonwealth, 2013). The *Commonwealth Class* (http://schoolsonline.britishcouncil.org/classroom-resources/commonwealth-class) education resource for schools and teachers produced by the British Council provides a range of online and downloadable activities and initiatives for engaging students in learning about the Commonwealth. The resource also provides online learning courses for teachers.

G7/G8: The G7/G8 refers to the group of seven/eight industrialised countries who meet regularly to discuss matters of international significance. The group originated in the 1970s as a group of six nations (France, Italy, Japan, West Germany, the United Kingdom and the United States), and then expanded to become the G7 (including Canada) and then the G8 (including Russia). Typically, the terms are used to refer to meetings of heads of government, but meetings also take place between ministers responsible for specific policy areas (for example, finance or the environment). Over the last twenty years, membership of the G8 has been under question. Meetings have frequently included five of the newly developed leading industrial nations – Brazil, China, India, Mexico and South Africa (though these nations have not officially become members of the G8 group). At the time of writing the future of the G8 is under threat from diplomatic tensions arising over the future of the Crimea between Russia and its other members. The tensions have led the German Chancellor, Angela Merkel, to declare that effectively the G8 no longer exists and as such that the organisation should be considered as the G7 (BBC, 2014).

Association of South East Asian Nations (www.aseansec.org): The Association of South East Asian Nations (ASEAN) is a political and economic group of ten nations that seek to support and promote economic growth, peace and stability and social development. ASEAN has sought to expand its co-operative relationships with its near neighbours, including working to establish close connections with China, Japan and South Korea, as well as developing a larger East Asia free trade agreement including Australia and New Zealand. ASEAN was central to the development of the annual East Asia Summit that brings together eighteen nations, including Russia and the United States.

Organization of American States (www.oas.org): According to its website, the Organization of American States (OAS) is the world's oldest inter-regional organisation having its roots in the then International Union of American Republics, established in the late 1800s. The OAS was established in 1948, and the first Article of its Charter (www.oas.org) sets out its being as 'an order of peace and justice, to promote their solidarity, to strengthen their collaboration, and to defend their sovereignty, their territorial integrity and their independence'. The OAS is structured around a range of institutions, overseen by its supreme organ – the General Assembly.

North Atlantic Treaty Organization (www.nato.int): Established in 1949, the North Atlantic Treaty Organization (NATO) is an intergovernmental political and military alliance. It comprises twenty-eight member nations who agree to work together as a combined operation in response to particular threats and situations. NATO's objectives include promoting and furthering democratic values, resolving disputes peacefully and managing crises effectively. NATO engagement in a conflict is on the basis of either the articles of its own treaties or in response to a UN mandate.

If we look across these various unions and organisations we can identify a number of important commonalities. First, and as we have suggested previously, each of the unions and organisations involves an inter-relationship *between* nation-states rather than a *replacement of* nation-states. As Beck and Levy (2013: 14) explain, when we are considering the relationship between nation-states and forms of global governance it is not an 'either-or' situation. Indeed, global governance 'grows out of nationalism'. Viewed in this way, the relationship is symbiotic, mutually beneficial and mutually reinforcing. Second, central to the work of unions and organisations are some common aims and commitments, underpinned by the principle of democracy. In their mission, aims and principles, the organisations set out here state their commitment to build and maintain economic stability, protect and ensure peace and security, support and guarantee human rights, and promote sustainable development.

Third, and of particular relevance to our focus on global learning, each of the unions and organisations make important contributions toward developments in education. These can be seen primarily by the work undertaken to support equality of access to education, of which the work of UNICEF is a leading example, and also through the educational resources produced to raise awareness both of the unions and organisations themselves and also of the various issues and concerns in which they are involved. The various resources that are available are too numerous to detail in full here – we have made reference to some of them already in this book, and continue to do so throughout its remainder, and we ask you to briefly familiarise yourself with these resources through the following activity.

Activity

Learning about global political institutions

From the list of organisations above, select two that you feel (1) provide a good illustration of global governance and (2) are of particular relevance to your context. Undertake web-based research to find educational resources that would support your teaching about these to students within your own context. Use the following prompts to guide your research:

- What educational resources for use in schools are provided by each of the organisations? These are usually provided by national agencies within constituent countries. For example, the European Parliament Information Office in the UK provides a range of teaching resources and CPD activities, including *Crisis Point* – an interactive scenario-based activity in which students take on key decision-making positions in the face of a fictional pandemic (www.europarl.org.uk/en/education/teachingresources.html).
- What additional resources are available that, as educators, you can use, adapt and reframe to support student learning about the organisations?

Global economics

One of the major megatrends of our time is the shift in global power from west to east, and from north to south – from a few to a handful, to a myriad. Fifty years ago, the emerging markets and developing economies accounted for about a quarter of world GDP. Today, it is half, and rising rapidly – and very likely to be two-thirds within the next decade. The diffusion of power also goes beyond country relationships, extending to a whole host of networks and institutions that inhabit the fabric of global society . . .

Multilateralism must be made more inclusive – encompassing not only the emerging powers across the globe, but also the expanding networks and coalitions that are now deeply embedded in the fabric of the global economy. The new multilateralism must have the capacity to listen and respond to those new voices.

(Lagarde, 2014)

If proof was needed, the global financial crisis (GFC), which shook the world in 2007 and 2008, provided compelling evidence of the interconnectedness and inter-dependency of national economies, global and national financial institutions, and multinational and national companies/organisations. The worst financial crisis since the Great Depression of the 1930s, the GFC resulted from difficulties experienced across a range of financial markets, and stemmed out of the credit crisis experienced by the United States housing markets. The easy availability of credit in many countries meant that financial institutions, businesses and consumers were affected around the world. Some financial institutions (most famously the US financial services organisation Lehman Brothers Holdings) collapsed, while others were in effect rescued by public funds (as for example in the United Kingdom). The GFC had a knock-on effect on reducing the value of leading stock markets, and has been a contributory factor in the adoption of policies of economic 'austerity' in many nations, particularly in Europe, influencing government spending and reducing the availability of credit within national economies of the countries concerned.

A further illustration of the globalised nature of contemporary economics is the role played by multinational corporations (MNC). MNCs are businesses that operate (either by purchasing or selling products and services) across more than one nation. While MNCs are not new to international commerce, their prevalence and size has undoubtedly increased over the last forty years, affecting us in different ways. Many of the products we purchase are produced, either entirely or partly, overseas. When we speak to a customer service centre this is just as likely to be located abroad as it is in the country we are calling from. When we visit other countries around the world a range of goods and services – ranging from fast food, to clothes, to electrical goods and mobile technologies – will be the same as those available to us in our home countries. Through the availability of the Internet the options for purchasing goods and services are no longer limited to local or national businesses; we can purchase products from around the world at the click of a button using internationally recog-nised payment methods. According to Lagarde (2014), multinational corporations (defined as a corporation that is registered and/or has operations in more than one country) now control two-thirds of the world trade. Indeed, for a large proportion of the world's population, multinational companies and organisations are a feature of daily life. Highly influential in structuring the global economy and its financial markets are a range of international intergovernmental organisations and institutions that work together toward a range of objectives, including economic stability, economic security, economic growth, development and human well-being. The leading international organisations in this regard are:

International Monetary Fund (www.imf.org): The IMF is an agency of the United Nations that supports growth and economic stability globally. The IMF was created in the context of the Second World War and, at the time of writing, the IMF has 188 member countries, with members contributing to the fund and influencing its direction through a complicated quota-based system that, according to the IMF is 'broadly based on their relative size in the global economy' (www.imf.org). The IMF's role includes advising member nations, providing policy advice, as well as lending finance to member countries. The latter has raised tensions regarding the conditions sometimes placed on loanee countries by the IMF.

The World Bank (www.worldbank.org): Established in 1944, the World Bank is an institution of the United Nations that works to support developing countries by providing funding. While the World Bank is its usual title, it actually consists of two separate institutions – the International Bank for Reconstruction and Development and the International Development Association. It has two goals to achieve by 2030: to 'end extreme poverty by decreasing the percentage of people living on less than US$1.25 a day to no more than 3%', and to 'promote shared prosperity by fostering the income growth of the bottom 40% for every country'. The World Bank forms part of the wider World Bank Group.

G20 – The Group of Twenty (www.g20.org): The G20 is a forum for economic thinking, co-operation and decision-making, consisting of nineteen individual countries and the European Union. Established in 1999 initially for national finance ministers and governors of Central Banks, the G20's role has expanded to include, since 2008, annual meetings of G20 leaders. Meetings typically include a range of other invitees, including representatives of countries outside of the G20 as well as representatives of other international financial and economic institutions. The G20 focuses on a range of items, including trade, taxation, development, energy and tackling corruption.

G24 – The Group of Twenty Four (www.g24.org): The G24 is an intergovernmental collective of nations that 'co-ordinates the position of developing countries on monetary and development issues', as well as advocating for developing countries in international financial affairs. Member nations are divided into three regions: Africa, Latin America and Asia. The Group is a sub-set of the G77 group of the United Nations that seeks to promote the interests of developing nations. All members of the G77 are invited to attend meetings of the G24, while China acts a 'Special Invitee'.

World Trade Organization (www.wto.org): The World Trade Organization (WTO) was established in 1995, replacing its fore-runner, the General Agreement on Tariffs and Trade, that had existed since 1948. As its name suggests, the World Trade Organization works to support, develop and regulate the operation of trade in order to 'sort out the trade problems' between member nations. The Organization lists the following as key aspects of its work: 'trade negotiations', the 'implementation and monitoring of agreements', 'settling disputes', and 'building trade capacity'. A core theme of the WTO's work is the liberalisation of trade.

Organization for Economic Co-operation and Development (www.oecd.org): Founded in 1960/1961, the OECD is a collective of thirty-four member nations. It works 'to promote policies that will improve the economic and social well-being of people around the world'. The OECD collects and analyses a wide range of data to inform policy discussions and initiatives that influence the work of national governments.

Free versus fair trade

A central aspect of the work of many of the organisations listed above – most clearly the World Trade Organisation – is the liberalisation of international trade. This refers to reducing (or even removing) government-imposed protections and regulations, such as tariffs and quotas, that restrict the free operation of the market. In other words, working towards what is often termed 'free trade'. The European Union and the North American Free Trade Agreement provide clear examples of the removal of trade barriers and the creation of open market free trade areas. Over the last twenty years, the liberalisation of international trade has come under a great deal of criticism from proponents of what can be broadly categorised as the 'fair trade' movement. Fair trade can mean different things in different contexts, but is defined by the Fair Trade Advocacy Office as a 'trading partnership, based on dialogue, transparency and respect that seeks greater equity in international trade' (www.fairtrade-advocacy. org/about-fair-trade).

In his analysis of what the fair trade movement comprises, Walton (2010: 432) draws on the coffee industry to illustrate the main concerns of fair trade advocates with liberal trade systems:

> It involves a buyer-driven commodity chain where power rests with an oligopoly of roaster corporations which, thanks to various developments in technology and transportation, are able to exercise control and promote price competition by demanding 'just-in-time' delivery and using 'mix-and-match' blending. Alongside other technological improvements and market restructuring this downward pressure on prices resulted, in 2006, in a 40-year low. In such a situation producers must often accept the first offer they receive for their produce.

Recognising this situation has had a number of results. First, a number of fair trade organisations have campaigned to protect the rights and well-being of producers and to raise awareness of their inequitable power relationship with major buyers. Leading examples of fair trade networks include the FINE network (comprising Fairtrade Labelling Organizations International, the World Fair Trade Organization (formerly the International Fair Trade Association), the Network of European Worldshops, and the European Fair Trade Association) and the Fair Trade Advocacy Office (comprising Fairtrade International, the European Fair Trade Association and the European Branch of the World Fair Trade Organization). Second is the role of ethical and responsible consumerism in engendering as well as responding to principles of fair trade. The extent to which consumers instigate demand for fair trade products as opposed to responding to its supply is contested. Nevertheless, there is an important sense in which fair trade products have become more popular and numerous in recent years. An illustration of this is the role now played by fair trade certification labels placed on particular products in a number of nations. Third, many organisations have recognised the value in developing more socially responsible relationships with their suppliers, including for example large supermarkets entering into or being legally compelled to work within codes of conduct with regard to their suppliers.

Activity

Reviewing fair trade resources

We have already touched upon how the issue of fair trade can be used effectively in global learning with reference to the practice of Lifeworlds Learning in Chapter 2. Many organisations – such as Traidcraft Schools (www.traidcraft schools.co.uk) and the Fair Trade Resource Network (www.fairtraderesource. org) – provide teachers with useful resources to support teaching about fair trade.

Critically review an example of a fair trade educational resource – this could be sourced locally or if not possible visit an international organisation such as the Fair Trade Resource Network website.

Consider how as an educator you are able to build upon these resources in order to avoid presenting the topic of Fair Trade unproblematically. How might you be able to encourage your students to engage critically and creatively with this topic through providing a variety of perspectives?

Global civil society

[The public sphere] is best understood as a dimension of social life, with its own norms and decision rules, cutting across sectorial boundaries: as a set of activities, which can be (and historically has been) carried out by private individuals, private charities and even private firms as well as public agencies. It is symbiotically linked to the notion of public interest, in principle distinct from private interests; central to it are the values of citizenship, equity and service. In it goods are distributed on the basis of need and not of personal ties or access to economic resources. It is a space, protected from the adjacent market and private domains, where strangers encounter each other as equal partners in the common life of society – a space for forms of human flourishing which cannot be bought in the market-place or found in the tight-knit community of the clan or family or group of intimates.

(Marquand, 2004: 7)

In the above quotation, the British intellectual David Marquand defines what he understands by the term 'the public sphere'. He does so largely in terms of how the public sphere is understood *within* contemporary nations, as a space between the state and individuals in which competing interests and perspectives are shared and become known. The highly influential German scholar Jürgen Habermas (1996: 360) conceives the public sphere as 'a network for communicating information and points of view'. Globalising processes have brought into question the extent to which a public sphere, expressed through a *global civil society* exists at a level beyond nations. That is, whether there is a space existing beyond nations in which a range of non-governmental organisations and individuals raise awareness of and campaign for issues of global concern.

Kaldor *et al.*, (2003: 4) provide the following definition of global civil society:

> the sphere of ideas, values, networks and individuals located primarily outside the institutional complexes of family, market, and state, and beyond the confines of national societies, polities, and economies ... [Global civil society is] about the meaning of human equality in an increasingly unjust world ... it is about private action for public benefit.

Central to the successful operation and maintenance of civil society is the development of a 'civic culture' (Oxhorn, 2007: 326), so here we are interested in considering the extent to which the various groups and organisations involved in global issues operate within a 'global civic culture'. As Jenlink (2007: 301) suggests, globalisation has been seen as 'presenting an opportunity for democratization from below through the articulation of radical and new forms of transnational citizenship and social mobilization'. Typically, global civil society is concerned with crises across the world, whether this be 'acts of terror, war, poverty, and perhaps most importantly by the way the world's economic and social systems are structured and managed' (Jenlink, 2007: 304). The thoughts raised by Jenlink have been echoed by Bennett (2003: 143), who cites the influence of globalised social justice activism characterised by its 'networked complexity, openness to diverse political identities, and capacity to sacrifice ideological integration for pragmatic political gain'. This last point is particularly significant. As we saw in Chapter 1, in relation to *Occupy*, global civic activism is increasingly being shaped by wider movements that act as a collective overarching framework for a plethora of groups, which, while likeminded, are often focused on different specific issues or are informed by a range of theoretical positions. Partly for this reason the addressees of global activism can be global political organisations, global economic institutions, national governments, multinational corporations, national corporations or trade organisations.

We must also be mindful, however, that groups and organisations that operate in a global space are likely to be related to those that have a national base and/or focus. As Oxhorn (2007: 325) suggests:

> many, if not all, of today's transnational social movements can trace their roots back to the mobilization of social movements at the national level, frequently long before anyone even realized that the process of 'globalization' that we take for granted today had even begun.

In a slightly differentiated version of this argument, Gillan and Pickerill (2008: 76) have explored and analysed transnational anti-war activism within and across Australia, the United Kingdom and the United States. Drawing on interviews, participant observations and analysis of web sites, they concluded that ' "being global" is less about building formal connections between international groups and far more about re-scaling the meaning of local actions to a global audience'. Central to their findings was recognition that the global movements operating in the space of civil society both direct 'flows of information' and 'mobilise opposition' (Gillan and Pickerill, 2008: 76). While the former is transnational in nature, the latter takes place within national and local contexts and as such represents a form of 'rooted cosmopolitanism'. Indeed, the term 'rooted cosmopolitanism' provides a useful prism through which we may consider global civil society as combining global mindedness and national/local action.

The organisations that work within the space of global civil society are, of course, too numerous to recount here. Elsewhere in this book reference is made to the extensive and compelling work of a number of such organisations, predominantly within the fields of human rights, development and environmental sustainability. For the most part, these organisations conform to the depiction offered by Oxhorn – that is, organisations that are transnational in scope, focus and operation but which are rooted in important ways within nations – and we ask you to reflect on this as you encounter different organisations in the other chapters. To provide a brief consideration of the potential to go truly beyond nations in the space of global civil society we focus briefly here on one particular movement – Avaaz – that, according to *The Guardian*, 'is only five years old, but has exploded to become the globe's largest and most powerful online activist network' (Pilkington, 2012). The term Avaaz means voice, and the movement was established in 2007 with the aim to 'organize citizens of all nations to close the gap between the world we have and the world most people everywhere want' (www.avaaz.org). The movement supports action through 'internet organising' and in doing so empowers campaigning on a wide range of global issues. Member-polls (at the time of writing there are nearly 35 million members) also enable the movement to set out its main priorities from a set of nine issues. In 2013, members ranked these as follows: (1) human rights, torture, genocide and human trafficking; (2) political corruption and the abuse of power; (3) climate change and the environment; (4) economic policy that benefits the common good over the elite few; (5) poverty, disease and development; (6) war, peace and security; (7) biodiversity and conservation; (8) democracy movements and challenging tyrannical regimes; and (9) food and health.

We should also consider that the individuals, groups and organisations that operate in the space of civil society may act in harmony or in conflict with states. The level of accord is, of course, influenced by a range of factors including the particular issue/concern, the prescience of this, and the position and actions adopted by the state with regard to the issue/concern. Mundy and Murphy (2001: 90) helpfully point out that the actual *influence* of organisations operating in the space of global civil society is not fully clear. They suggest that:

> Most scholars agree that their greatest impact to date has been 'at the level of agenda setting, the spreading of norms and changes in intergovernmental and

governmental discourse'. But very different assessments have been offered of their success in holding nations and international organizations accountable to new agendas, or in achieving the deeper democratization of international organizations and intergovernmental forums, which is so often a key part of their agenda.

The nature and operation of global civil society raises a number of questions for educators, and these relate back to our focus and exploration in Chapters 1 and 2. Moreover, the way in which global civil society continues to develop is heavily influenced by the availability of recent technologies – most clearly the Internet – that have fundamentally altered the ways in which people can interconnect globally (UNDP, 2013: 111). We explore the nature and impact of global technologies in the next section.

Global technologies

As we interconnect ourselves, many of the values of a nation-state will give way to those of both larger and smaller electronic communities. We will socialize in digital neighbourhoods in which physical space will be irrelevant and time will play a different role. Twenty years from now, when you look out a window, what you see maybe five thousand miles and six time zones away. When you watch an hour of television, it may have been delivered to your home in less than a second. Reading about Patagonia can include the sensory experience of going there. A book by William Buckley can be a conversation with him.

(Negroponte, 1995: 7)

Mobile broadband Internet and other modern technologies are opening new channels through which citizens, particularly young people, can demand accountability. They also enable people in different countries to share values and experiences, bringing them closer together.

(UNDP, 2013: 91–2)

The above words of Nicholas Negroponte were written twenty years ago. When we consider statements written before the Internet was truly global in its usage, it is very easy to cast our eyes back in hindsight and make judgements about their accuracy (or sometimes more aptly their inaccuracy). It is perhaps more suitable to consider the accuracy of the sentiment underpinning the statement – in Negroponte's case that the world would be irrevocably changed by the Internet, making human stories more accessible and fundamentally altering how time and particularly space are conceived and experienced. In simplistic terms, the Internet has changed how we source information, how we communicate with friends and strangers, how we shop, how we work, and how we spend our leisure time.

Drawing on the work of Wellman (2000), Bennett (2003) describes the contemporary condition of 'networked individualism'. This term refers to the interconnectedness available to people as a result of new technologies, and is defined by Bennett (2003: 147) as 'the ease of establishing personal links that enable people to join more diverse and more numerous political communities than they would ordinarily join in the material world'. Against a general backdrop of a perceived deficit in young people's political participation, it is argued by some commentators that as 'digital natives' young people are helping to lead new forms of online engagement in the public sphere (Jenkins, 2006; Palfrey and Gasser, 2008; cf. Bennett, Wells and Freelon, 2011). At the time of writing, however, research on online youth civic engagement remains somewhat tentative, and precludes generalisable judgements about its scope, nature and impact (Bennett, Wells and Freelon, 2011).

This may reflect the varied nature of, and possibilities for, political engagement on the Internet. Vromen (2008: 81; emphasis in the original) summarises three primary uses of the Internet as a political space for participation. First, the Internet acts as an '*information source*' through which political institutions, interest groups and various forms of the media raise awareness of particular issues and concerns. Second, the Internet acts as a '*communication medium*' through which people can converse with each other through a range of different forums (emails, blogs, forums etc.) and at a range of different levels. Third, the Internet acts as a '*virtual public space*', enabling users to come together to share ideas and to discuss them in a critical manner to develop and form opinions as a collective.

In the last ten years, two growth areas relating to the Internet have been particularly important to global interconnectedness and interdependency. First, the development and proliferation of social and digital media and, second, the growth in mobile technologies as evidenced for example by smart phones and tablets (IGS, 2014). The way in which these two elements of growth have interacted with global events bears some comparison with the advent in the late 1980s and early 1990s of rolling, 24-hour televised news, and in particular the ability to show television images less than two hours old (Jakobsen, 2000). This ability has fundamentally changed the production and consumption of television news. This change is evident when we consider the following reflection from a former journalist for Independent Television News in the UK written in the 1990s:

> Once, there were long delays in getting news videotape through fighting and roadblocks to a distant television station and on to air. In the 1980s, footage of the war in Lebanon had to be sent by boat to Cyprus. Pictures were often out of date when they were transmitted. No more. Bosnia and Somalia represent the new generation of instant television war. Mobile satellite dish transmitters mean the delay in receiving pictures from the battlefield can be measured in minutes. Frequently, there is no delay at all. Much coverage is real-time.
>
> (Gowring, 1994)

Today, and as we discuss later, transmission is not only instant but has diversified in its authorship, with reporters, members of the military, and civilians able to relay events instantly using smartphones, tablets and other mobile technologies.

The CNN Effect?

At the time of Gowring's reflection, and since, the growth in 24-hour televised news as well as technological advancements that enabled ongoing live transmission of key world events – perhaps most notably the fall of the Berlin Wall, the Tiananmen Square protest, and the Gulf War – led some commentators to talk of 'The CNN Effect' (Robinson, 1999). Named after Cable News Network (CNN), one of the world's leading news channels based in America and the first to launch a 24-hour rolling news station, the CNN Effect refers to the extent to which such stations have not simply reported the news, but have provoked 'major responses from domestic audiences and political elites to global events' (Robinson, 1999: 301). Drawing on Jakobsen's (2000: 132) analysis, the flow of the CNN Effect is depicted in Figure 3.1.

While its actual effect is hotly contested, the CNN Effect does raise questions about the role media plays in shaping and affecting the course of international events and international political responses to them in Western democracies. Writing in the mid-1990s, James Hoge (1994) suggested that 'today's pervasive media increases the pressure on politicians to respond promptly to news accounts that by their very immediacy are incomplete, without context and sometimes wrong'. The main premise behind the CNN Effect is rather compelling, particularly where humanitarian issues are concerned. In circumstances resulting from war, famine, drought or natural disaster the images and media representations of human suffering often act not only to raise awareness, but also to engender certain cognitive and emotional responses (as depicted in Figure 3.1). This said, it is very difficult to ascertain the precise impact that media has had, either on policy makers themselves or on the wider public. Former

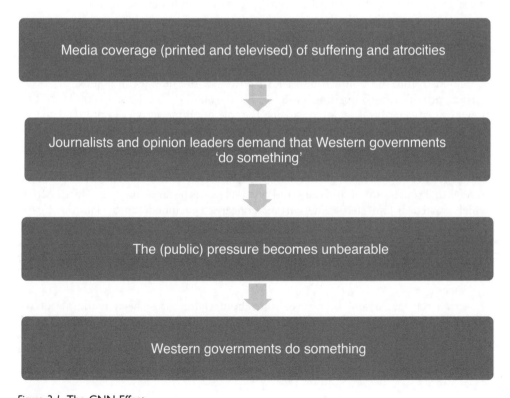

Figure 3.1 The CNN Effect

Source: Adapted from Jakobsen (2000: 132).

Secretary General of the United Nations, Kofi Annan, has explained the impact in the following way: 'when governments have a clear policy . . . then television has little impact', but when 'there is a problem, and the policy has not been thought through they have to do something or face a public relations disaster' (cited in Robinson, 1999: 305).

In more recent times, commentators have sought to make similar claims with regard to the effect of new forms of social media – in particular Facebook and Twitter. We considered earlier in this chapter that the events surrounding the killing of Osama Bin Laden were reported on Twitter before they had been officially covered. The ability of social media networks such as Facebook, Twitter and YouTube, according to Gillmor (cited in Newman, 2011: 10), has meant that: 'Big media has lost its monopoly of the news. Now that it is possible to publish in real time to a worldwide audience, a new breed of grassroots journalists are taking the news into their own hands.'

As Newman (2011: 10) highlights, an increasing range of outlets are available to support 'citizen journalists' to publicise and share images often captured by mobile technologies in addition to traditional news outlets. Sites such as Storyful (www.storyful.com), Demotix (www.demotix.com) and Citizenside (www.citizenside.com) each use slightly differentiated models for such purposes. Demotix, for example, markets its service as involving a three-point process – 'sign up', 'upload your media', 'we sell your news and split profits 50:50 with you' (www.demotix.com/community).

The Arab Spring

Of all the events that have occurred in the world in recent years that have been cited as demonstrating the political and social power of the new technologies, the 'Arab Spring' provides a compelling case study, particularly because of the fact that previously 'much of the debate regarding the role of online activity in political change had focused on Western democracies' (Tufecki and Wilson, 2012). Indeed, according to the UK television broadcaster, Channel 4 (2011), 'while demonstrators in the Arab world and further afield seem to have been ignited by "people power", the influence of the Internet on young revolutionaries is undeniable'. The term 'Arab Spring' is used to refer to a succession of uprisings and protests in Arab states, many in North Africa, which started in late 2010. The nations concerned included Libya, Tunisia, Egypt, Yemen, Iraq, Syria, Algeria and Jordan, and it is important therefore that we caution against understanding its causes and process as a singular event. As Anderson (2011) suggests, 'although they shared a common call for personal dignity and responsive government, the revolutions . . . reflected divergent economic grievances and social dynamics'.

Across the media and literature, some bold claims have been made about the influence of the Internet and social media on events that took place during the Arab Spring uprisings. Terms such as 'Facebook Revolution' and 'Twitter Revolution' are commonly used, while in the UK the British Broadcasting Corporation (BBC) broadcast a two-part documentary on the events of the Arab Spring entitled *How Facebook Changed the World*.

Among a range of other factors – there is some evidence that the Internet and social media – including blogs, Facebook, Twitter and YouTube – *did* play an important influencing factor on awareness of the uprising, in spite of censorship in some of the countries concerned. This influence took a number of forms, including: the distribution of video and still images; the provision and dissemination of information about events both internally and internationally; and the development of group identities and networks. Tufecki and Wilson (2012: 364) explain this with regard to Egypt:

> During the protests, protestors steadily produced and disseminated content in real time. The shutdown of Internet service between January 25 and February 2 slowed, but did not stop, the flow of information out of Tahrir Square, as a small but technologically savvy group of protestors continued to disseminate information and videos.

The proliferation of images appearing on social media during the Arab Spring was undoubtedly helped by the availability and affordability of mobile technologies, as well as by the availability of an Arabic language service on Facebook (Tufecki and Wilson, 2012). A notable feature of the content appearing online was that it interacted with, and often provided the content for, more traditional televisual and print media. Indeed, there is some evidence to suggest that rather than replacing traditional news media (whether television or newsprint) social media is developing a symbiotic relationship with them. For example, most, if not all, traditional news journalists have Twitter accounts and keep track of news stories on social media. It is also the case that social media networks such as Facebook and Twitter act as gateways and referral systems to traditional media (Newman, 2011).

The Arab Spring illustrates that the advent and proliferation of new social media means that many of us are now consuming news in a very different way to how we would have done ten years ago. According to Chris Anderson (cited in Newman, 2011: 11) of *Wired* magazine:

> We're tuning out television news, we're tuning out newspapers. And we still hear about the important stuff . . . I figure by the time something gets to me it's been vetted by those I trust. So the stupid stuff that doesn't matter is not going to get to me.

In this statement, Anderson is making a bold claim about the accuracy of information on online social media. There are, of course, potential problems with this view. Some high profile examples of false stories appearing on Twitter suggest that, while perhaps quickly redressed, the accuracy of trending news items on social media is not always guaranteed. In the UK, for example, there have been a number of cases in which public figures have been subject to false allegations or have been publicly named on social networks in breach of court injunctions. Further complexity is added to this by the sometimes unclear rules around libel and discrimination laws on social media as well as the ability of people to hide behind anonymous profiles. Speaking in light of such instances, the Lord Chief Justice, Lord Judge, commented that he was 'not giving up on the possibility that people who in effect peddle lies about others using modern technology may one day be brought under control. It may be through damages; it may even be through injunctions to prevent the peddling of lies' (Burrell, 2011).

Activity

News diary

Keep a news diary over a period of three to four days. In your diary, note down the news items/stories you have become aware of. For each news item/story, note down the following:

- the medium (including how instantly the transmission on the issue was produced);
- date of access;
- time of day;
- the length of your engagement with the media;
- where you were and who you were with;
- how the access came about (intentional? unintentional? recommended to you by a person or linked through another form of medium?).

After you have collected the data over the course of three to four days, review your diary and identify any patterns of your engagement. What patterns can you identify? Are there any patterns that surprise you? How could you adapt this activity for your students in your context?

Political action and new technologies

Despite the prevalence of social media across the Arab Spring, insufficient evidence exists to make any uncontested claims about the interactions and inter-relationships between political action (whether global, national or local) and new technologies. The claims and ideas we have considered so far in this section should not, therefore, be read as definitive, but rather as raising important questions about how people engage with technologies in relation to their political participation. In concluding this section it is worth spending a short time considering what some of the current research says about new technologies and young people's participation. In their study, Davide Calenda and Albert Meijer (2009: 883) suggest that two models can be proposed with regard to the relationship between the Internet and political participation. The 'techno-deterministic' perspective views new technologies as changing the extent and nature of political participation. Here, technologies result in a 'shift from more traditional to newer forms of politics since the medium characteristics have a better fit with new forms of participation'. In contrast, the 'voluntaristic' perspective sees political participation online as simply a reproduction of offline, more traditional forms of engagement. In her research into young people's political participation on the Internet, Vromen (2008: 94) concluded that the Internet was 'important in facilitating young people's political spaces', and that 'young people connect and form on-line and off-line communities in complex and myriad ways'. Interestingly, her research also found that young people 'are engaged by political information that has been generated by young people themselves'. An excellent example of this in practice is provided by the work of Dr Ian Cook at Exeter University as outlined below:

Case study

followthethings.com

The followthethings website coordinated by Ian Cook at Exeter University is an example of how Internet technology can be used by students to explore their global interconnectedness through commodity chains. The site reveals how our lives are intertwined through the making, trading, consumption and disposal of things. It illustrates all three of Vromen's primary uses of the Internet as a space for civic participation. Through its use of Web 2.0, the site acts as an information source, communication medium and virtual public space where students as researchers come together to share information about how everyday items are sourced and made.

Called followthethings.com, the website represents a spoof 'online shop' that currently has fifty-eight different items spread across eight different departments: grocery, fashion, electrical, health and beauty, gifts, money, security and auto. Rather than merely describing these items for consumption, the site showcases and researches films, art work, books, journalism and other sources that follow the production journey of the commodities themselves, illuminating the human and social context of how each has been made. One example is *Bananas!**, a documentary by the filmmaker Fredrik Gertten documenting a courtroom drama in the US where South American banana workers sued the Dole corporation for using banned pesticides that had allegedly made them impotent. The site involves students as 'civic detectives' engaging in crowd-research to understand the making and impact of examples like this and to co-create new narratives to be posted on the site, exposing previously hidden stories of how commodities reach us. Recent student research projects have included a group in the UK creating a cartoon telling the surprising story of the chemical ingredients in paracetamol, and a group of students in the US researching the making of laptops specifically designed for use by children growing up in some of the poorest areas of the world. In many cases the items in the online shop powerfully reveal the exploitation of other people or the environment within their global production and present this in a personal, artistically creative and deliberative way.

followthethings.com illustrates a global civil society in action not only in terms of the worldwide reach of this communication but through detailing the global links of everyday products. As already touched upon in this chapter, the web technology it uses provides a platform for the social mobilisation of students both as researchers and civic communicators. Since its creation in 2011, the website has received over 26,000 visitors from over 150 different countries. It also has over 1200 followers of its Twitter feed (@followthethings). The site can be used by teachers as an effective means for engaging learners with topics relating to global interconnectedness such as trade justice, poverty, exploitation, inequality and sustainability.

To view the site visit www.followthethings.com.

To read more about the creation of and rationale for followthethings.com see Ian Cook *et al.* (in press).

We should also consider how technological changes relating to the Internet have impacted on extending opportunities to participate. Writing in the late 1990s, Shenk (1997: 23), for example, suggested that 'the Internet does allow previously disenfranchised groups to communicate cheaply without geographic limitation'. This view gained a good deal of support in the United Nations Development Programme's Report in 1999 (UNDP). While it emphasised the extent to which the Internet was enabling rapid globalisation in a number of ways, the report made clear that access to and engagement with the new technology was far from equitable. For example, data obtained in 1998 suggested that 93.3 per cent of Internet users came from the world's richest 20 per cent of people, with 6.5 per cent from the middle 60 per cent and 0.2 per cent from the world's poorest 20 per cent (UNDP, 1999: 2). The report also details issues with access, cost and educational disadvantage as central reasons for the vast inequalities in Internet use at the time. By contrast, the most recent UNDP *Human Development Report* (2013: 14–15) makes clear that, partly as a result of more efficient and cheaper mobile broadband Internet, 'the digital divide is rapidly narrowing'. The report states that:

> There has been an exponential rise in the number of people in the [global] South with access to the world wide web (Internet). The takeoff has been especially notable in the past decade. Between 2000 and 2010, average growth in Internet use surpassed 30% in around 60 developing countries with a population of 1 million or more.

Still, as Davies *et al.* (2012: 295) point out, 'arguments for technology as a democratizing force are not persuasive if it is concentrated in the hands of those who are already privileged'. As educators we must though reflect on the extent to which this statement is apt within our local contexts, our national contexts, and also within global contexts. For example, while most statistical analyses point to the exponential growth in access to the Internet in many nations, there is an important sense in which we should keep these in perspective. Consider the following statistics: figures provided by Internet Growth Statistics (IGS, 2014) show that in December 1995 there were 16 million users of the Internet worldwide. Ten years later, in 2005, this figure had grown to 1018 million users. According to the latest figures produced in March 2013, the figure stood at 2749 million. These figures are impressive and speak of the extent to which access to the Internet has grown rapidly.

Now consider the following statistics: figures provided by Internet Growth Statistics (IGS, 2014) show that in December 1995 0.4 per cent of the world's population were users of the Internet. In 2005 that figure was 15.7 per cent. The latest figures from March 2013 put the figure at 38.8 per cent. Of course, every set of figures raises questions about context and interpretation. By showing them, we are not suggesting that the influence of the Internet has been in any way trivial or has not affected most, if not all, nations around the world. What we are suggesting, however, is that as educators we need to give some critical thought as to which countries and which citizens have access to, and indeed actually use, the Internet.

Conclusion

In this chapter we have explored the main factors that influence global interconnectedness and interdependency in the world today. As with many of the organisations, issues and events considered throughout this book, these factors are not static but are fluid and dynamic. As the example of tensions within the G8 over Russia's relations with the Crimea and Ukraine illustrates, unforeseen events arise that change how (in this case) global governance operates. At the time we write this, a range of possibilities remain about this particular conflict. International diplomacy may produce a settlement that appeases the interests and concerns of all, maintaining the current structure and composition of both the G8 and the UN Security Council. If this fails, the composition and nature of both organisations may be changed for the foreseeable future. This highlights the importance of an implicit understanding that has underpinned this chapter. This is the recognition that a key constituent of global learning is *systems thinking and political literacy*. In other words, if students are to understand global events and issues, and if they are to engage as global citizens, they need to know and comprehend the key global political, economic and civic organisations and worldwide flows of interconnection. Again, the situation with the Crimea and the Ukraine is useful for illustrative purposes, given that students need to understand the diplomatic roles of both the G8 and the UN Security Council if they are to interpret the news and views expressed within the media, as well as make informed decisions about their own opinions and actions as global citizens.

Questions for further investigation

1   What do you think is the difference between global interconnectedness and global interdependency, and how significant is this difference?
2   What are the key global political and economic organisations and institutions within your context and what educational resources do these provide?
3   In what ways can and should global learning involve students working with social media and other new technologies?

Further reading

Global Voices (http://globalvoicesonline.org)
An international community of bloggers and translators that report on blogs and citizen media to raise awareness and profile of stories from around the world, and to act as a filter and information source for those seeking to learn more about people's stories and reports.

Palfrey, J. and Gasser, U. (2008) *Born Digital: Understanding the First Generation of Digital Natives*. New York, NY: Basic Books.
An interesting book that adopts a sociological approach to considering and exploring the ways in which young people engage and perceive the digital media they have been brought up with.

United Nations Association of the United Kingdom (2012) *The United Nations Matters Teacher's Handbook*, www.una.org.uk/sites/default/files/Teacher's%20Handbook.pdf (accessed 10 March 2014).
A clear and thorough handbook for teachers exploring the mission, structure and activities of the United Nations. Includes a range of ideas for teaching about the United Nations.

Chapter 4

Cultural diversity

Chapter objectives

By the end of this chapter you should have:

- considered some of the main processes that have contributed to living in diverse communities and a diverse world, as well as some of the issues raised by this;
- reflected on the role of schools and teachers in supporting student learning about and for living in diverse communities and in a diverse world;
- reflected on different approaches to teaching and learning about and for diversity, giving particular thought to their applicability within your own contexts.

Introduction

In this chapter we will explore and consider the nature and challenges of living in a diverse world. It is important from the outset to make clear that diversity exists around a number of factors, which include age, gender, socio-economic status and ethnicity/culture. While we would not wish to neglect any of these factors (indeed, they often inter-relate), we focus here on the latter given the effect of globalising processes on ethno-cultural diversity increasing in most nations around the world. Where appropriate, we make links to other forms of diversity as they relate to ethnicity and culture, and of course we touch upon these too elsewhere in this book. A key feature of the heterogeneity of modern communities is that the diversity brought about by global processes is often felt and experienced at the level of the local community. According to one of the leading writers about diversity and education, Audrey Osler (2008: 21):

> Our everyday citizenship is most commonly experienced at the local level. Individuals will have multiple and changing identities and multiple and changing allegiances to local, national and transnational communities. Educators cannot assume that their students will identify first and foremost with the national community or that they will necessarily see this as their primary focus of allegiance.

The various communities with which young people identify are likely to reflect a range of values, beliefs, both religious and secular.

A key theme within this chapter, and something that as educators we need to take seriously, is the recognition that, while diversity brings a number of benefits to local communities, it also raises specific and important challenges, not least how people with different ethnic and cultural identities, beliefs and values can live together in harmony. This is one of the challenges we consider as we progress through this chapter. It is not an overstatement to say that education has been commonly identified as being at the forefront of political attempts to support an understanding of diversity as well as to work towards greater mutual understanding of different ethnicities and cultures.

As educators we must think about the role of education in relation to diversity, including how we might develop apt pedagogies for students learning about and for living in diverse communities within a diverse world. As Banks *et al.* (2008: 68) suggest from a US context, this involves a multitude of areas, not least the recognition that 'continuing education about diversity is especially important for teachers because of the increasing cultural and ethnic gap that exists between the nation's teachers and students'. This requires teachers once again to consider a range of educational processes – including organisation, mission and ethos of the school, the content of the curriculum, and its relationships with families and the community – as well as exploring their own perceptions and understandings of race, ethnicity and culture. Banks *et al.* (2008: 74) continue:

> Diversity in . . . schools is both an opportunity and a challenge. The nation is enriched by the ethnic, cultural, and language diversity among its citizens and within its schools. However, whenever diverse groups interact, intergroup tension, stereotypes, and institutionalized discrimination develop. Schools must find a way to respect the diversity of their students as well as help to create a unified, superordinate nation-state to which all citizens have allegiance.

The ways in which we as educators conceive and approach the processes will need to respond to the particular needs of the particular contexts (national, local, neighbourhood, etc.) within which we work, so as you read through the chapter we ask that you think about how each of the ideas discussed relates to your own particular context/s. We close this introduction with the following quotation from the writer and human rights activist, Mahnaz Afkhami (n.d.):

> We have the ability to achieve, if we can master the necessary goodwill, a common global society blessed with a shared culture of peace that is nourished by the ethnic, national and local diversities that enrich our lives.

Cultural diversity in globalised communities

Worldwide migration has increased diversity in most nation-states and is forcing nations to rethink citizenship and citizenship education. National boundaries are eroding because millions of people live in several nations and have multiple citizenships … Millions have citizenship in one nation and live in another. Others are stateless, including millions of refugees around the world. The number of individuals living outside their original homelands increased from approximately 33 million in 1910 to 175 million in 2000.

(Banks, 2008a: 132)

Diversity today

The effects of greater diversity within nation states throughout the world today are felt in a number of ways. One of these, for example, is the plurality and diversity of the languages spoken by inhabitants of major cities. Recent official figures show, for example, that London is one of the most ethnically diverse cities with fifty non-indigenous groups being part of its population (London Councils, 2014). This diversity is evidenced by the fact that it has the largest number of community languages spoken of any European city, with 'over 300 languages … spoken in London schools with Bengali, Gujarati, Punjabi, Cantonese and Mandarin most common' (London Councils, 2014). Greater levels of diversity have also brought about major changes to a range of cultural experiences – including eating, shopping, the sorts of music we hear and listen to, the sorts of films that are available to see, and the television programmes we watch. Items that once used to be available only in specialist shops are now commonly available at the local supermarket. The centres of western cities are no longer home to cathedrals and churches, but also to synagogues, mosques, temples, gurdwaras and a range of other places of worship.

One of the central global processes that has led to greater levels of diversity is migration. According to the most recent figures from the United Nations Department of Economic and Social Affairs (UN-DESA) and the Organisation for Economic Cooperation and Development (2013: 1), there were 232 million international migrants worldwide. As a consequence most cities are no longer predominantly mono-cultural, but instead are home to a rich diversity in a number of ways, including ethnic, racial and religious (Kymlicka, 1995). Indeed, the fact of diverse and plural societies is a feature of everyday lived experience for most students living in most modern cities throughout the world. Migration between nations occurs for a number of reasons, and typically these are divided into *pull* and *push* factors. Pull factors influencing migration include employment opportunities, seeking better living standards, family connections, education and health. Push factors influencing migration include low living standards, political and religious persecution, natural disasters and civil war. Freedom of movement within and between nations is governed by international declarations and treaties, as well as by the particular legislative instruments in individual nations. The United Nations Universal Declaration of Human Rights (1948), for example, makes provision for freedom of movement within and between countries, as well as the right to leave and return to one's own country (International Organization for Migration, 2014).

One of the most important aspects of educating students about diversity is to ensure that they understand key terms, and this is particularly true of terms relating to migration. Frequently in public discourse, terms such as asylum seeker, refugee and illegal immigrant are used interchangeably, masking significant differences between them. The following is a list of some of the key terms students will need to understand (for definitions of a wider list of key terms related to migration, visit the International Organization for Migration website, www.iom.int):

Asylum seeker: an individual who seeks refuge in a country other than their own in order to be protected from some form of persecution. Seeking asylum requires a formal application that is considered in relation to the relevant international and national laws governing asylum.

Brain drain: a term used to refer to the phenomenon of educated individuals from poorer nations migrating for economic reasons to wealthier countries. Figures suggest, for example, that one in nine (Africa), one in thirteen (Latin America and the Caribbean) and one in thirty (Asia) individuals with a tertiary qualification have moved to live in OECD countries (UN-DESA/OECD, 2013: 1).

Forced migration: the process through which individual/s move as a result of persecution, coercion, fear and/or natural disaster. This may be within a nation or across nations.

Illegal immigrant: the term for a migrant who moves across national borders in contravention to the laws and regulations of the destination country. The UN Refugee Convention allows an individual to enter a destination country by any means as long as they are seeking asylum through legal measures.

Immigration: occurs when individuals move from a nation to another nation in which they are not nationalised citizens in order to live and settle.

Internally displaced person: individuals who are forced to migrate from their homes but stay within the borders of their nation-state. Reasons for the forced migration of internally displaced persons include natural disasters, civil wars and persecution.

Migration: the general term used with regard to the pattern of movement by individuals. Migration can occur within a nation-state or across nation-state boundaries. As well as the different forms of migration and the different reasons for migration, official bodies frequently look to analyse the nature and level of migration between and within hemispheres (i.e. North–South, South–North, North–North, South–South). Figures suggest that approximately half of all international migrants reside in ten countries: USA (45.8 million; 20 per cent); Russian Federation (11 million); Germany (9.8 million); Saudi Arabia (9.1 million); United Arab Emirates (7.8 million); UK (7.8 million); France (7.5 million); Canada (7.3 million); Australia (6.5 million) and Spain (6.5 million) (UN-DESA/OECD, 2013: 2). Figures also suggest that half of the migrants living in OECD countries come from sixteen countries, with the most emigrants deriving from Mexico (11 million); China (3.8 million); United Kingdom (3.5 million); India (3.4 million); Poland (3.2 million); and Germany (3.2 million) (UN-DESA/OECD, 2013: 3).

Refugee: is defined by the 1951 Convention relating to the Status of Refugees (UNHCR, n.d: 14) as a person who:

> owing to well-founded fear of being persecuted for reasons of race, religion, nationality, membership of a particular social group or political opinion, is outside the country of his nationality and is unable or, owing to such fear, is unwilling to avail himself of the protection of that country; or who, not having a nationality and being outside the country of his former habitual residence as a result of such events, is unable or, owing to such fear, is unwilling to return to it.

> Figures suggest that there are 15.7 million refugees in the world, comprising 7 per cent of all international migrants. (UN-DESA/OECD, 2013: 2)

Stateless person: is an individual who is not recognised as a national by any state. A stateless person is not, therefore, protected by the laws and regulations of a nation-state, often meaning that they lack education, healthcare and a range of other services provided by nation-states.

As well as supporting students to understand different forms of migration, as educators we must think carefully about the effects of migration on students themselves. Extensive research suggests that experiences of schooling play a major role in the well-being of refugee children (Richman, 1998). An extensive review of literature on the experiences and needs of refugee and asylum seeking children in the UK is provided by Hek (2005). The review makes clear that schools and teachers must consider a wide range of factors that influence refugee students, including language needs, potential barriers to parental involvement, student confidence and self-esteem, levels of isolation/integration, socio-economic status, as well as students' social and emotional needs.

Case study

'Giving voice to refugee and asylum seekers' – Global Link, Lancaster, UK

> Everyone has the right to seek and to enjoy in other countries asylum from persecution.
> (Article 14 of the Universal Declaration of Human Rights)

Global Link (www.globallink.org.uk) is a development education centre and a charity based in the North of England. It uses creative experiential learning methodologies and resources to encourage learning for a more just and sustainable world. The charity works with students and teachers in schools and also with people of all ages through community initiatives.

A key global learning area for Global Link has been human rights and diversity and in particular working to challenge the stereotypical perspective in Britain

continued ...

that asylum seekers are not genuinely fleeing persecution, but are merely seeking a 'better life' in Europe. They have attempted to do this through a variety of projects, each giving refugees and asylum seekers a voice. As explained by Gisela Renolds, who has led Global Link's work in this area, the aim has been to encourage learners to consider the perspective that 'refugees are ordinary people in extraordinary circumstances' and that asylum seekers are survivors who are seeking 'safety' and 'refuge'. Global Link seeks to achieve this through the power of survivor testimony as a means of encouraging students to connect more personally to the issue with a sense of common humanity.

Towards this aim Global Link created 'Escape to safety', a multimedia experiential learning exhibition. The exhibition was built into a 12.5 metre box trailer and transported to schools across the country. It involved students going through a labyrinth of eight stations each depicting a different stage that a refugee might experience as they sought asylum. As students went through the labyrinth they listened to a soundtrack on an MP3 player that followed the voices of three asylum-seekers from Rwanda, Afghanistan and Palestine as they escaped their countries and sought refuge in the United Kingdom. Working with over 14,000 young people, this exhibition sought to be holistic in the sense of communicating key points of information, but at the same time providing an emotive experience to empathically engage people. The power of this learning space is illustrated by the following two evaluations from participating educators:

'Thanks for the exhibition, breaking stereotypes and apathy is priceless.'

'An hour in the Escape to Safety Exhibition is worth a day in the classroom.'

Since creating this exhibition, Global Link has gone on to develop other innovative work in this area of global learning. They have developed an outdoor learning experience where students become refugees for a day and experience a simulation of 'escaping' their country, crossing borders and seeking asylum in the UK. Most recently, Global Link has teamed up with a group of NGO partners from Hungary, Turkey, Italy and Germany with a project called IntegrArt. This seeks to use arts methodologies to enable refugees and asylum seekers to give voice to their own experiences. This has involved Gisela Renolds and colleagues working with an Asylum Refugee Community in order to create a number of digital stories. They have also used participatory theatre methods to work with a group of refugees and asylum seekers to devise and perform their own piece of theatre exploring refugee issues.

More information about the projects can be found at www.globallink.org.uk.

Cultural diversity   79

Activity

Researching refugee and asylum seeker councils

Most nations have at least one non-governmental organisation that works to support refugees and asylum seekers, campaign on their behalf, raise awareness of the issues faced by refugees and asylum seekers, and combat many of the myths and prejudices sometimes held about refugees and asylum seekers. In the UK, United States, Ireland and Australia the Refugee Council in each nation is perhaps the main example. In addition to these nationally based organisations, there are a range of international and local organisations that have similar aims.

Select and research three such organisations – one local, one national and one international. What specific prepared resources do they provide for educators? How useful are these resources for *your* context, and why? Through your review of these organisations are you able to identify a possible resource that you could adapt or that sparks your own ideas for creating an innovative practice that you could trial with learners in your own context.

Diversity and recognition of indigenous populations

Another notable aspect of diversity within a number of nations over the last fifty years has been the greater importance given to reconciling and recognising indigenous populations. In Australia, for example, until 1967 the Constitution included the following statements regarding its indigenous population:

> 51. The Parliament shall, subject to this Constitution, have power to make laws for the peace, order, and good government of the Commonwealth with respect to:
> . . . (xxvi) The people of any race, other than the aboriginal people in any State, for whom it is necessary to make special laws.
> 127. In reckoning the numbers of the people of the Commonwealth, or of a State or other part of the Commonwealth, aboriginal natives should not be counted.

(National Archives of Australia, n.d.)

As a result of a referendum in which 90.77 per cent voted in favour, the words 'other than aboriginal people in any State' and the whole of section 127 were removed from the Australian Constitution. Aboriginal peoples in Australia were only given the right to vote in federal elections in 1962. While the constitutions of most states and territories gave Aboriginal peoples the right to vote in state/territory elections, this was not given in Western Australia until 1962 and in Queensland until 1965. It was not until 1971 that the first Indigenous Australian – Neville Bonner – sat in any Australian Parliament (Australian Electoral Commission, n.d). More recently, there has been a cross-party commitment to amending the Constitution further to give greater recognition to the rights, languages and advancement of Aboriginal and Torres Strait Islander Peoples with the Australian Parliament passing the Aboriginal and Torres Strait Islander Peoples Recognition Bill in 2012. One of three cross-curricular priorities in the new Australian Curriculum is a focus on Aboriginal and Torres Strait Islander histories and cultures.

Similar issues related to giving proper recognition and respect to indigenous populations have been a central theme within public policy and debates in a number of other nations, including Canada, New Zealand and South Africa. In Canada in 1971, for example, the Canadian Prime Minister at the time, Pierre Elliot Trudeau, drew on the concept of 'multiculturalism' to support and inform the acceptance of bilingualism: 'a policy of multiculturalism within a bilingual framework is basically the conscious choice of individual freedom of choice. We are free to be ourselves' (cited in Meer and Modood, 2011: 180). The 1988 Canadian Multicultural Act explicitly commits the Government of Canada to promote multiculturalism, including recognising and protecting Canada's multicultural heritage and recognising aboriginal rights (Kymlicka, 1995).

Education about and for diversity and wider public concerns

As teachers there is a need for us to recognise and celebrate the benefits and experiences that greater diversity brings, while being mindful of the challenges and tensions that might also result. We consider the problem of striking the balance within the work of teachers and schools in celebrating diversity while dealing with its tensions further in the next section. For the remainder of this section, we will begin to explore these tensions, using the context of England as a case in point. Within this we draw links between significant, high-profile public events over the last twenty years and the ways in which they have informed and shaped education policy and practice. Doing so reminds us that education policies relating to diversity can seldom – if ever – be separated from events and concerns in wider society. Indeed, education is often seen by governments and policy makers to be a central mechanism through which tensions stemming from greater diversity can be managed and reduced.

1   On 22 April 1993, Stephen Lawrence, a young black British man from South East London was murdered in a racially motivated attack while waiting for a bus. Five white British men were investigated and arrested, but the Crown Prosecution Service judged that there was insufficient evidence to take the case to trial (in 2012 two of the men were convicted of Stephen Lawrence's murder). Amid concern about the standard of the investigation, a public enquiry was established in 1998 under the chair of Lord William MacPherson. One of the MacPherson Report's most important and highly publicised findings was of a culture of *institutional* racism within the Metropolitan Police Service. The Report defined institutional racism as:

> The collective failure of an organisation to provide an appropriate and professional service to people because of their colour, culture or ethnic origin. It can be seen or detected in processes, attitudes and behaviour which amount to discrimination through unwitting prejudice, ignorance, thoughtlessness and racist stereotyping which disadvantage minority ethnic people.
>
> (MacPherson Report, 1999: 49)

As Arora (2005) suggests, the MacPherson report was influential in recognising that racial discrimination was not only something possible of individuals, but could also be possible within whole organisations. The MacPherson Report recommended directly that the curricula in UK schools should do more to value cultural diversity and reduce racial discrimination. The subsequent Race Relations Amendment Act (2000) had a number of implications for education and educational policy. Once again, the relative lower attainment levels of students from black and minority ethnic (BME) communities were questioned with extensive policy interest and support aimed at addressing this gap. Through the work of a range of organisations – including the Office for Standards in Education (the school's inspectorate), the Qualifications and Curriculum Authority, and the Teacher Training Agency – schools were expected to place a greater focus on meeting the needs of BME students, valuing diversity within the school and its curriculum, and challenging prejudice and discrimination. Statutory guidance for the National Curriculum, for example, required that schools meet students' diverse needs, enabling them to participate effectively in lessons (for example, DfEE, 1999; QCA, 1999).

2   In 2001 separate disturbances occurred in three northern towns and cities – Oldham, Bradford and Leeds. For different reasons, each of the disturbances occurred against a backdrop of racial tension between communities (Keating and Benton, 2013). Concern was expressed that the tensions that sparked the riots had been growing over time. In light of the disturbances, an independent review was established to explore 'community cohesion' under the chair of Professor Ted Cantle (Home Office, 2001). The findings of the report start with the following summation:

> Whilst the physical segregation of housing estates and inner city areas came as no surprise, the team was particularly struck by the depth of polarisation of our towns and cities. The extent to which these physical divisions were compounded by so many other aspects of our daily lives, was very evident. Separate educational arrangements, community and voluntary bodies, employment, places of worship, language, social and cultural networks, means that many communities operate on the basis of a series of parallel lives. These lives often do not seem to touch at any point, let alone overlap and promote any meaningful interchanges.
>
> (Home Office, 2001: 9)

The report (2001: 10) went on to recommend that there was an 'urgent need to promote community cohesion, based upon a greater knowledge of, contact between, and respect for, the various cultures' within Great Britain. The report also identified an urgent need for a shared sense of citizenship and values to be developed – something which we will return to later. The focus on community cohesion formed a central strand of education policy from the publication of the report until the end of the Labour government's period in office in 2010. Since 2007, English state schools have been legally required to promote community cohesion (Keating and Benton, 2013), which has been defined officially as:

> working towards a society in which there is a *common vision* and *sense of belonging* by all communities; a society in which the diversity of people's backgrounds and circumstances is appreciated and valued; a society in which

similar *life opportunities* are available to all; and a society in which strong
and positive relationships exist and continue to be developed in the workplace,
in schools and in the wider community.

(DCSF, 2007: 3; emphasis in original).

3   On 7 July 2005 in London, in a co-ordinated series of four attacks, suicide bombers
killed 52 people and injured more than 770. The attacks focused on the London
Transport system, targeting underground trains (Russell Square, Aldgate and
Edgware Road) and a bus (Tavistock Square). All four bombers were British
citizens, three of them born in the United Kingdom. The bombers claimed their
actions were in the name of Islam, and their actions raised serious concerns within
public debates about the radicalisation of British Muslims. As a result there was
a call for education to be part of a wide-ranging set of policy responses: (1) to
help prevent the radicalisation, and (2) to prevent the stereotyping and misrepre-
sentation of both Islam as a religion and British Muslims. In large part informed
by the debates which followed the July Bombings, the Department for Education
and Skills launched a review of Diversity and Citizenship in the curriculum under
the chair of Keith Ajegbo, a leading school headteacher in London. Drawing
on its research in schools, one of the key recommendations of the Ajegbo Report
(DfES, 2007: 97) was that a further strand be added to the curriculum for citizenship education in English state secondary schools entitled 'identity and diversity:
living together in the UK'. This recommendation was taken up in the revised
National Curriculum published and taught in England between 2008 and 2014
(the latest instantiation of the citizenship curriculum in England to be taught
from September 2014 requires that 14–16 year olds be taught about the 'diverse
national, regional, religious and ethnic identities in the United Kingdom and the
need for mutual respect and understanding' (DfE, 2013)).

Each of the three examples we have outlined here signifies some of the tensions
relating to diversity – evidenced further by the extensive consternation, enquiries and
debates invoked by each about what it means to live in a multicultural nation in the
early twenty-first century. Different contexts will have their own examples – whether
national or local in scope and profile – which evidence the interconnectedness between
tensions related to diversity and the ways in which these tensions impact on
educational policy and initiatives at national and local levels.

Activity

Reflecting on your own context

We have briefly outlined here the ways in which, in the recent past, events related
to diverse communities have come to influence public policy *and* educational
practice within England. Now, reflect on your own context. Are there any global,
national or local events or other factors that *you* will need to take into account within
educational practice concerned with helping students to live in a diverse world? How
do these affect the educational institutions with which you are involved?

Balancing plural interests with shared values

The various events and tensions outlined above – including the debates to which they have led and the possible solutions identified – are underpinned by a central question facing diverse communities, societies and nations. The question can be formulated as follows: How can modern nations recognise, respect and celebrate diversity while at the same time having a sense of shared values, commitment and unity?

Most democratic nations are grappling – at both national and local levels – with this question, and in doing so are attempting to find some ground between the ethnocentrism of forced assimilation (where group identities and cultural differences are subordinated to national identity) and forms of cultural relativism, which eschew any sense of allegiance and shared interest beyond one's own ethnic/cultural group (an idea that serves a theoretical purpose, but which is not viable in practice). The balance to be aimed for, then, is one which recognises and embraces difference *but at the same time* enables unity through some sort of shared commitment. One of the leading scholars on education and diversity, James Banks (2008a: 130–1), explains this tension:

> Global immigration and the increasing diversity in nation-states throughout the world challenge ... assimilationist conceptions of citizenship. They raise complex and divisive questions about how nation-states can deal effectively with the problem of constructing civic communities that reflect and incorporate the diversity of citizens and yet have an overarching set of shared values, ideals, and goals to which all of the citizens of a nation-state are committed.

Another leading writer on living in diverse nations and communities – Bhikhu Parekh (2000b: 231) – has written that in recent times there has been a political focus on shared national identity in Western democracies because of the 'need to cultivate a common sense of belonging among ... diverse communities'. As part of his presidential campaign in 2008, Barack Obama touched upon similar themes in a speech on the subject of 'race' in Philadelphia, in which he explained:

> I chose to run for the presidency at this moment in history because I believe deeply that we cannot solve the challenges of our time unless we solve them together – unless we perfect our union by understanding that we may have different stories, but we hold common hopes; that we may not look the same and we may not have come from the same place, but we all want to move in the same direction – towards a better future for our children and our grandchildren.
>
> (New York Times, 2008)

These views raise important questions regarding the role and nature of educating about and for diversity in contemporary contexts, and in particular about how plural interests can be recognised alongside a commitment to common and shared values. In the next section, we consider some of the key terms that have shaped contemporary thinking, political discussions and education practice in this area. But before doing so it is important that we reiterate one further point that we raised in the introduction to this chapter. In our exploration we are focusing on living in a diverse world, something which necessarily involves living in diverse local communities. While we separate out diversity here within our analysis, we recognise that diversity inter-relates in important ways with a range of other factors, which affect how lives are lived. For example, and perhaps most significantly, questions relating to diversity are not fully distinct from questions relating to socio-economic status. In their work Keating and Benton (2013) consider whether tensions concerning cohesion are really about diversity or whether they are really about poverty. They cite the work of Laurence and Heath (2008: 41) as evidence that 'ethnically diverse areas tend to be *more* rather than less cohesive and that it is "deprivation that undermines cohesion, not diversity"'. In their tentative analysis of data obtained from the extensive Citizenship Education Longitudinal Study conducted in England between 2001 and 2012, they suggest that 'the overall level of ethnic diversity in a school appears to have little or no relationship with the cohesion attitudes, behaviours and attachments of its students' (Keating and Benton, 2013: 173).

Multiculturalism, interculturalism and cosmopolitanism

In this section we will explore three concepts relating to living in a diverse world; namely multiculturalism, interculturalism and cosmopolitanism. It is important to restate here a key point that we introduced in the introduction to this chapter – that forms of diversity brought about by the processes of *globalisation* are often experienced at the *local* level of communities and, as we have explored in the previous section, give rise to complex issues within and for *nations*. The three concepts on which we focus in this section are in many ways inter-related, although there is sufficient difference between them to make it possible and worthwhile to consider them separately. Each involves an empirical sentiment about the world in which we live (for example, that we live in cosmopolitan communities). But the concepts do more than this: for some they also offer a normative goal or hope (for example, that we should be cosmopolitan in our outlook).

Multiculturalism and education

> It does not make sense to encourage strong multicultural or minority identities and weak common or national identities; strong multicultural identities are a good thing – they are not intrinsically divisive, reactionary or subversive – but they need the complement of a framework of vibrant, dynamic, national narratives and the ceremonies and rituals which give expression to a national identity. It is clear that minority identities are capable of exerting an emotional pull for the individuals for whom they are important. Multicultural citizenship, if it is to be equally attractive to the same individuals, requires a counterbalancing pull.
>
> (Modood, 2007)

Of all the concepts and terms used to refer to the plural and heterogeneous nature of diverse communities, multiculturalism has received by far the most attention, both within the academic literature and within public policy and debate. Multiculturalism is a concept that has recently received critical attention for being somewhat limited, although as we shall see later, for some of its leading proponents this criticism has been misguided and unhelpful. Part of the reason for the different interpretations of the usefulness of multiculturalism is that 'different models of multiculturalism can be followed, so in this sense there are many multiculturalisms' (Osler, 2008: 16).

A simple definition would view multiculturalism as the awareness and acceptance of different cultural identities within society such that 'immigrant and minority groups can retain important aspects of their languages and cultures while exercising full citizenship rights' (Banks, 2008a: 132). Because of this, it is generally recognised that in such multicultural societies singular forms of identity are no longer viable and that identities are fluid and often characterised by their hybridity. As Ladson-Billings (2004: 112) suggests:

> The dynamic of modern . . . nation-states makes identities as either an individual or a member of a group untenable. Rather than seeing the choice as either/or, the citizen of the nation-state operates in the realism of both/and . . . People move back and forth across many identities, and the way society responds to these identities either binds people to or alienates them from the civic culture.

This last point is worth reiterating – the ways in which society interacts with and responds to multiple identities can result in either *affiliation* or *alienation*. In his influential work, *The Future of Multi-ethnic Britain*, Bikhu Parekh (2000a: 36) raised serious concerns about the extent to which such alienation was felt in the British context, suggesting that Britain 'continues to be disfigured by racism; by phobias about cultural difference . . . by institutional discrimination; and by a systematic failure of social justice'. In similar remarks, the then Chair of the UK's Commission for Racial Equality Trevor Phillips (2005) argued that Britain was 'sleepwalking to segregation' and that there had been too much of a focus 'on the "multi" and not enough on the common culture'.

Recognition of multiple identities within a common framework has been a key feature of educational policies concerning diversity. In England, for example, guidance from the Department for Education and Skills published in 2004 made clear that:

> Pupils need to know and feel confident in their own identity, but also be open to change and development, and to be able to engage positively with other identities. All pupils need to be comfortable with the concept of multiple identity and with hyphenated terms such as Black-British, British-Muslim and English-British.
>
> (21)

The American education scholar James Banks (2008b) identifies *five dimensions* of multicultural education. The dimensions are:

1 *Content integration*: The ways in which teachers make use of different examples, events and individuals drawn from a range of cultural groups and identities.
2 *The knowledge construction process*: The co-construction of knowledge between teachers and students, including an examination of ways in which central texts and assumptions reflect dominant, partial and perspectival forms of knowledge.

3   *Prejudice reduction*: The method of teaching and supporting students to develop democratic attitudes and dispositions in order that they act to reduce, challenge and combat prejudice.

4   *An equity pedagogy*: The explicit and implicit processes through which curriculum, teaching and learning are brought together in ways that reflect the needs of diverse cultural groups – including relating to the life-worlds of students.

5   *An empowering school culture and social structure*: The establishment of school structures and processes – including mission and ethos – based on equity for all students, including democratic structures and respectful relationships.

If one were to review virtually all official government reports, programmes and initiatives relating to multicultural education, aspects of these dimensions would be found. The emphasis that Banks provides, however, is that *all of the dimensions are required*, none sufficient alone, to ensure that education is truly multicultural. This recognition is reflected in the criticisms some have aimed at initiatives like Black History Month or African American History Month. In regard to the former, Tikly *et al.* (2004) critique the use of Black History Month by some schools as the only instance of content integration. In their commentary of such criticisms, Maylor and Read (2007: 19) suggest that:

> Diversity presented in this partial manner, through the use of a few additional texts on diversity, suggests that 'diversity' is not viewed as mainstream and is indeed at the margins of 'normal' or mainstream British history . . . writers also observe that there are contributions made by other minority ethnic groups to British society that need to be included within the curriculum.

Activity

The five dimensions – evaluating the school and its curriculum

Banks' five dimensions highlight that educators need to consider a range of educational processes and content in educating about and for diversity. This is a recurring theme throughout this chapter. In relation to an educational institution you know, ideally a school or early childhood centre, consider the ways and extent to which the setting demonstrates or does not demonstrate each of Banks' five dimensions.

Multiculturalism, however, has not been without its critics, particularly in terms of public policy and debate. In their analysis of the British context, Meer and Modood (2011: 176) present a number of reasons as to why multiculturalism has fallen from favour, including the perception that it has 'facilitated and enhanced social divisions' and that it has 'encouraged a moral hesitancy among "native" populations'. Illustrative of the rejection of multiculturalism as a useful political term is a speech on radicalisation and Islamic extremism made in Munich in 2011 by the UK Prime Minister David Cameron. In the speech, Cameron (2011) claimed:

> In the UK some men find it hard to identify with the traditional Islam practised at home by their parents whose customs can seem staid when transplanted to modern Western countries. But they also find it hard to identify with Britain too, because we have allowed the weakening of our collective identity. Under the doctrine of state multiculturalism, we have encouraged different cultures to live separate lives, apart from each other and the mainstream. We have failed to provide a vision of society to which they feel they can belong. We have even tolerated these segregated communities behaving in ways that run counter to our values.

In educational terms, while the concept of multiculturalism continues to hold currency in some jurisdictions (particularly the United States, Canada and Australia), in others it has received a good deal of criticism (particularly in Europe). In England, for example, a dominant (and as we suggest later, misguided) interpretation of multiculturalism views it as somewhat naïve – concerned with celebrating differences, but not enabling an insightful and meaningful dialogue between different groups. Many critics of approaches to multicultural education in England portray it in negative terms. The reasons for this are varied, and include the criticisms of it made by leading public figures, like David Cameron. In addition, multiculturalism for some has become synonymous with a naïve and uncritical form of education in which different cultures are celebrated, but in which differences and commonalities are not explored in a meaningful way. This uncritical multiculturalism has been characterised as celebrating 'saris, samosas and steel-bands'. While we would take issue with the view that multiculturalism is *necessarily* uncritical, there has been a movement within both public policy and education toward embracing what is proposed as a better alternative – interculturalism. It is to this concept that our attention now turns.

Interculturalism and education

> Intercultural dialogue is the best guarantee of a more powerful, just and sustainable world.
>
> (Robert Alan Silverstein, unsourced)

For some commentators, interculturalism represents an important alternative to multiculturalism (Wood *et al.*, 2006), whereas for Lentin (2005: 394) interculturalism is an 'updated version' of multiculturalism. For some advocates of multiculturalism (Meer and Modood, 2011; Kymlicka, 2012), the movement away from multiculturalism to interculturalism, particularly as it has occurred within the European Union, is mainly polemical and as such interculturalism does not really involve anything that cannot be found in properly constituted forms of multiculturalism, and therefore owes more to political expediency than to real differences. As educators it is worthwhile exploring, therefore, what interculturalism is and whether it is useful in helping teachers respond to the pluralism that is a common feature of communities and classrooms.

In their analysis of the relationship between multiculturalism and interculturalism, Meer and Modood (2011: 177) identify fours ways in which the former has been contrasted to the latter in public discourse: (1) that whereas multiculturalism involves different cultural groups living together in a respectful way, interculturalism encourages and requires greater dialogue and interaction between different cultural groups; (2) that owing to this greater dialogue and interaction, interculturalism involves an explicit aim for some sense of 'synthesis' between groups; (3) that more so than multiculturalism, interculturalism involves a fundamental commitment to shared commitments as citizens; and (4) that while multiculturalism may be 'illiberal and relativistic', interculturalism challenges perspectives and is therefore better able to address 'illiberal cultural practices'.

In considering these four points of contrast between multiculturalism and interculturalism, we can see the central role afforded to dialogue and interaction within the latter. Wood *et al.* (2006: 7) explain that:

> Multiculturalism has been founded on the belief in tolerance between cultures but it is not always the case that multicultural places are open places. Interculturalism on the other hand requires openness as a prerequisite and, while openness in itself is not the guarantee of interculturalism, it provides the setting for introduction interculturalism to develop.

In Europe, the recent focus on intercultural dialogue has represented a distinct movement away from the perceived outdated and unhelpful concept of multiculturalism. For example, the Council of Europe's White Paper on intercultural dialogue *Living Together as Equals in Dignity* claims that:

> Whilst driven by benign intentions, multiculturalism is now seen by many as having fostered communal segregation and mutual incomprehension, as well as having contributed to the undermining of the rights of individuals – and, in particular, women – within minority communities, perceived as if these were single collective actors . . . a recurrent theme of the consultation was that multiculturalism was a policy with which respondents no longer felt at ease.
>
> (Council of Europe, 2008: 18).

In the White Paper, the Council of Europe (2008: 17) provide an underpinning definition of intercultural dialogue, which they present as:

> a process that comprises an open and respectful exchange of views between individuals and groups with different ethnic, cultural, religious and linguistic backgrounds and heritage, on the basis of mutual understanding and respect. It requires the freedom and ability to express oneself, as well as the willingness and capacity to listen to the views of others. Intercultural dialogue contributes to political, social, cultural and economic integration and the cohesion of culturally diverse societies. It fosters equality, human dignity and a sense of common purpose. It aims to develop a deeper understanding of diverse world views and practices, to increase co-operation and participation (or the freedom to make choices), to allow personal growth and transformation, and to promote tolerance and respect for the other.

The significance attached to interculturalism at a policy level is further evidenced by 2008 being adopted by the European Union as its *Year of Intercultural Dialogue*. The year, which involved a range of EU-wide projects, events, debates, and initiatives, had three overarching aims:

1   *raising public awareness* in Europe and beyond of the need for intercultural dialogue to help us adapt to an increasingly mixed and complex world;
2   *involving many people* in exploring what intercultural dialogue means in their daily life;
3   *promoting the role* of intercultural dialogue in:

- increasing mutual understanding
- exploring the benefits of cultural diversity
- fostering active European citizenship and a sense of European belonging.

(European Commission, 2013)

In education, there has been a burgeoning of interest in the role that education can and should play in developing interculturality. The field of intercultural education, for example, has its own international, peer-reviewed journal. Writing in this, David Coulby (2006: 246) makes clear that interculturalism should not be considered as a curriculum subject, but as a 'theme, probably a major theme, which needs to inform the teaching of all subjects'. The context of Australia provides an apt example of this, and also demonstrates how multiculturalism and interculturalism are not always viewed as mutually exclusive. We considered in the first section of this chapter that multiculturalism has been, and continues to be, an important policy focus in Australia. In education – where policy has traditionally been the preserve of the individual states and territories, but has over the last few years developed a federal national curriculum – the overall approach of multiculturalism is accompanied by a recognition of the need for, and importance of, intercultural understanding. This attachment to intercultural understanding can be evidenced at both a federal and an individual state level. For example, in their strategy document *Education for Global and Multicultural Citizenship*, the Department of Education and Early Childhood Development in Victoria, Australia identifies intercultural understanding as a key constituent of global and multicultural citizenship:

An interculturally literate person possesses the skills, knowledge, understanding and attitudes required to form relationships and collaborate with others across cultures. They value, respect and explore cultural difference, critically reflect upon varied cultural traditions (including their own) and participate fully in cross-cultural interactions. They are able to communicate effectively in contexts both familiar and unfamiliar.

(DEECD, 2009: 5)

At a federal level, *intercultural understanding* forms one of seven 'general capabilities' that sit across the Australian National Curriculum. The scope of the capability is set out as follows:

Intercultural understanding combines personal, interpersonal and social know-ledge and skills. It involves students in learning to value and view critically their own cultural perspectives and those of others through their interactions with people, texts and contexts across the curriculum.

Intercultural understanding encourages students to make connections between their own worlds and worlds of others, to build on shared interests and common-alities, and to negotiate or mediate difference. It develops students' abilities to communicate and empathise with others and to analyse intercultural experiences critically. It offers opportunities for them to consider their own beliefs and attitudes in a new light, and so gain insight into themselves and others.

Intercultural understanding stimulates students' interest in the lives of others. It cultivates values and dispositions such as curiosity, care, empathy, reciprocity, respect and responsibility, open-mindedness and critical awareness, and supports new and positive intercultural behaviours. Though all are significant in learning to live together, three dispositions – expressing empathy, demonstrating respect and taking responsibility – have all been identified as critical to the development of intercultural understanding in Australia.

(ACARA, 2012: 1)

We have consciously repeated the scope of intercultural understanding in full as it provides a clear, succinct and thorough depiction of the key elements and intended outcomes of intercultural education: empathy, respect, care, open-mindedness and sharing one's own interests and perspectives while learning and hearing those of others. These are important learning outcomes in educating about and for diversity that we will return to later on in this chapter.

Whether we accept that significant differences exist between them, or we view intercultural understanding as an important part of multiculturalism, both terms are centrally concerned with the nature of citizenship, identity and belonging in nation-states as a result of the diversity brought by increased levels of global movement of peoples and greater recognition of the rights and cultures of indigenous populations. At times linked to these discussions, but often unhelpfully separate from them, is a further conceptual approach – cosmopolitanism – which brings into question the relationship between membership and belonging within a nation-state and affiliations and connections to global humanity. We consider this next.

Cosmopolitanism and education

As previously discussed in Chapter 1, in recent years a significant body of literature in the fields of political science (for example, Nussbaum, 1994, 1996; Appiah, 2006; Held, 2010) and a growing corpus in the field of education (for example, Osler and Starkey, 2003; Merry and de Ruyter, 2011) has identified 'cosmopolitanism' as a meaningful and useful concept for understanding contemporary citizenship in diverse local and global communities. A core tenet of cosmopolitanism – which finds expression across various political, economic, cultural and moral forms – is that globalisation means that civic identities focusing solely on the nation-state are increasingly being transcended as a result of increased movement (whether physically, technologically or mentally) across boundaries and borders. For supporters of cosmopolitanism, there is a need for people to view themselves as citizens of the world either as well as, or instead of, citizens of the nation-state. This view invokes a principle which draws on the Cynic Diogenes' assertion, when asked from where he came, that 'I am a citizen of the world [*kosmopolitês*]'.

A central idea within cosmopolitanism, particularly those forms that include a focus on moral relationships transcending borders, is the acknowledgement that 'common humanity . . . translates ethically into an idea of shared or common moral duties toward others by virtue of this humanity' (Lu, 2000: 245). Such a position is exemplified in Held's (2010: 69) assertion that '[H]umankind belongs to a single "moral realm" in which each person is regarded as equally worthy of respect and consideration'. This requires citizens living in one particular nation-state having a moral obligation to consider and account for the needs of others in the world. For Nussbaum, there is a need to 'work to make all human beings part of our community of dialogue and concern' (1996: 9). This means that we should treat all human beings – wherever they live in the world – as ends in themselves. This requires us to recognise a shared human dignity. While this point is philosophical, it has clear real world implications. For example, it might be argued that if a consumer buys a product made in another country by an under-paid and neglected child labourer they are not appropriately recognising and respecting the dignity of the child labourer. Rather, they are in effect using the child as a means to their own ends – gaining pleasure from purchasing and owning the product.

That cosmopolitanism provides a meaningful concept, which can guide and shape educational practice, has received increasing levels of attention in educational discourse. Nussbaum, for example, contends that 'world citizenship, rather than democratic or national citizenship, [should be] the focus for civic education' (1996: 11). According to two of the leading educational proponents of a cosmopolitan approach, a defining characteristic of the educated cosmopolitan citizen is to 'work to achieve peace, human rights and democracy within the local community and at a global level, by . . . *accepting personal responsibility* and recognising the importance of civic commitment' (Osler and Starkey, 2003: 246; emphasis added). This once again highlights the importance of inter-relationships between the local and the global. According to Osler (2008: 22):

> [E]ducation for cosmopolitan citizenship . . . requires us to re-imagine the nation . . . as cosmopolitan and to recognise local communities and the national community as cosmopolitan. It implies a sense of solidarity with strangers in distant places but it also requires solidarity, a sense of shared humanity and dialogue with those in the local community and the national community whose perspectives may be very different from our own.

For two further advocates of a cosmopolitan approach within education, Michael Merry and Doret de Ruyter, it is not enough for students to be taught about their inter-relationship with others and the need to recognise the common humanity in others (wherever they live in the world); students need to be taught that they must account for these in their own actions. They suggest, for example, that 'at a minimum the struggle against injustice entails that one reduces the suffering of others, as far as one is able, irrespective of pre-existing desires or relationships, but also geographical proximity, of those in need of help' (2011: 2).

Activity

Educating about and for diversity: multiculturalism, interculturalism and cosmopolitanism

As we have progressed through this chapter we have hopefully made clear that while it is frequently analytically important and often politically expedient to distinguish between multiculturalism, interculturalism and cosmopolitanism, as educators there may be elements of each that strike us as being useful or significant to our practices and contexts. Now we ask you to reflect on the following statement:

> Schools should help students to understand how cultural, national, regional, and global identifications are interrelated, complex and evolving . . . These identifications are interactive in a dynamic way. Each should be recognized, valued, publically affirmed, and thoughtfully examined in schools. Students should be encouraged to critically examine their identifications and commitments and to understand the complex ways in which they are interrelated and constructed.
>
> (Banks, 2008a: 134)

Which of the concepts do you think provides the best response to Banks' call on schools? Is it one of the concepts in isolation or a combination? What is the basis for your judgement?

Developing pedagogies for diverse communities, schools and classrooms

We would argue that at the heart of educators' work in developing effective pedagogies for diverse communities, schools and classrooms is the concept of *recognition*. Each of the aspects of pedagogy touched upon in this chapter so far – developing empathy, sharing interests, practising tolerance, understanding context etc. relates in important ways to *recognition*. As educators, it is important that we think about the ways in which teaching, learning and the curriculum recognises – or indeed may often fail to recognise – different perspectives and plural interests. Charles Taylor (1992: 25–26; emphasis in original), for example, says the following about the importance of recognition:

Our identity is partly shaped by recognition or its absence, often by the *mis*recognition of others, and so a person or group of people can suffer real damage, real distortion, if the people of a society around them mirror back a confining or demeaning or contemptible picture of themselves. Non recognition or misrecognition can inflict harm, can be a form of oppression, imprisoning some in a false, distorted, and reduced mode of being.

This reminds us that identities are not fixed, but rather are fluid and can be affected in positive and negative ways by a complex range of experiences and interactions. Such experiences and interactions occur between the state and individuals/groups as well as between individuals/groups.

The focus on recognition and the necessity of dialogue raises important questions for schools and teachers about the extent to which, and the ways in which, students can be supported to engage in deliberation and discussion in order to share their own interests and to come to understand the interests of others. Links between deliberation and education have been made in a number of countries, and Gutmann and Thompson (1996: 359) suggest that '[I]n any effort to make democracy more deliberative, the single most important institution outside government is the educational system'. As part of this endeavour, students are involved in articulating their interests, and coming to know the interests of others, through dialogical processes. This broadly deliberative approach to dialogue within education is encapsulated by the Swedish National Agency for Education (2000: 8) who contend that:

> [D]ialogue allows differing views and values to confront one another and develop. Dialogue allows individuals to make their own ethical judgements by listening, reflecting, finding arguments and appraising, while it also constitutes an important point of developing an understanding of one's own views and those of others.

Democratic communication within civic education involves students in deliberating both with peers and with those in positions of power (whether in the school or the wider political community) (Barton and Levstik, 2004). The work of Walter Parker (2003, 2006) and of Diana Hess (2009) reminds us that communication and deliberation can adopt two main purposes within classrooms. Hess (2009: 85; emphasis in the original) suggests that educators may aim at 'teaching *for* and *with* discussion' and that communication 'is both a desired outcome and a method of teaching', while Parker (2006: 12), on whom Hess draws, remarks that the 'two kinds of discourse are complementary in school practice, and neither is sufficient alone'. For Parker, discussion aims at both 'enriching the mind and cultivating a democratic political community'. This is particularly important and apt for dialogue between diverse groups. Indeed, as Walter Parker (2004: 453) reminds us: 'diversity figures as the most deliberative asset'.

Peterson (2012) has outlined six 'capacities' that need to be developed to support students' effective engagement in meaningful dialogue:

1 *civic commitment*: Students need to have a desire to participate in open and unforced dialogue. Such dialogue is likely to be ineffective if it is forced or tokenistic;

2   *civic knowledge*: Students need not only to know and understand certain facts, but to apply such learning to their actions and deliberations. It is not a sufficient condition of democratic and deliberative civic education simply for students to know – they must be able to apply such knowledge appropriately in their discursive interactions;

3   *civic speaking*: In their verbal communication students need to employ reason, but not eschew the use of rhetoric and rhetorical devices in order, and when appropriate, to stir the emotions of others. Civic speaking is a particular brand of talk which aims at making clear one's own position and interests, but in a way which invites others to respond to these in the spirit of civic commitment. The skills, confidence and self-esteem necessary for civic speaking are not innate, and take time to cultivate;

4   *civic listening*: The clearest illustration of civic listening comes from Benjamin Barber (1998: 118), who asserts that '[T]he public not only has a voice, but an ear: the skills of listening are as important as the skills of talking', and that '. . . talk as communication . . . involves receiving as well as expressing, hearing as well as speaking, and emphasizing as well as uttering' (2003: 174).

5   *civic empathy*: Students engage in dialogical forums in order that they come to understand the perspectives and interests which others hold dear. Students should learn to empathise not only with the interests of others, but also with the public interest, particularly when these may be in conflict with their own. As citizens interact, they are required to take on board and reflect upon how their actions and interests affect other citizens, as well as the manner in which other citizens are affected by actions of the State. Empathy should not degenerate into sympathy or, worse still, pity;

6   *internal-reflection*: Involved in each of the other five elements, internal-reflection aims at more than a simplistic evaluation of what went well and what did not. Rather it tends to the process which Dewey (1933: 9) describes as the 'active, persistent and careful consideration of any belief or supposed form of knowledge in the light of grounds that support it and further conclusions to which it tends'. This reminds is that when students engage in dialogue with each other, they are likely to be involved in reflecting upon and amending their views, based on the interests and evidence which they are subjected to. This will inevitably involve a number of complex, and not always comfortable, stages including the challenging of prejudices, and the changing of opinions as a result of new ideas and information. The processes involved are likely to be demanding on students, and will involve both cognitive and affective domains.

At the heart of deliberative dialogue is the acceptance that it is a co-operative and shared endeavour rather than one which is competitive and individual. Elizabeth McGrath (cited in Nash, 1997: 147) makes the observation that:

> Many people seem compelled to jump into a heated argument the moment they have sensed a different opinion . . . This tendency may be natural, but it need not be controlling. We can learn to acknowledge, without feeling threatened, the value of ideas that do not fit our system . . . [when I acknowledge the other] I am simply offering to that person the dignity, support, and encouragement that I myself need

as I inch my way along the path. In short, we can choose to act as effective catalysts and staunch supports for one another or we can make [dialogue] even more difficult and painful by fuelling the fires of self-doubt in ourselves and others.

In Chapter 2 you were introduced to a range of deliberative pedagogies. This pedagogy is particularly apt for informing educators' practice within diverse class-rooms, as illustrated in the following case study.

Case study

A role for inter-faith dialogue?

One of the key dimensions of cultural diversity is the closer proximity and interaction of people of different faiths and/or people of no faith. Faith – and the diversity of religious and non-religious life-worlds this includes – raises a number of questions for global learning as well as for public policy and public life. Such questions include the forms and nature of faith positions within culturally diverse communities, the official constitutional relationship between religion and politics in individual nations, the place and nature of faith in political life, and the extent to which issues concerning faith should – and actually do – remain private.

While these questions have been prevalent for centuries, their precise nature has been influenced in recent years by the complexities of greater religious diversity brought about by a range of factors, including migration and changing patterns of religious practice across many nations. According to many leading theorists of religion, such as Berger (1999) and Martin (2005), the condition of religion world-wide evidences two particular patterns; first, the rise of secularization (typically depicted in terms of reporting of religious commitment as well as regular religious worship) in Western Europe, Canada and Australia, and the maintenance, and even growth, in religion elsewhere.

Given this religious diversity, as well as some of the tensions to which it has led, a number of educationalists have looked to draw on the wider field of inter-faith dialogue as a strand within intercultural dialogue. Inter-faith dialogue has been defined as:

> the different faith communities not just living harmoniously side-by-side . . . but actively knowing about and respecting each other and each other's beliefs in fair and honourable competition.
>
> (Cahill and Leahy, 2004: 12)

Two examples of initiatives that draw on inter-faith dialogue are:

*   *Harmony Day:* Celebrated on 21 March every year since 1999, Harmony Day is an annual event organised by the Federal Government in Australia. Harmony Day coincides with the United Nations International Day for the

continued . . .

Elimination of Racial Discrimination. Events celebrating Harmony Day are organised in a range of public organisations, including schools, around the theme 'Everyone Belongs'. The website provides a range of educational resources for schools and teachers (www.harmony.gov.au).

- *Redbridge Ambassadors of Faith and Belief*: A local initiative led by Newbury Park Primary School in London in which older students (16–19 year olds) from local schools 'have been trained to support religious education and promote social cohesion by sharing their faith experience with children in local primary schools' (OfSTED, 2013: 1). Many of the project's aims are particularly pertinent, including 'to promote community cohesion (intergenerational, as well as in relation to religion, belief (and non-belief), culture and ethnicity)', 'to ensure young people develop skills that will enable them to live constructively in and with this diversity', and 'to provide an opportunity for young people to listen to each other without prejudice, of discovering the common ground, of accepting the differences and of building confidence in their own identity' (Newbury Park Primary School, 2013: 2). The project website provides details of the current ambassadors and their profiles (www.redbridgeafab.org.uk).

Conclusion

In this chapter we have discussed and explored the reasons for increasingly diverse communities, some of the educational challenges these bring, and some potential educational responses to them. As with other key elements of global education, there is an important sense in which schools cannot simply teach students *about* certain principles, whether that be human rights or recognising and respecting diversity; they must do more. Schools must embrace and enact these commitments in order for them to be meaningful. As Audrey Osler (2008: 18) writes in relation to diversity:

> if schools are invited to promote a depoliticised multicultural approach which does not encourage political literacy or critical analysis of democracy and diversity there is a real danger that this will leave unchallenged (and possibly disguise) the considerable inequalities within schools.

While throughout this chapter we have focused on the role of education in supporting social cohesion, as educators we must be mindful that 'social cohesion and social justice cannot be separated . . . social cohesion (whether it concerns ethnicity, gender, age or any other social grouping) cannot occur where inequalities in housing, education, economic well-being, health and policing persist' (Cremin and Warwick, 2008: 37). As educators we need to reflect on these and how we can respond to them when planning for students living and learning with diversity.

Questions for further investigation

1 To what extent does 'multiculturalism' look similar or different within different contexts (either between places in one nation or across nations)?
2 How do these differences relate to educational policies and practices concerning diverse interests and shared values?
3 What are the key dispositions and skills you think students should learn in order to participate effectively in diverse communities?

Further reading

Banks, J. (2008) *An Introduction to Multicultural Education*. Boston, MA: Pearson.
An interesting and insightful account of multicultural education written by one of the leading education scholars in the field.

Hess, D. E. (2009) *Controversy in the Classroom: The Democratic Power Discussion*. Abingdon: Routledge.
An excellent account and exploration of deliberation around controversial and sensitive issues in the classroom.

Intercultural Education. Published by Taylor & Francis.
This journal is an excellent resource, containing articles on a range of areas related to intercultural education and – importantly – includes contributions from a wide range of different contexts. The following article from the journal provides a good overview of intercultural education: Coulby, D. (2006) 'Intercultural education: theory and practice', *Intercultural Education*. 17 (3): 245–57.

Social justice

Introduction

Writing in 2007, David Cameron (now Prime Minister of the United Kingdom) argued that 'without good education there can be no social justice' (Cameron, 2007: 84). In this chapter we will explore and analyse two key elements of global social justice – human rights and development – as well as the particular and varied forms of education related to them. We have separated the two fields out deliberately in this chapter. Our contention is that both human rights education and development education are distinct and meaningful strands within the wider field of global education, and that both relate fundamentally to issues of global justice. However, this does not mean that the two fields are unrelated. Indeed, questions of human rights are frequently bound up with issues related to development. The connection between the two is central to the work of the highly influential economist Amartya Sen. In his seminal text *Development as Freedom* (1999: xii) he argues that 'expansion of freedom is . . . both . . . the primary end and . . . the principal means of development', and that 'development consists of the removal of various types of unfreedoms that leave people with little choice and little opportunity of exercising their reasoned agency'. Similarly, Thomas Hammarberg (2008), then the Council of Europe's Commissioner for Human Rights, points out that poverty is not 'only a question of low income, but also of marginalisation, vulnerability and powerlessness. Poor people ha[ve] very little access to the system of justice and generally [lack] the means of being heard and claiming their rights.' Where possible and appropriate we will highlight the connections between human rights/human rights education and development/development education, asking you to consider their educational implications.

Human rights and human rights education

Where, after all, do universal human rights begin? In small places, close to home – so close and so small that they cannot be seen on any maps of the world. Yet they are the world of the individual person; the neighbourhood he lives in; the school or college he attends; the factory, farm, or office where he works. Such are the places where every man, woman, and child seeks equal justice, equal opportunity, equal dignity without discrimination. Unless these rights have meaning there, they will have little meaning anywhere. Without concerted citizen action to uphold them close to home, we shall look in vain for progress in the larger world.
(Eleanor Roosevelt, cited in Ministry of Justice *et al.*, 2008: 3)

In this section we will explore different understandings of human rights, key human rights declarations and legislation, and different ideas within the broad term of 'human rights education'. Many of the examples that will be considered as we progress through the chapter focus either on general issues concerning human rights or on human rights issues in particular contexts. It is, of course, not possible to consider human rights in their entirety within this chapter. Our view is that it is vital for all educators to engage in a process of conscious reflection about the context of their work and its links to issues of social justice and human rights, for as Tibbitts (2002: 160) reminds us, 'every society has human rights problems'. As we will consider, human rights have many features and this raises a range of issues relating to defining them, valuing them, respecting them, protecting them, and advocating for them.

What are human rights?

Human rights are a key feature of contemporary life. Hardly a week passes without a number of 'human rights issues' appearing in the media. The continued existence of conflict around the world, the plight of asylum seekers and refugees, as well as contentious domestic policies practised in a number of nations – such as capital punishment or the extradition of prisoners to states that may gain evidence through the use of torture – mean that questions to do with human rights are all around us. Rights also relate to young people's lives in schools. Students are often keen to draw on their rights to justify particular actions or to challenge those of others. But what are human rights and on what basis can appeals to human rights be made? As with many of the concepts within this book, 'human rights' is not an unambiguous concept. For Bowring (2012: 53), for example, human rights are 'always and necessarily scandalous and highly contested'. In addition – and perhaps because of this – we might also add that human rights are by their very nature ever-changing. According to Osler and Starkey (2010: 93), human rights 'have gained widespread currency through a process of cultural interaction and exchange yet they are in a constant process of development as they are interpreted, negotiated and accommodated in different cultural settings'. So how within our professional capacities as educators can we start to make sense of what human rights are?

Broadly speaking, human rights refer to a set of principles – often set out in the form of a declaration – which are common to all humans within a given jurisdiction (a nation-state, a collective of nation-states, or the world). An important distinction within human rights is between those rights that are *absolute* and those that are *non-absolute*. Absolute rights – such as freedom from torture – refer to rights that should never be restricted, while non-absolute rights may justifiably be restricted in some situations. Non-absolute rights fall within two categories. First, certain human rights can be *limited* in given, specific situations. For example, the right to liberty can be restricted if someone has been found guilty of committing a crime. The other category of non-absolute human rights is *qualified* rights, which are those rights that need to be balanced in relation to those of others and of society. While qualified rights can justifiably be controlled, this control must be *lawful, legitimate, necessary* and *proportionate* (British Institute of Human Rights, 2010). For example, while children may have a right to education the government can restrict this by deciding on the age range of those entitled to compulsory education.

Beyond this, there are number of different ways to define and understand what human rights are. The first way of identifying what human rights are is to think about their *key characteristics*. Typically, human rights have been seen as constituted by being (1) *inherent* – they intrinsically belong to all people because they are human beings and as such are not given or earned; (2) *inalienable* – they are part of the human condition and as such cannot be removed or retracted; (3) *universal* – they apply to all human beings; and, (4) *indivisible* – to realise one's human rights requires the realisation of all human rights; countries cannot pick and choose which rights are important. The following definition of human rights provided by the UK Ministry of Justice in its teaching resource *Right Here Right Now* (Ministry of Justice *et al.*, 2008: 7; cf. Bowring, 2012) makes reference to these various key characteristics:

> Human rights are the basic rights we all have simply because we are human; they are the fundamental things that human beings need in order to flourish and participate fully in society. Human rights belong to everyone, regardless of their circumstances . . . The ideas behind human rights have been present throughout history in many different societies and civilisations.

A second way of defining human rights is to identify *different types* of rights. In their *Manual for Starting Human Rights Education*, Amnesty International (2001: 9) distinguish between three categories of rights: (1) *civil and political rights* – such as the right to life, to participation in political life, to freedom of assembly and the right to protest; (2) *economic and social rights* – such as the right to work, to education and to food; and (3) *environmental, cultural and developmental rights* – such as 'the right to live in an environment that is clean and protected from destruction'.

A third way of defining human rights is to start by thinking about their justifications; that is, why human rights are important. Drawing on the work of Wenar (2005), McCowan (2012: 68) distinguishes between 'status-based' and 'instrumental' justifications for human rights. The former are based on the idea considered above that human rights are 'inalienable' – they are possessed by virtue of being human. In contrast, instrumental justifications see human rights as valuable because of what they bring about for individuals and societies, namely the extent to which human rights increase general welfare and happiness. Because they focus on the benefits of general welfare and happiness, rather than on rights as an inherent individual property, instrumental justifications allow for the infringement of some rights if it is clear that this will protect certain other rights.

In addition to these categories of defining human rights, we might also expect certain things to be in place in order (1) for human rights to make practical sense and/or (2) for it to be possible to make claims to human rights. It is often thought, for example, that some form of political community is necessary. Kiwan (2012: 2), for example, argues that 'in terms of practice, clearly the possession and exercise of human rights cannot occur outside of a political community'. An interesting perspective on the importance of the political community for making sense of human rights is provided by the American political scientist James Bohman. Bohman (2004) considers the basis for the protection of human rights in a global context, critical of arguments that justify human rights as solely inalienable characteristics of human beings. Bohman (2004: 341) contends that '. . . when national states break down, liberals can only appeal to some abstract notion of human rights', and that human rights can only be maintained when 'rights are located within a particular community (in this case international)'. In cases where national states are not able to protect human rights, citizens have only the global political community to which they can appeal. From this perspective, human rights exist as 'rights of membership' rather than as an eternal or natural feature of humanity. Individuals are therefore able to appeal to the global political community for the protection of human rights, subject to certain conditions agreed and maintained by that political community. For Bohman (2004: 344), such conditions are three-fold. First, the rights claim must be *legitimate*. Second, the individual making the claim must have *standing* in the sense that they are recognised by the political community to which they are making the claim. Third, the claim must have an *addressee*, namely the political community in which the individual has membership. In this sense, the rules and rights of membership of the global political community represent a socially and politically established system.

Activity

Reflecting on your own experiences

Reflecting on your own life experiences, what would you consider to have been the essential human rights that you have enjoyed and that have provided the conditions that have supported your own sense of well-being?

Using the theoretical frameworks outlined above, what has been the nature and sources of these human rights? What or who has perhaps threatened or compromised your experiences of these human rights over time?

Human rights – a recent sphere of concern?

Contemporary interest in human rights is located within the immediate period following the end of the Second World War, and in particular the United Nations Universal Declaration of Human Rights (1948). Indeed, a common starting point for teaching students about human rights is to work through some of the international declarations, treaties and conventions, as well as key domestic instruments that set out and inform the protection of human rights. Perhaps in the above activity you may have referred to some of these as influencing and informing your own experiences of human rights. What follows is a chronological list and simple explanation of these, all of which relate to the different types of rights identified above:

The United Nations Universal Declaration of Human Rights (1948): Perhaps the leading and most influential charter to protect human rights is the UDHR. Heavily informed and shaped by the suffering and human rights abuse witnessed during the Second World War, the UDHR consists of thirty articles for the protection of human rights. It was adopted by the General Assembly on 10 December 1948. Together with the ICCPR and the ICESCR (see below), the UDHR forms part of the International Bill of Human Rights.

The Geneva Convention (1949): The Geneva Convention of 1949, which followed the Second World War, was the fourth in a series of conventions (1864, 1906, 1929) that set out the basis of humanitarian treatment during times of war. This includes the rights and protections for soldiers, prisoners of war and civilians.

European Convention on Human Rights (signed 1950/effective from 1953): The ECHR is a treaty that protects human rights within Europe ratified by all Council of Europe members. A central part of the convention was the establishment of the European Court of Human Rights to which people within Europe can seek redress for violation of their rights.

International Covenant on Economic, Social and Cultural Rights (signed 1966/effective from 1976): The ICESCR is an international treaty adopted by the United Nations General Assembly. The covenant requires signatories to respect and protect key economic, social and cultural rights, including the right to education, the right to health, and the right to work.

International Covenant on Civil and Political Rights (signed 1966/effective from 1976): The ICCPR is an international treaty adopted by the United Nations General Assembly. The covenant requires signatories to respect and protect key civil and political rights, including due process, the right to life, and freedom of speech.

United Nations Convention Against Torture (signed 1984/effective from 1987): The Convention Against Torture and Other Cruel, Inhuman or Degrading Treatment or Punishment is an international treaty adopted by the United Nations General Assembly. It commits nation-states to prevent torture and other forms of cruel, inhuman and degrading punishment within their borders, while preventing them from extraditing anyone to a nation-state where they are likely to be tortured.

United Nations Convention on the Rights of the Child (1989): The Convention on the Rights of the Child is a human rights treaty under the auspices of the United Nations, which recognises and respects the rights of children generally under the age of 18 (an exception is made in states in which the age of majority is lower). Article 12 of the Convention, for example, provides children with the right to express themselves in relation to matters that affect them. Signatory states are compelled by international law to uphold the provisions of the convention. While the United States helped to write the Convention, and signed up to its provisions, at the time of writing it is one of only three UN member states (the other two are Somalia and South Sudan) that has not ratified the Convention.

To support and enforce many of these agreements a number of international judicial systems and courts have been established, including the European Court of Human Rights, the Inter-American Court of Human Rights and the International Criminal Court.

The list of declarations, covenants and treaties above are all post-Second World War. While there is some truth in the statement that the 'rise of "human rights" can be situated in the context of post-World War II, with the adoption of the Charter of the United Nations in 1945, followed in 1948 by the passing of the Universal Declaration of Human Rights' (Kiwan, 2012: 2), we should not necessarily view the development of human rights and human rights protection as a *solely* recent occurrence. For example, in different ways and for different reasons, issues related to human rights can be found in each of the following: the Magna Carta (1215), the United States Declaration of Independence (1776), the French Declaration of the Rights of Man and the Citizen (1789) and the United States Bill of Rights (1789/1791).

In addition to these international treaties, conventions, declarations and institutions are a wealth of constitutional and legislative frameworks that protect (or indeed do not protect) certain human rights. In the United Kingdom the 1994 Criminal Justice and Public Order Act was criticised for removing or altering certain central rights within the UK. The Act altered the right to silence, for example, with the police statement on arrest changing from the words 'you have the right to remain silent' to 'you do not have to say anything. But it may harm your defence if you do not mention when questioned something which you later rely on in Court'. More high-profile has been the Human Rights Act 1998 (HRA) that came into effect in 2000. The HRA codified into UK law the protections contained within the European Convention on Human Rights, and requires all public bodies in the UK to comply with these rights. The HRA affects a wide ranging set of rights, including the right to life, the right to a fair trial, freedom of thought, belief and religion, and freedom of expression. (A full copy of the HRA can be found at www.legislation.gov.uk/ukpga/1998/42/contents). One of the rights contained within the Act is the right to education. Protocol 1, Article 2 of the HRA (1998) states that:

> no person shall be denied a right to education. In the exercise of any functions which it assumes in relation to education and to teaching, the State shall respect the right of parents to ensure such education and teaching in conformity with their own religious and philosophical convictions.

A further significant element of the HRA is that individuals can now seek redress in respect of human rights cases within the UK legal system, rather than having to appeal to the European Court of Human Rights. In addition to the HRA are a range of other acts that protect particular elements of human rights, such as acts relating to discrimination on the basis of gender, race or disability (similar national legislative acts are found within other democratic nations).

The case of the UK is interesting as it does not have a codified constitution, and instead depends largely on legislation, conventions and precedents for its rules of governance. In countries where these rules are largely found in a written document, human rights often feature as a central part of a codified constitution. In the United States, for example, human rights are protected through the different elements of its Constitution. Of particular importance are specific Amendments to the Constitution – notably the first ten Amendments (known collectively as the Bill of Rights) and subsequent Amendments such as the 13th (abolition of slavery in 1865), 14th (equal rights and protection of the laws), 15th (right to vote for all races) and the 16th (right to vote for both sexes).

However, the protection of human rights within a codified constitution is not wholly straightforward. Throughout its history the US Constitution has been subject to interpretation by the Supreme Court. For example, based on interpretation by the US Supreme Court, the rights provided for in the Constitution did not in themselves prohibit slavery. In the landmark ruling Dredd Scott v. Sandford, 1857, the Court ruled that African Americans, whether slaves or free, could not be American citizens. This principle held until it was overturned by the 13th and 14th Amendments to the US Constitution. The relevant parts of these Amendments read respectively that 'neither slavery nor involuntary servitude, except as punishment for crime whereof the party shall have been duly convicted, shall exist within the United States, or any place subject to their jurisdiction' and that:

> all persons born or naturalized in the United State, and subject to the jurisdiction thereof, are citizens of the United States and of the State wherein they reside. No State shall make or enforce any law which shall abridge the privileges or immunities of citizens of the United States; nor shall any State deprive any persons of life, liberty, or property, without any due process of law; nor deny to any person within its jurisdiction the equal protection of its laws.
>
> (www.archives.gov/exhibits/charters/constitution_
> amendments_11-27.html)

Even these Amendments were open to interpretation. For example, a further Court ruling (Plessy v. Ferguson, 1896) in effect legally endorsed segregation until that ruling was overturned by the later Brown v. Board of Education of Topeka, 1954, ruling. Still today a range of human rights issues persist in the United States – most notably the use of capital punishment in some states and the treatment of non-citizen prisoners – that are either not provided for in the Constitution or are dependent for their remedy on particular interpretations of the Constitution. The examples of the UK and the US, then, remind us that even where nations include the protection of human rights within their laws and/or written constitutions, interpretation of these items by the judiciary plays a key role in the extent of their realisation.

Activity

From where do human rights come?

In his exploration of human rights and public education, Bill Bowring (2012: 59) – a human rights lawyer, professor and advocate – makes the following statement:

> I do not find human rights empirically in the plethora of human rights instruments and their ratification by the majority of states . . . nor do I find them in human nature; nor simply in the fact of citizenship. Instead, I understand human rights as the highly contested products of great historical upheavals, social capital identified in instruments, and brought back to life constantly in the context of real struggles.

Reflecting on this statement and on the definitions of human rights set out in this chapter so far, write a short statement in response to the following question:

Human rights are . . .

In writing your statement, you might like to consider the following:

- Are human rights natural or given?
- How important are international/national conventions, charters, treaties and laws in determining and understanding human rights?
- Do human rights necessarily require or entail action?
- Does one need to be a citizen of a particular nation-state in order to have human rights?
- Can human rights only be understood through the contexts and circumstances in which they arise?
- Are human rights agreed or are they inherently contested?

Once you have written your statement, reflect on how this particular understanding of the basis of human rights might impact on how you would teach students about human rights. It will be useful for you to think about this question further as you work through the next section on human rights education.

One of the questions we need to consider as teachers is the role that the international conventions, treaties and charters can – and should – play in *formal* human rights education. Both Baxi (1994) and Bowring (2012: 55) remind us that we should remember the view expressed in the Preamble to the 1948 Universal Declaration of Human Rights that 'a common standard of achievement' of these values, nationally and globally, requires 'that every individual and organ of society, keeping this Declaration in mind, shall try by teaching and education to respect for these rights and freedoms'. Indeed, the UDHR contains a number of aims for education in relation to human rights, including promoting understanding and respect for human rights (McCowan, 2012).

Activity

Enacting a Human Rights Charter in schools

To coincide with global Human Rights Day, in December 2013 the British Institute of Human Rights launched their Human Rights Charter (www.bihr.org.uk/charter). The Charter starts with the following pledge:

> We are committed to helping build a culture of respect for human rights here at home because we believe that human rights are the cornerstone of a healthy democracy. Human rights ensure the Government plays fair and they help us to live well in communities where each person's dignity is equally respected. The Human Rights Act is the foundation for making this a reality, ensuring our rights and freedoms are protected by the law of the land.
>
> (British Institute of Human Rights, 2013)

To supplement this pledge, the Charter suggests the following actions:

1   All people in the UK, no matter our background, need to know what our human rights are and how they are protected, respected and fulfilled here at home.
2   All levels of government and services, such as local councils, the police, health services and schools, are supported to consider human rights when developing and delivering laws, policies and services.
3   Strong leadership and active communities are needed to ensure recognition of the role of human rights in providing a basic safety net for us all.

Think about, and list, the ways in which the work of schools and teachers in your own context relate to this example of a Human Rights Charter. How might aspects of this particular charter be useful for informing the work of schools and teachers? When preparing your list, you might like to think about the following areas: school mission and aims, school ethos, school policies, the taught curriculum and extra-curricular activities.

Before we end this section and turn our attention to human rights *education*, it is worth us noting that there are commentators who are critical of human rights. Similar to the critics of globalisation considered in Chapter 1, these criticisms can be divided into those who are critical of human rights *per se* and those who are critical of the turns that the discourse and practice of human rights have taken. Common concerns for critics of human rights typically perceive that – either in theory or in practice – human rights: are a Western construct; are patriarchal in nature; or they lack the 'natural' basis often ascribed to them (for a clear overview of these criticisms see Dickinson *et al.*, 2012; McCowan, 2012).

An interesting critique of human rights is provided by David Kennedy. Kennedy (2002: 101) commences his critique of human rights by making clear that the international human rights movement 'has done a great deal of good, freeing individuals from great harm, providing an emancipatory vocabulary and institutional machinery for people across the globe'. He continues, however, to express his concern that 'the human rights movement might, on balance, and acknowledging its enormous achievement, be more part of the problem in today's world than part of the solution' (2002: 101). Kennedy details a list of hypotheses as to why this is the case. His list includes that human rights discourse has become a dominant hegemony against which all other forms of emancipation have to be considered, resulting in a neglect of other approaches. For example, Kennedy cites recent thinking on development, which he suggests has become determined largely through the prism of human rights; in other words, that development is attained through greater recognition and protection of human rights, and is measured by this. Kennedy (2002: 111) also claims that because they are viewed as universal and general, human rights shut off discussions of 'what it means to be human, who is human, of how humans might relate to one another', something which leads to a focus on individual identities as rights-holders rather than participants in a communal and shared life. A further interesting perspective on the nature of human rights discourse is provided by the British political philosopher David Miller. For Miller (2002: 81), the claim that human beings are of equal worth (a central element of human rights discourse) is simply 'platitudinous' for the reason that very few would disagree with the principles of human equity and dignity. Miller continues, 'there is a gap between our moral assessments of states of affairs and the reasons we have for acting in relation to those states of affairs'. In other words, the claim that human beings are equal in and of itself tells us very little about how we should act and what our obligations are in respect of protecting human rights.

Our purpose in raising these criticisms of human rights is not to undermine their importance or to suggest that they should not be a central element of global education. It is rather to highlight that – as educators – we should adopt a critical approach to human rights, aware of the criticisms made of them and cognisant of what it is we might be seeking to achieve when questions of human rights are explored in education, which we consider now.

Human rights education

While this section focuses specifically on *human rights education*, we start it by exploring briefly some wider issues relating to education as a human right. This reflects the recognition that human rights can be found and expressed within education in a number of ways. In his analysis, McCowan (2012: 70) helpfully identifies three of these. The first is the right *to* education – the idea that access to and participation in education is a fundamental human right. The second is rights *through* education –

students learning about the human rights and the conventions set out to protect them. The third is rights *in* education – the ways in which the rights of students are upheld and recognised within education and schooling. In this section we are particularly interested in the second and third of McCowan's triad, both of which relate to human rights education.

The right to education

Before turning to this it is worth briefly considering the nature of the first of the triad – the right *to* education. Figures from UNICEF in 2008 suggested that 93 million children were not in school (UNICEF, 2008). In 2012, figures from UNESCO (2012a) in an Education for All monitoring report suggested that this figure was down to 61 million, but was also stagnating. Also, as McCowan (2013) reminds us, these figures do not necessarily give the true picture of levels of engagement of those who were denoted as attending school. For many children, attendance at the start of the year may not necessarily mean a long-term and consistent opportunity of engagement.

Issues with meeting the right of access to education have come in spite of a concerted concern and effort to reduce – if not eradicate – inequalities in access to education. Article 28 of the United Nations Convention on the Rights of the Child (1989), for example, includes the following provision in relation to the right to education:

1 States Parties recognize the right of the child to education, and with a view to achieving this right progressively and on the basis of equal opportunity, they shall, in particular:

(a) Make primary education compulsory and available free to all;
(b) Encourage the development of different forms of secondary education, including general and vocational education, make them available and accessible to every child, and take appropriate measures such as the introduction of free education and offering financial assistance in case of need;
(c) Make higher education accessible to all on the basis of capacity by every appropriate means;
(d) Make educational and vocational information and guidance available and accessible to all children;
(e) Take measures to encourage regular attendance at schools and the reduction of drop-out rates.

(UNHR, www.ohchr.org/en/professionalinterest/pages/crc.aspx)

The Millennium Declaration (UN, 2000), which built on two UNESCO *Education for All* conferences (Jomtein in 1990 and Dakar in 2000), required countries to (1) universalise primary education and (2) eradicate gender inequalities in school enrolments by 2015 (Sundaram, 2012). In her analysis of gender inequalities Sundaram draws on a range of data from UNICEF (2006), which suggests that 32 million (roughly 28 per cent) out of 113 million children of primary age in sub-Saharan Africa were not in school. This compared with a world average of 5 per cent for boys and 8 per cent of girls. It is these sorts of disparities and inequalities that the UNESCO-led movement *Education for All* seeks to monitor, challenge and address. There is, of course, insufficient space and scope to do full justice to issues and debates concerning the right *to* education here – the further readings identified at the end of this chapter provide one potential way for you to engage further with these. We turn our attention now to the other two elements of McCowan's triad – human rights *through* education and *in* education.

Human rights through education

Human rights education is defined by Amnesty International (2014) as a 'deliberate, participatory practice aimed at empowering individuals, groups and communities through fostering knowledge, skills and attitudes consistent with internationally recognized human rights principles'. The definition of human rights education provided by the United Nations points toward its perceived benefits:

- the strengthening of respect for human rights and fundamental freedoms;
- the full development of the human personality and the sense of its dignity;
- the promotion of understanding and tolerance . . . among all nations and groups; and
- the enabling of all persons to participate effectively in a free society.
  (General Assembly Resolution 1997; cf. Tibbitts, 2002)

The need for, and importance of, human rights education has been a longstanding international commitment (a clear overview of this is provided by Bowring, 2012). For example, in 1974 UNESCO published the *Recommendation Concerning Education for International Understanding, Co-operation and Peace and Education Relating to Human Rights and Fundamental Freedom* (UNESCO, 1974). The document took a wide view of the term education – viewing it as including both formal schooling as well as a range of other educational and socialising processes within the modern nation-state. In 1993, UNESCO published the *World Plan of Action for Education on Human Rights and Democracy* (UNESCO, 1993), which directly informed the *United Nations' Decade for Human Rights Education* that ran between 1995 and 2004 (Bowring, 2012). In late 2013, the *2020 Global Coalition for Human Rights Education* was established to monitor and promote human rights education around the world by 'supporting and strengthening the implementation of existing international standards and commitments' (HREA, 2013). The Coalition is informed by the UN's *Declaration on Human Rights Education and Training* as well as the *World Programme for Human Rights Education*. The former, adopted in 2011, is not legally binding on member nations and does not itself contain any new rights, but it does further cement international commitment to human rights education. Human rights education has also been a key concern of bodies within the European Union. In 2010, the Council of Ministers accepted the *Charter on Education for Democratic Citizenship and Human Rights Education*. In addition, the Council of Europe's Commissioner for Human Rights publishes regular reports about human rights in member states – many of which contain information about education for democratic citizenship and human rights education.

In her analysis, Tibbitts (2002) presents the following three models of human rights education:

1   A *values and awareness model* in which the aim is to ensure a basic knowledge and understanding of human rights – through formal education and raising awareness among the general public – as well as aligning a concern for human rights with societal values. The intended outcome of this approach is 'that mass support for human rights will continue to bring pressure upon authorities to protect human rights' (Tibbitts, 2002: 163). To do so requires the development of critical learning and thinking in order that people are able to engage with issues concerning human rights.

2   An *accountability model* in which learners are active participants in guaranteeing human rights through their 'professional responsibilities'. This involves either '(a) directly monitoring human rights violations and advocating with the necessary authorities; or (b) taking special care to protect the rights of people . . . for which they take some responsibilities' (2002: 165). This model is typically one used for educating professionals and activists working in the field of human rights.

3   A *transformational model* is one which seeks to empower 'the individual to both recognize human rights abuses and to commit to their prevention' (2002: 166). According to Tibbitts, the model 'assumes that the learner has had personal experiences that can be seen as human rights violations' (166). For this reason, the model is typically employed in programmes in various situations – including post-conflict or with victims of domestic abuse.

While Tibbitts' (2002: 167) analysis views each model as primarily connecting to particular groups of learning, she argues that this need not always be the case, suggesting that 'even in schools, it is possible to attempt a transformational model of HRE, if links are made between school and family life'. Given the central tenets of the transformational model, this is a controversial claim – something we pick up on in the activity below.

Activity

How useful is Tibbitts' typology?

Tibbitts (2002) presents her typology largely as one in which the aims and methods of human rights education are adapted to and dictated by the intended audience. Tibbitts asks us to envisage the model in a triangular form, with the values and awareness model at the bottom (given its wider audience and applicability), the accountability model on top of this, and the transformational model at the pinnacle of the triangle. As we have said above, Tibbitts does not view the methods and intended audiences of these models as mutually exclusive. When she writes that the transformational model *could* be used in formal education, Tibbitts (2002: 167) has the following to say:

> Should the school chose to do so, the agenda is extensive: the curriculum should include participation in family decision-making; respect for parents but rejection of family violence, particularly mother (wife) battery; equality

continued . . .

of parents within the home; and consideration of sexuality as a form of social relations rather than as a manifestation of man's nature.

Here, Tibbitts is clearly drawing on a feminist standpoint to explore the possibilities of what human rights education in schools might involve. We should also remember that Tibbitts is talking about human rights education across nations, rather than in one specific nation. As such, Tibbitts' view provides a useful catalyst for thinking about the aims and boundaries of human rights education in schools.

Consider whether the forms and focus of learning identified by Tibbitts are appropriate for school age students within your own contexts. If so, why, and is this restricted to particular age groups? If not, why not, and what are your thoughts about this? What are the school-level contextual factors that will influence your responses that might need to be taken into account?

Most human rights-based NGOs provide a range of educational resources, activities and initiatives to support schools and teachers in human rights education. One of the best examples of these materials is the *Right Here, Right Now* resource produced by the UK Ministry of Justice, the British Institute of Human Rights, Amnesty International and the former Department for Children, Schools and Families (2008). Looking at a comprehensive resource like this is a good way of thinking about human rights education. The resource provides an overview of human rights and human rights education as well as a range of lesson plans and resources linked to particular themes. These include school rules, human rights in the UK, the UN Convention on the Rights of the Child, child poverty and homophobic bullying. Other leading organisations that provide resources include: Amnesty International; Human Rights Watch; Human Rights Foundation; Liberty; Campaign for Nuclear Disarmament; World Vision; Breakthrough; and Human Rights Education Associates.

Activity

Educational resources produced by human rights organisations

The organisations identified above share similar aims relating to development and global justice. Select the website of two of the organisations (where available, it may be useful for you to visit the organisations' sites in your own country as well – for Amnesty International, for example, go to www.amnesty.org.uk; www.amnestyusa.org; www.amnesty.org.au; www.amensty.ca) and reflect on the following:

1   How are the aims of each organisation similar and how do they differ?
2   How are the methods used by each organisation and the projects they are involved in similar and how do they differ?
3   How does each organisation support and advocate for human rights?
4   What pedagogical approaches do each of the organisations encourage to engage learning in human rights education?

Human rights in education

It is important that we also think about whether schools themselves are places that recognise and respect human rights; that is, how human rights are protected *in* education. From this perspective 'educational institutions and spaces [are] arenas of society in their own right' and as such are '*instantiations* of society, and not just sites of preparation for it' (McCowan, 2012: 72; emphasis in original). This perspective is one which is shared by Fielding and Moss (2011). They speak of the importance of there being congruence between the emancipatory and democratic educational aims of the school and how the school actually goes about seeking to achieve this in the very essence of its organisational structure, ethos and relational engagement with students and parents, as well as in its curriculum. Speaking of one pioneering example, Fielding and Moss (2011: 9) suggest that 'one of the key consequences of taking democracy really seriously was that it formed the bedrock of all that went on in the school, for democracy was understood and practised not primarily as a mode of decision-making; it was a way of living and learning together'.

A number of international NGOs run programmes that recognise schools' work in relation to human rights. Amnesty International's *Human Rights Friendly Schools* initiative, for example, awards schools that place human rights at the centre of schooling and school life. The following definition, which comes from the initiatives website, provides a good insight into what such a school looks like (www.amnesty.org/en/human-rights-education/projects-initiatives/rfsp):

A Human Rights Friendly School is founded on principles of equality, dignity, respect, non-discrimination and participation. It is a school community where human rights are learned, taught, practised, respected, protected and promoted. Human Rights Friendly Schools are inclusive environments where all are encouraged to take active part in school life, regardless of status or role, and where cultural diversity is celebrated. Young people and the school community learn about human rights by putting them into practice every day. Through an approach which goes beyond the classroom and into all aspects of school life, commonly called a 'whole-school approach,' a 'holistic approach' or 'rights-based approach', both schools and young people become powerful catalysts for change in their wider communities.

Case study

A rights-respecting school – Holywell Primary School, Loughborough, UK

Similar to Amnesty's Human Rights Friendly Schools scheme is an initiative launched by UNICEF UK called the Rights Respecting School Award (RRSA). This scheme aims to put the United Nations Convention on the Rights of the Child (CRC) at the heart of a school, in terms of its planning, policies, practice and ethos. So it seeks to ensure all three aspects of McCowan's triad for human rights education are in place, assessing the quality of respectful relationships between staff and students as well as the extent to which children are being taught about human rights. For a school to be accredited as rights-respecting it must provide evidence that it is meeting the following four standards:

- *Standard A*: Rights-respecting values underpin leadership and management.
- *Standard B*: The whole school community learns about the Convention on the Rights of the Child.
- *Standard C*: The school has a rights-respecting ethos.
- *Standard D*: Children are empowered to become active citizens and learners.

Below is a case study of a primary school that recently received the RRSA award.

Holywell Primary School is a school within a particularly cosmopolitan catchment area resulting in over one third of its students speaking English as an additional language, and as many as twenty-nine different languages being spoken by its children, who are aged between four and eleven years old.

The school received the Rights Respecting School Award in April 2013 after two years of developmental work. The UNICEF award required that the school complete a self-evaluation and impact evaluation audit along with passing an assessment visit by a UNICEF representative to observe the school in action and to meet with both staff and students.

The school's headteacher Christine Linnitt states that the RRSA and CRC are now 'central to the ethos of the school' and offer 'a format to what we wanted to be'. Through both formal and extra-curricular activities the school seeks to celebrate its cultural and ethnic diversity and encourage awareness of its global links with reference to active citizenship and sustainable development. One particularly innovative approach is that each year the school holds a number of focus weeks that are topic based and in the past these have centred on global citizenship dimensions such as fair trade, human rights and partnership working through their school links in India and China. The spirit of care and the right for all children to feel safe is supported by a range of initiatives including, for example, a playground buddy scheme with 'playtime friendship stops' being run by the older children in the school. Children are empowered to have a say over their own education as active citizens through school council and eco-committee processes where elected students will consult with their peers about decisions within the school. They are also empowered through a homework policy that includes a democratic and active learning pedagogy where students are encouraged to explore their own topics of interest and to creatively choose how they wish to present their learning.

Following whole-school staff training about the UNCRC, teachers in all classes lead students in a dialogic activity each year to consider these rights for themselves and draw up their own class charter for how they will carefully respect themselves and one another while living and learning in the school. This work then feeds into the school's overarching statement of aims that are referred to in whole-school meetings and assemblies. Homework activities also touch upon the human rights agenda as a means of consolidating the students' understanding, but also as a means of informing and engaging with parents as important stakeholders in the whole initiative.

The school regularly undertakes school improvement planning procedures that are informed by the CRC framework in order to seek to give consistency in practice across the whole school.

Crucially, students at the school describe the classroom charters and range of RRSA linked practices as making a difference to their experience of school. Students describe the charter as providing a structure that they have a strong sense of ownership over, because they helped write it. The charter also helps to ensure that nobody feels left out and provides a respect structure that the children feel they can hold each other to account by. As one student describes, when someone has not behaved in line with the charter they felt confident to be able to say 'Why have you broken it when you agreed to it?' Overall, this UNICEF initiative is felt to be providing young children within the school the language and procedures to help them build and maintain good relationships with each other and to be able to lead restorative approaches to disagreements and conflict if and when they do occur.

For more information about this award scheme visit www.unicef.org.uk/ Education/Rights-Respecting-Schools-Award.

To view an academic evaluation of the impact of this scheme on children's sense of well-being following a three year study of twelve schools visit www. unicef.org.uk/Documents/Education-Documents/RRSA_Evaluation_Report.pdf.

To summarise, human rights relates to education in a number of ways – including issues concerning the right to education, rights within education, and learning about human rights. While there is a genuine international commitment to human rights education, approaches can differ in important respects. One of our challenges as teachers is to consider the nature of human rights within our educational work and to seek clarity regarding our aims and purposes in this area. As some of the issues we have explored suggest, this may be somewhat harder in principle than in practice. Nevertheless, it is an important and worthwhile undertaking.

Development and development education

In this section we will explore the nature of development and development education. While development is a long-standing and internationally recognised field, the area of development education is somewhat contested. As such, we will explore what is meant by development education and, indeed, whether the term development education is one that is still useful within global education.

Development

> Change in the societies at the very bottom must come predominantly from within; we cannot impose it on them.
>
> Paul Collier (2007: xi)

> Development is about transforming the lives of people, not just transforming economies.
>
> Joseph Stiglitz (2006: 50)

> The objective of development is well-being for all. Well-being can be described as the experience of good quality of life.
>
> Robert Chambers (2005: 193)

According to Bailey and Dolan (2011: 30), 'development co-operation arose in the context of the cold war, the process of de-colonisation and the on-going nature of globalisation'. Development is a broad and complex term that usually refers to economic development and increased welfare. The stage of a country's development is often viewed on a continuum from 'more developed' to 'less developed'. This simple definition belies, however, the complexity of development for a number of reasons. First, there is a danger that 'more developed' is interpreted in economic terms simply as 'richer', and 'less developed' simply as 'poorer'. Even if this were a sound interpretation (which we would strongly suggest it is not), interpreting what is meant by 'richer' and 'poorer' is far from simple. Standard measures include overall GDP, GDP per capita and purchasing power parity, all of which differ in important ways. A fuller understanding of development understands it not only in economic terms, but also as involving a range of other measures relating to education, healthcare and the protection of human rights. As the United Nations' *Human Development Report* (1996: 1) states: 'human development is the end – economic growth is a means'. This recognition is important, and highlights the inter-relationship between the development of countries and human development. These sentiments were echoed in a speech made by the UK Prime Minister, David Cameron, to the United Nations General Assembly in 2012. In the address, Cameron (2012) stated unequivocally the UK government's commitment to aid spending:

> I am convinced that we need to focus more than ever on the building blocks that take countries from poverty to prosperity. The absence of conflict and corruption. The presence of property rights and the rule of law. We should never forget that for many in the world the closest relative of poverty is injustice. Development has never been just about aid or money.

A second – and related – complexity is whether development can really be conceived as a continuum within which those countries that are 'less developed' should aim to become like those countries that are 'more developed'. There are tensions with such a position regarding ethnocentric and Western-imposed standards, and also with adopting a singular sense of what development needs and aims are. This is in light of postcolonial theory in particular, which argues for the importance of challenging 'western assumptions, stereotypes and ways of knowing and offers its own alternatives' (Sharp, 2009: 7). Postcolonial theory very much supports the view that multiple voices and perspectives need to be embraced in representations of the world in order to avoid the cultural imperialism of a singular narrative. Instead, individual countries have their own diverse needs and priorities regarding their development relative to their specific contexts. Partly on the basis of this, Bailey and Dolan (2011: 30) identify a 'shift in the language of development co-operation . . . which now encompasses terms such as "participation", "empowerment", "poverty reduction" . . . and more recently "partnership"'. Some have questioned the very use of the term 'development', identifying within it an inherently structural, impositional and unequal relationship (for example, Kothari, 1989; cf. Bailey and Dolan, 2011). In their 2014 Gates Foundation letter, Bill and Melinda Gates (2014: 6) adopt a different perspective, returning in some way to an economic focus (although it should be stated that they clearly view development in more than purely economic terms):

> So the easiest way to respond to the myth that poor countries are doomed to stay poor is to point to one fact: They haven't stayed poor. Many—though by no means all—of the countries we used to call poor now have thriving economies. And the percentage of very poor people has dropped by more than half since 1990. That still leaves more than one billion people in extreme poverty, so it's not time to celebrate. But it is fair to say that the world has changed so much that the terms 'developing countries' and 'developed countries' have outlived their usefulness . . . Some so-called developing countries have come so far that it's fair to say they have developed. A handful of failed states are hardly developing at all. Most countries are somewhere in the middle. That's why it's more instructive to think about countries as low-, middle-, or high-income.

This point of view is also animated by the work of the Gapminder Foundation and its co-founder – the statistician Hans Rosling. The Gapminder website (www.gapminder.org.uk) provides a wealth of fact-based material to try and improve the general public's understanding of basic global patterns and macro trends. Their time-lapsed statistical maps of a range of global indicators, beyond just income per person, challenge the present-day validity of using simplistic and polarised terms such as developed and developing countries.

One way of gaining a fuller understanding of the principle of development is to consider the nature of the Millennium Development Goals (MDGs). These were introduced by the United Nations in the year 2000 and were agreed upon by all member states. The MDGs comprise eight goals to be achieved by the year 2015. These are:

1 To eradicate extreme poverty and hunger;
2 To achieve universal primary education;

3   To promote gender equality and empower women;
4   To reduce child mortality rates;
5   To improve maternal health;
6   To combat HIV/AIDS, malaria, and other diseases;
7   To ensure environmental sustainability;
8   To develop a global partnership for development.

(United Nations, n.d.; www.un.org/millenniumgoals)

Progress towards achieving the MDGs has been varied. Nevertheless, there have been notable areas of positive progress. For example, the first of the MDGs influenced leaders of the G8 nations at the 2005 Summit (held in Gleneagles, Scotland) to agree to fund the cancellation of the debt owed to the IMF, the World Bank and the African Development Bank by some of the world's poorest countries. In 2013, the UN reported that the proportion of people living in extreme poverty had been halved at the global level well ahead of schedule. It also reported significant progress in the target area of access to drinking water, estimating that over the last twenty-one years over 2 billion people gained access to improved drinking water (UN, 2013a).

With progress towards these targets seeming at times to be far too slow and insufficient, the MDGs have also provided a useful global reference point for a variety of campaigns concerned with advocating for bolder action in pursuit of well-being for all. One such example is the *Make Poverty History* campaign established in a number of nations – including the United Kingdom, the United States, Australia, Canada, Norway, Ireland, Nigeria and South Africa. This sought to raise awareness and influence policy change through petitions around fair trade, poverty/debt and international aid, bringing together a range of different organisations. Along similar lines, the movement *Global Call to Action Against Poverty* (www.whiteband.org) is a collective of civil society organisations that campaigns for an end to poverty. Indeed, there are a wide range of international non-governmental organisations that also work in various ways to support those living in poverty and to campaign about issues around development and aid. There is not space or scope to detail all of these organisations here, but the following list provides a few examples of the sorts of organisations involved, their aims and their methods. Each of the organisations provides a number of educational resources connected to development education:

Oxfam International (www.oxfam.org): Oxfam International seeks to fight and overcome poverty using a six-sided strategy: the belief that when basic human rights are claimed, people can escape poverty; the belief that women drive human development; supporting people when disaster occurs; lobbying governments and international organisations for action on poverty and sustainability; working to secure global food supplies; and working for finance to be aimed at essential services such as education and health. Underpinning this strategy is a commitment to *working in partnership* with a range of stakeholders.

CAFOD (www.cafod.org.uk): The Catholic Agency for Overseas Development (CAFOD) is the official Catholic aid agency for England and Wales, and works with a range of partner organisations to support those living in poverty and suffering from injustice. CAFOD's work revolves around the following areas: helping people make a living; disaster and emergency response; campaigning and advocacy; and education. Similar organisations exist in other nations (Caritas in Australia, www.caritas.org.au; Catholic Relief Services in America, www.crs.org; Canadian Catholic Association for Development and Peace www.dvp.org).

Action Aid International (www.actionaid.org): Action Aid International works in forty-five countries and campaigns to reduce poverty and injustice in a number of areas: food rights, women's rights, democratic governance, education, emergencies and conflicts, climate change, HIV/AIDS and Youth.

CARE International (www.careinternational.org): CARE International is a confederation of fourteen member organisations that works in eighty-four countries and campaigns to support development and humanitarian aid projects in a number of areas: emergency response; climate change; maternal health; economic development; water sanitation and hygiene; advocacy; education; HIV and AIDS; food security; and a focus on women and girls.

Activity

Educational resources produced by local development organisations

The four organisations we have just identified share similar aims relating to development and global justice, and each are widely known internationally. In this activity we ask that you undertake a scoping exercise to research smaller, local charities and organisations that provide development education support and resources to educators. The following questions may be useful in structuring your approach to the activity:

1   What are the aims of each organisation?
2   What methods are used by each organisation? What projects are they involved in?
3   How does each organisation support and advocate education within developing countries?
4   What educational resources does each organisation provide for teachers and students to learn about development?

Each of the four organisations works to overcome a range of issues related to development through direct programs and a range of lobbying activities. We must, though, in our engagements with these organisations be mindful as educators not to oversimplify the possible solutions to development. As Stiglitz (2006: 26) makes clear:

There are no magic solutions or simple prescriptions. The history of development economics is marked by the quixotic quest to find 'the answer', disappointment in the failure of one strategy leading to hope that the next will work. Development is a process that involves every aspect of society, engaging the efforts of everyone: markets, governments, NGOs, cooperatives, not-for-profit institutions.

Solutions to development are likely to come from a range of sources, policies and processes and must focus not only on economics and finance, but also on education and healthcare. Moreover, there is an important role to be played by national governments in allocating aid budgets to the appropriate resources as well as to raising awareness of development issues. An example of this is provided by the Conservative–Liberal Democrat Coalition government's policy on aid. Since coming to power in 2010, and in part resulting from the effects of the global financial crisis, the Coalition government has entered a period of austerity budgeting, with large cuts to most department budgets. Despite these cuts, the Coalition has protected the UK's aid budget. Figures released in 2013 suggest that the UK will be the first of the G8 nations to meet the target of spending 0.7 per cent of gross national income (Provost and Tran, 2013). In a more debated move, they have also looked to shift resources away from general awareness-raising of issues relating to global poverty among the general population, while stating an ongoing commitment to development education work in schools (O'Brien, 2011).

Given that they have different histories, contexts and needs, different solutions are needed to address development issues in different countries. Partly for this reason evidence suggests that experiences of development across different regions of the world are not identical. Stiglitz (2006: 59) provides us with the following summary of the need to find solutions to development. This raises important points for critical debate with regard to notions of positive discrimination, interdependent growth, and appeals to self-interest:

> The rest of the world cannot solve the problems of the developing world. They will have to do that for themselves. But we can at least create a level playing field. It would be even better if we tilted it to favour the developing countries. There is a compelling moral case for doing this. I think there is a compelling case that it is in our self-interest. Their growth will enhance our growth. Greater stability and security in the developing world will contribute to stability and security in the developed world.

As problematic as the term 'development' and its pursuit has been shown to be, it has nonetheless pointed towards the need for change, and the aspiration of such change being sustainable, for the better and serving the well-being of all; an agenda that we will return to again in Chapter 6. Increasingly, it is being recognised that apt and effective development is linked into partnership and empowerment processes allowing for a co-ownership of change strategies and actions at the local and regional levels (Chambers, 2005). This facilitation of personal and collaborative change, the critical literacy and creative capacities that it requires of us all as citizens, very much brings our attention back to the vital role that can be played by education.

Development education

Given that the terms have often been used interchangeably, an initial question that we need to consider is whether development education is actually distinct from global education. For our purposes here (and similar to human rights education) we would suggest that development education is both a distinct field in its own right *and* is a key strand within the wider umbrella field of global education. As Doug Bourn – the Director of the Development Education Research Centre at the Institute of Education, University of London – suggests, development education as a distinct field is characterised by 'its relationship to development and consequent support from aid ministries and international non-governmental organisations, with an emphasis on linkages between learning and action within a social justice perspective' (Bourn, 2012: 255). The European Consensus on Development (2007: 5) defines development education in the following way:

> The aim of Development Education and Awareness Raising is to enable every person in Europe to have life-long access to opportunities to be aware of and to understand global development concerns and the local and personal relevance of those concerns, and to enact their rights and responsibilities as inhabitants of an interdependent and changing world by affecting change for a just and sustainable world.

Bourn (2012) identifies different approaches to development education within different periods of time. During the 1960s and 1970s the predominant approach adopted in Europe and North America was one informed by the processes of decolonisation and which aimed to 'educate for support a "largely ignorant or disinterested public" through an information-delivery model of learning' about poverty and the role of international aid in other countries (Bourn, 2012: 255). From the late 1970s onwards, approaches to development education took a more critical turn, aiming not only to raise awareness but also to empower people to adopt a critical approach to perceptions of poverty and the aims and practices of international aid programmes. In another of his analyses, Bourn (2011) reminds us that development education can mean different things to people in different national contexts. For example, he draws on the work of Hoppers (2008) in South Africa for whom development education is primarily about 'promoting indigenous knowledge', and the work of Kumar (2008) in India whose perspective is that it is essentially concerned with dialogue and reflection.

Bourn (2012) also provides us with four compelling reasons as to why there has been an increase in focus and attention on development education since 2000. First is the high profiles afforded to the Millennium Development Goals and the related Make Poverty History initiative; second is the impact of globalisation in reducing the immediacy and awareness of the global north to the experiences of countries in the global south. Awareness of these experiences is no longer the result of singular events, campaigns or even news items, but rather it has become part of everyday life and, increasingly, of everyday education too. Third is the increased sense of recognition in the value of development education programmes; and fourth, development education has benefited in turn from the increased attention being given to the wider field of global education.

Activity

What is development education?

In summarising the contested nature of development education, Bourn (2012: 258) suggests that:

> Development education could be seen as an area of education such as the environment or human rights, if you see it as an area of educational practice located within and around discourses of development. It could also be seen as an approach towards learning that once had value but should now be subsumed within concepts such as global learning, global education, global citizenship or education for sustainable development. There is another interpretation of development education, which is that it includes methodology and approach that has relevance to broader theories of learning, particularly critical pedagogy.

Reflecting on this quotation, what do you consider the purpose and nature of development education to be?

In an interesting analysis, Bourn and Brown (2011: 7) identify three general assumptions that are often adopted in relation to young people's learning about development, and for which there is 'little robust research to support'. These are: (1) that the motivations of young people in engaging in issues related to development are driven by their 'concern for international poverty'; (2) that young people typically engage in development issues through 'specific, targeted projects or activities'; and, (3) that such engagement is 'purely in terms of taking action (for example, campaigning or raising money)'. Bourn and Brown (2011: 7–8) draw on the work of Standish (2008) in relation to Geography education in the UK to highlight the risks that blind acceptance of these assumptions may run. Standish claims that Geography teaching 'has become too dominated by organisations and academics who are trying to inculcate in young people a specific moral and political standpoint based on environmentalism, social justice and human rights'. Now, the argument that Standish makes is itself contentious, and neglects that the standpoints he criticises are generally accepted as important aims of education and schooling. But Standish does raise an issue that as teachers we should bear in mind – and which we considered in Chapter 1 – namely, what is the relationship between active student engagement in global issues and the students' *own volition*? As Kumar (2008: 44) argues, 'one of the larger global goals of development education is to ensure that development is not pro-rich, monopolised and manipulated'. The case study that follows exemplifies one attempt to meet the challenge that Kumar sets.

Case study

Developing sustainable partnerships in the Philippines – an Australian based foundation

AFFLIP – Australian Foundation for Fostering Learning in the Philippines (www.afflip.com)

AFFLIP is a voluntary, non-governmental, not-for-profit foundation based in South Australia. The Foundation works to contribute to the educational development of young people in some of the poorest areas of the Philippines. AFFLIP's key focus is on learning – and its various programmes are built around this principle – and the Foundation understands education to be central to the social, political, economic, environmental and cultural health of any society. On its website, the Foundation sets out its philosophy and rationale. An important feature of this – and extremely pertinent to our exploration in this chapter – is the following statement which is one of the assumptions underpinning the Foundation's work:

> Although AFFLIP has a Philippines wide brief, the Foundation believes that it is best to start its work with a small group of disadvantaged neighbouring schools in a severely disadvantaged part of the Philippines. This allows the schools to collaborate and to build sustainability, and provides a practical and 'doable' focus for AFFLIP as it develops its infrastructure and expertise.
>
> (www.afflip.com/#!our-philosophy-/c1cj9)

A central element of the Foundation's philosophy and rationale is its educational philosophy. Through this the Foundation aims to 'contribute to a range of facilities, resources, programs and activities, which develop the capabilities of each child necessary for living a full and productive life' (www.afflip.com/#!our-philosophy-/c1cj9). Allied to this is a further – and highly important – underpinning assumption that 'there must be an equal relationship between AFFLIP and the schools with which it is working where both parties have agency' (www.afflip.com/#!our-philosophy-/c1cj9). Because of this, the Foundation aims to build sustainable programmes based on enduring and mutual partnerships rather than a dependent 'helping hand' approach.

The Foundation has a range of initiatives, including the following flagship programmes: developing high quality *curriculum resources*; building *health and nutrition*, by supporting agriculture and aquaculture activities to support schools' feeding programmes and enriching their learning; a *scholarship programme* to support the most impoverished students in participating in elementary schooling; working with teachers in the Philippines to provide *professional development* activities and support for teachers to enhance their knowledge and skills in teaching literacy; and facilitating a *schools network* for the twinning of South Australian primary schools with schools in the Philippines (www.afflip.com/#!our-philosophy-/c1cj9).

Conclusion

We started this chapter by saying that while we have separated them out as distinct fields – and indeed they are distinct fields – there are clear and relevant links between human rights/human rights education and development/development education. We end this chapter by drawing the following passage from the United Nations Development Programme's *Human Development Report* (2000: 1) that demonstrates the connection between human rights and human development:

> Human rights and human development share a common vision and a common purpose – to secure the freedom, well-being and dignity of all people every-where.
>
> To secure:
>
> Freedom from discrimination – by gender, race, ethnicity, national origin or religion.
> Freedom from want – to enjoy a decent standard of living.
> Freedom to develop and realize one's human potential.
> Freedom from fear – of threats to personal security, from torture, arbitrary arrest and other violent acts.
> Freedom from injustice and violations of the rule of law.
> Freedom of thought and speech and to participate in decision-making and form associations.
> Freedom for decent work – without exploitation.

This passage not only extends the relationship between human rights and development but makes clear the needs and challenges of both. This relationship is one that is also central to the recent *Report of the High-Level Panel of Eminent Persons on the Post-15 Developments Agenda*. Tasked by the UN Secretary-General, Ban Ki-Moon, to reflect on development needs following the end of the period of the MDGs, the Report (United Nations, 2014: 5) has envisaged that their vision and responsibility is to 'end extreme poverty in all its forms' and to address the 'universal challenges of the 21st century: promoting sustainable development, supporting job-creating growth, protecting the environment and providing peace, security, justice, freedom and equity at all levels'. The report (2014: 7–10) sets out 'five transformative shifts' that are needed: 'leave no one behind', 'put sustainable development at the core', 'transform economies for jobs and inclusive growth', 'build peace and effective, open and accountable public institutions', and 'forge a new global partnership'.

The task for the teacher – using the range of resources available as support – is to think carefully about how these aims can be considered, explored and perhaps even enacted in schools. This involves more than just the taught curriculum. School ethos, mission and extra-curricular activities also have a crucial role to play. This undertaking is not a simple one, but it is one that is not only a central part of global education. It is also of the highest importance.

Questions for further investigation

1   What should be the aims of human rights education?

2   Is development an outdated notion? If so, in what ways? If not, for what reasons?
3   Is development education a useful term in its own right or should it be subsumed fully into global education?

Further reading

Bourn, D. (ed.) (2008) *Development Education: Debates and Dialogues*. London: Bedford Way Papers.
Contains a range of insightful and thought-provoking contributions from some of the leading commentators on development education.

Gapminder (www.gapminder.org)
An interactive, not-for-profit initiative that promotes sustainable development and the achievement of the Millennium Development Goals founded by Anna Rosling Rönnlund and Hans Rosling. A central feature of the site is its display of statistical information through animated and interactive graphs.

McCowan, T. (2013) *Education as a Human Right: Principles for a Universal Entitlement to Learning*. London: Bloomsbury.
A philosophical exploration of the aims and purposes of education as a human right. The book challenges the work of organisations in relation to protecting the right to education.

UNESCO (2012) Reaching Out of School Children is Essential for Development. *Education for All Global Monitoring Report*. Policy Paper 04. Paris: UNESCO.
A wide-ranging report from UNESCO that suggests that the numbers of children out of school globally are stagnating and which argues for the central link between access to education and development.

Chapter 6

Sustainable development

Chapter objectives

By the end of this chapter you should have:

*   considered the nature of Education for Sustainable Development, including debates and issues about this reform agenda;
*   explored the meaning of holistic and participatory approaches to Education for Sustainable Development;
*   identified and analysed the key contemporary issues in Education for Sustainable Development within your own context.

Introduction

A central aspect of global learning in and for the twenty-first century is recognition of the need for sustainable change. This is in light of an increasing awareness of manifold threats to well-being in both human and environmental terms. Citizens today require critical and creative competencies to be resilient and innovative in the face of pressing issues of global crisis, the extent of which transcend international boundaries and stretch across generational periods of time. This is prompting increasing numbers of people to consider the need for compassionate societal transformation, and subsequently to consider the need to reform the ways in which young people are educated to participate in creating more sustainable futures.

Interest in the concept of sustainable development has been prevalent since at least the 1960s, and the term has received a great deal of attention within education nationally and internationally over the last twenty years (Huckle, 2012). As a reform agenda, Education for Sustainable Development (ESD) raises important debate over the need for ecological literacy alongside notions of social justice when conceptualising educational frameworks for meeting the challenges of life in the twenty-first century. In this chapter, we consider a range of educational responses to the challenges of sustainability, and in particular the recent United Nations *Decade of Education for Sustainable Development* (2005–2014). This frames ESD as life-long learning that enables people to meet the needs of themselves, each other (including future generations) and the environment. We also present a model of ESD that emphasises the centrality of learning through values that are orientated towards an active concern for the common good. This model suggests that ESD is as much about participatory and active pedagogical *processes* as it is about interdisciplinary subject *content*.

It is important from the outset to state that ESD remains a broad and contested priority within education. In congruence with ESD's overarching aim to encourage students to be 'critical creatives', we provide here, as we have done in previous chapters, reflective learning activities to encourage your own critical and creative engagement with this significant area of educational innovation. We also provide examples of ESD in practice that should resonate with the pedagogical approaches to global learning that were first introduced in Chapter 2.

Growing up in the midst of crisis

The recent global interest in Education for Sustainable Development can be traced to a growing awareness of significant threats to present and future well-being. It is commonly recognised today that young people are growing up in the midst of an array of complex sustainability challenges, which go beyond the space of international boundaries and across generational periods of time. These systemic problems lie across the environmental, social, economic and political spectrum. Listed below are the global issues introduced in Chapter 2, briefly reframed here as questions of challenge for sustainability:

1   *Climate change*: How can we mitigate climate change? How can we improve the resilience and adaptability of our communities in the face of climate change? How can we meet growing energy demands in ways that are carbon neutral?
2   *Environmental degradation*: How can we provide food for all without weakening terrestrial ecosystems and reducing soil quality? How can we value the health of the environment within our economic decision-making processes? How can we tackle root problems of poverty that contribute to unsustainable and environmentally exploitative behaviours?
3   *Biodiversity loss*: How can we have a more complete picture of where human lifestyles and population growth are impacting detrimentally on the bio-diversity of the planet? How can we advance behaviour change that conserves habitats and reduces the threats of extinction to species? How can we pursue a quality of life for all, in ways that are more harmonious with nature?
4   *Pollution and waste*: How can we clean up our industrial process of production? How can regenerative systems of a circular economy dominate over linear flows of 'resource to waste'?
5   *Fresh water scarcity*: How can everyone have access to clean water, free from conflict and without overharvesting natural water supplies for future generations? How can the burden of water collection be eased, for women in particular, and technology harnessed to improve access to local water supplies?
6   *Extreme poverty*: How can the progress made with regard to reducing poverty levels worldwide (through the pursuit of the Millennium Development Goals) be not only maintained but increased?

7   *Inequality*: How can the currently widening gap between the economically rich and poor be reduced both within and between countries? How can ethical economic systems provide fairer working conditions for the most vulnerable employees? How can we protect the liberty and human rights of all, regardless of gender, religion, sexuality or socio-economic background?

8   *Food and nutrition insecurity*: As the human population continues to rise how can we grow and supply enough food for all? How can food supplies be made resilient in the long term against the impact of megatrends such as climate change?

9   *Disease and health risks*: How can access to existing treatments for disease and illness be made available to all? How can the threat of new, more resistant strains of diseases be responded to in the future? How can citizens be supported in healthy lifestyle choices in order to reduce the rising risk of non-communicable diseases or problems such as obesity?

The phenomena of these and other interlinked sustainability challenges highlights that we are living in unprecedented times of global change that together represent manifold threats to our quality of life. For young people today, such narratives of global challenge and crisis represent an increasingly familiar reality; prevalent in a variety of forms within the media, debated at length by politicians and forming central topic areas of exploration in both scientific research and technological development. But our understanding of these challenges and their interlinked systemic nature remains partial and unfolding, as does our vision of more preferable futures and our capacity for nimbly moving towards such futures. Crucially, this raises not simply the need for education for all, but asks much deeper questions around what *kind* of education.

The emergence of sustainable development

Across the world there has been a surge of interest in the concept of sustainable development. This term brings into question the integrity of dominant models of development and calls for more humane approaches to be advanced. The recent origins of this concept can be traced back to the 1970s, such as at the UN Conference on the Human Environment in 1972, and the growth of environmental and conservation movements articulating the threats to the natural world posed by human lifestyles. In 1980, the International Union for the Conservation of Nature and Natural Resources (IUCN) published the 'World Conservation Strategy: living resource conservation for sustainable development' (IUCN, 1980). In partnership with the United Nations Environment Programme and the World Wildlife Fund, this strategy proposed a safeguarding of the biosphere in recognition of human development patterns causing dramatic environmental degradation, highlighting particular issues such as tropical deforestation. It outlined sustainable development as involving radical changes to the management of living resources in order to:

*   maintain essential ecological processes and life support systems;
*   preserve genetic diversity; and
*   ensure the sustainable utilization of species and ecosystems.

(IUCN, 1980)

In 1987, the term 'sustainable development' was popularised at a much greater level through the World Commission on Environment and Development (WCED). Their report 'Our Common Future' defined sustainable development as:

> Development which meets the needs of the present without compromising the ability of future generations to meet their own needs.
>
> (WCED, 1987)

Although criticised for being anthropocentric in its focus, this seminal definition was useful for highlighting the temporal dimension of patterns of development impacting on the well-being of future generations. It gave emphasis to the concept of needs, in particular the essential needs of the world's poorest people whom the report argued should be given greater priority. It also drew attention to the concept of limitation upon certain patterns of development due to their lasting detrimental impact upon the environment.

Over twenty-five years on from this report, the term sustainable development remains contested with a proliferation of definitions and descriptions. However there is growing consensus that the objective of sustainable development is *well-being for all*. Achieving this will require that we better balance environmental and societal considerations in the pursuit of improved quality of life. In turn this is seen to require creative engagement in lifelong learning processes of transformation and change, hence the perception that once again education has a vital role to play.

Education for sustainable development

The co-ordinated international movement towards Education for Sustainable Development began in earnest following the United Nations Conference on Environment and Development held in Rio de Janeiro, Brazil in 1992. You may remember from our introduction to this book that this is the very same conference at which Severn Suzuki gave her famous speech. Commonly referred to as the first Earth Summit, this resulted in the publication of Agenda 21, a comprehensive plan of action for reducing the impact of human behaviour on the environment. Agenda 21 (UNCED, 1992) identified education as being a key tool for achieving these sustainable development targets and identified four priority areas of educational action:

- improve the quality of basic education;
- reorient existing education programmes to address sustainable development;
- develop public awareness and understanding; and
- provide training for all sectors of private and civil society.

Adopted by over 178 countries, Agenda 21 led to a Commission on Sustainable Development being established to ensure that plans of action were put into place at global, national and local levels. A decade later, at the second World Summit on Sustainable Development (WSSD) in Johannesburg in 2002, the monitoring and evaluation processes of Agenda 21 revealed that despite some progress in ESD, much still needed to be achieved, and this prompted the conception of the UN Decade of ESD.

United Nations Decade of Education for Sustainable Development (2005–2014)

At an international level, the collective will to respond to well-being threats from mainstream global lifestyles led to the United Nations embarking upon its Decade of Education for Sustainable Development (DESD) from 2005–2014. The UNESCO-led DESD sought to:

1   facilitate networking, linkages, exchange and interaction among stakeholders in ESD;
2   foster an increased quality of teaching and learning in ESD;
3   help countries progress towards and attain the Millennium Development Goals; and
4   provide countries with new opportunities to incorporate ESD into education reform efforts.

(UNESCO, 2009a: 8)

The DESD has supported five fundamental types of learning – learning to know, learning to be, learning to live together, learning to do and learning to transform oneself and society. The last of these learning types recognises that lifestyle-induced environmental and social justice threats require students to be supported in transformative ways of thinking and acting. Transformative learning approaches have stemmed from the pioneering work of adult education scholars such as Jack Mezirow (2000), and also have strong links to the critical literacy work of Paulo Freire (1995). It is a learning process that engages students in not simply maintaining the societal status quo, or even improving the rationality of current practices, but fundamentally reconsidering core values, assumptions and attitudes and reflexively exploring new, more sustainable ways of perceiving and acting (Sterling, 2011). Through these transformative processes

Table 6.1 National interpretations of ESD

Country	Meaning of ESD
Chile	A fundamental part of citizenship education, an opportunity to satisfy human needs through a pedagogy that fosters the cultural transformation towards a sustainable society and which permits education to re-think itself and to work in favour of the democratization of knowledge, the collective construction of an ethic of human action, which promotes the development of participatory and supportive educational communities.
Botswana	ESD is education that places emphasis on equipping learners and the public with skills that will sustain them in future. It involves the acquisition of knowledge, skills, right attitudes and values in such a way that learners will be able to use their environment productively and in a sustainable manner so as to improve the quality of their life and to become productive members of their society.
China	In accordance with common scientific understandings, ESD is viewed as a kind of education that develops values that support sustainable development, with the intention to help people learn relevant knowledge and values and to develop the right and healthy habits and lifestyle which will lead to sustainable development for the whole society (adapted from Asia-Pacific regional report).

Source: Adapted from UNESCO (2009a: 26).

ESD is seen to encourage rigorous autonomous thinking and empower students to consider making a vital contribution towards achieving lifestyles based on justice, equality, integrity and respect.

We should reflect, however, that ESD has been interpreted and put into practice differently in different nations. One way of thinking about this is to consider national interpretations of ESD highlighted in UNESCO's (2009a) *Review of Contexts and Structures for Education for Sustainable Development*. To introduce these different interpretations we reproduce the 'meaning' of ESD operationalised in three nations as explained within the report (see Table 6.1 above).

Activity

Contextualising ESD for ourselves

As noted in the Bonn Declaration (UNESCO, 2009b: 3): 'the progress of ESD remains unevenly distributed and requires different approaches in different contexts'.

Review the current national framing of the meaning of Education for Sustainable Development within your own specific context and consider the following:

1   How does it differ to the above national interpretations of ESD?
2   How visible is ESD as a priority within your own national, regional or institutional contexts?

The core dimensions of Education for Sustainable Development

Despite these international differences in interpretation and approach, through building upon earlier work by Warwick (2011), and from our review of the literature and in particular material published since the launch of the DESD, we propose here a number of core elements to ESD (Selby, 2006; Vare and Scott, 2007; Chalkley *et al.*, 2009; Stibbe, 2009; Jones *et al.*, 2010; Tilbury, 2011; UNESCO, 2012b). In Figure 6.1 we represent these in the form of a butterfly model of ESD, consisting of a wing of holistic relational dimensions and a wing of pedagogical dimensions that both stem from the value base of an active concern for well-being.

This model of ESD starts by acknowledging the centrality of extrinsic values such as care and compassion. The United Nations Economic Commission for Europe (UNECE, 2012: 6) frames ESD as being underpinned by 'an ethic of solidarity, equality and mutual respect'. At the heart of ESD is explicit attention to critically exploring notions of the common good, and the exploration of values oriented towards an active concern for the well-being of ourselves, each other and the planet. ESD is based upon the premise that not only can we help others in their pursuit of a quality of life, but that we ourselves need the help of others – once again pointing towards the

Figure 6.1 The Education for Sustainable Development butterfly model

interconnected nature of how our lives are bound together in the world today. It is important to emphasise, in line with the broader discussions around notions of global learning and education, that while this particular educational agenda is not value neutral, neither does it advocate a simplistic values transmission agenda. Rather it raises the need for learning spaces that first and foremost enable learners to critically consider a diverse range of perspectives and interpretations with regard to these values, their nature, level of prioritisation and outworking. It also requires the reflexive exploration of the self, with students discovering their own values and ways of being and belonging. With this in mind we refer you back to the spaces of global learning we introduced toward the end of Chapter 2 and ask you to reflect on these in relation to the core dimensions of ESD as shown in Figure 6.1.

From this starting point, unfold the two wings of ESD. The first is concerned with the subject *content* of ESD, while the second is concerned with the pedagogical *processes* that are deemed to be congruent with achieving its educational objectives.

The model of ESD in Figure 6.1 simplifies each ESD wing to consist of three core dimensions. The dimensions are:

1 Biosphere dimension

Recognising the interconnectivity between the well-being of people and the natural environment

This educational content dimension seeks to acknowledge that human problems and ecological problems are inextricably intertwined and need to be understood in relation to each other. This dimension gives greater emphasis to interdisciplinary learning and systems thinking approaches (Sterling, 2005; Stone and Barlow, 2005; Morris and Martin, 2009). This is in order to help students understand the dynamic and interconnected nature of sustainability challenges, and to develop the capacity to navigate the risks and unpredictable consequences of these challenges as they unfold. The biosphere dimension reflects Selby's (2006) claim that we require within education a much greater integration of lessons from nature:

> Lessons of cycles, flows, networks, partnerships, diversity and . . . unpredictability, uncertainty and turbulence can, and should, infuse both the curriculum and process of our learning and teaching, as well as the way our learning institutions work.
>
> (Selby, 2006: 363)

This raises the importance of a twenty-first-century educational system that nurtures new forms of ecological literacy that go beyond the political, social and economic. As Stone (2009: 4) suggests:

> This generation will require leaders and citizens who can think ecologically, understand the interconnectedness of human and natural systems and have the will, ability and courage to act.

In this way ESD presents the need for a form of global learning that goes beyond anthropocentric considerations and that seeks to draw out from all students the capacity to critically consider human relationships with, and responsibilities towards, the natural environment.

2 Spatial dimension

Recognising the interconnectivity of life across place and landscape

As already discussed in greater depth within Chapter 3, this aspect of ESD involves learners in considering their local, national and global interdependency. It seeks to raise students' awareness of how, through environmental processes, as well as global processes of communication, industrialisation and consumerism, our lives today are caught up in a network of mutuality that goes beyond local neighbourhoods and nation-states. This dimension involves students considering the implications of concepts such as the 'global village' and exploring their personal connections to worldwide issues of justice, rights, equality, inclusion and environmental stewardship.

3 Temporal dimension

Recognising the interconnectivity of life across time

This dimension involves a consideration of the links between the past, present and future, and the connections that exist across generations. It encourages examination of the historical roots to the issues we currently face as well as consideration of the implications of our lifestyles on future generations and landscapes. It also advocates, rather than a short term mentality, a long-term view within policy and lifestyle decision-making processes. Drawing in particular from the Futures Studies work of David Hicks (2001), which we focus on in more detail in the conclusion to this book, it is a dimension that seeks to engage students in notions of possible and preferable futures.

4 Critical dimension

Space to support people in thinking critically about themselves and their place in the world

This first of the pedagogical process dimensions presents the need for learning opportunities where sustainability issues can be considered critically through engagement with multiple perspectives. As outlined in Chapter 2, the complex and systemic nature of global issues requires students to think critically through the lenses of environmental, social, economic and political consideration, as well as encounter less dominant points of view, such as those from indigenous cultures. It encourages students to carefully consider: why are things as they are; in whose hands does power reside; and what systems of inclusion/exclusion are in operation? Within this dimension the aim is not simply to raise students' political literacy through awareness of 'the other' but to also provide a consciousness raising opportunity for critical literacy, where individuals reflexively consider their own perspectives, their sources, assumptions and the sustainability of their implications. As identified by Vare and Scott (2007), this critical dimension ensures that ESD is not simply about the unproblematic transmission or promotion of certain sustainable behaviours.

5 Creative dimension

Space to imagine new sustainable futures

This pedagogical dimension supports a re-conception of the importance of education nurturing people's creative capacities. It holds as being of fundamental importance the need to encourage students in the process of generating and exploring what Robinson (2011) refers to as 'original ideas that are of value'. This is based upon the view that young people today have a vital role to play in creating sustainable futures. While as educators we can share much useful current thinking around more sustainable policies and practices, it is impossible for us to foresee entirely how global challenges are going to play out in the lifetimes of our students. In order for our students to flourish as future citizens, ESD seeks to provide creative learning spaces that give explicit attention to drawing out their ability to collaboratively problem solve, imagine new ways of being and successfully navigate unpredictable global change events.

6 Active learning dimension

Space to act and reflect collaboratively on sustainable living

This pedagogical dimension recognises that while a wide variety of educational approaches can be employed within ESD (as we shall touch upon in the next section of this chapter) emphasis needs to be given to providing holistic learning spaces where people are able to *experientially* explore sustainability challenges. In her review of ESD learning processes for the DESD, Tilbury (2011) cites over twenty studies from scholars worldwide that highlight the alignment of ESD with active and participatory approaches. Through the active learning processes of conceptualising, planning, acting and reflecting, students are better able to engage holistically with the values, skills and knowledge areas of sustainable development. In so doing, the space is provided to develop what Wayman (2009) refers to as 'informed purposive action' where critical thinking is combined with the creative act of interpreting preferable images of the future. This collaborative dimension helps students to develop the social and civic consciousness and wisdom necessary for engagement with pressing sustainability challenges, whether that be at personal, community or institutional levels.

Activity

Developing personal concepts of ESD

How does the butterfly model resonate with your own concept of ESD – are there any dimensions that you would remove or add?

This model places as much emphasis on the active and participatory pedagogical processes within ESD as it does on sustainability content areas. Do you agree that the learning approach is as important as the subject matter in ESD?

Putting ESD into practice

Education for Sustainable Development needs to be a life-long process. International policy in this area recognises the need for ESD within primary, secondary and tertiary education, as well as within informal community education services, industry and business knowledge transfer systems (Samuelsson and Kaga, 2008). The United Nations reports that thousands of ESD projects have now been instigated worldwide (UNESCO, 2012b). More specifically it reports:

> A noteworthy pedagogical shift seems to be occurring in ESD as the DESD unfolds. It is marked by a rise in alternative/innovative forms of teaching and learning. The M&E literature review (Tilbury, 2011) identified four key processes under-pinning ESD: processes which stimulate innovation within curricula as well as through teaching and learning experiences; processes of active and participatory

learning; processes which engage the 'whole system,' and processes of collaboration and dialogue (including multi-stakeholder, and intercultural dialogue).

(UNESCO, 2012b: 25)

In line with the pedagogical approaches we have already considered in Chapter 2, the global monitoring and evaluation survey of the DESD has revealed nine main forms of learning associated with ESD. The definitions of these are found in full in the report (UNESCO, 2012b: 25–26). In summary terms they are:

- *discovery learning*: learning that includes elements of mystery to engender curiosity and exploration;
- *transmissive learning*: learning that includes the provision of information through teacher exposition and supporting materials;
- *participatory/collaborative learning*: learning that requires working actively with others on joint tasks and issues;
- *problem-based learning*: learning that requires students to solve problems about global issues;
- *disciplinary learning*: learning that starts from key foci in particular subject-disciplines (such as Science or Geography);
- *interdisciplinary learning*: learning that includes perspectives from different subject disciplines to support arriving at a conclusion;
- *multi-stakeholder social learning*: learning that brings together people with a range of interests and concerns to investigate and solve problems;
- *critical thinking-based learning*: learning that seeks to explore the values of stakeholders, challenging them when appropriate; and
- *systems thinking-based learning*: learning that includes an explicit focus on interconnections to understand and explore systems holistically.

These learning approaches utilise a variety of creative activities such as storytelling, simulations, role-play and community action. ESD can also be seen to be largely supporting a student-centred approach in order for learning to be provided in ways that are personally accessible, locally relevant and culturally appropriate. This is in order for the practice of ESD to be congruent with its underpinning values such as equity, as illustrated by UNESCO (2012c: 15):

Meeting the learning needs of all pupils in the classroom is a form of social equity, which is a core concept of sustainability . . . using a variety of teaching techniques to meet the learning needs of pupils can address equity in the classroom.

Towards a pedagogy of hope

Increasingly, student surveys reveal young people's interest in sustainability being included within the curriculum (e.g. Drayson *et al.*, 2013). But a key challenge for educators is that exposure to global issues can, in their vastness and potentially devastating implications, all too easily nurture in students a sense of despair, powerlessness or even confused complacency about addressing unsustainable ways of living (Hicks and Bord, 2001). A transformative agenda for ESD therefore becomes providing opportunities for learning that manifest a spirit of optimism. This might involve educators giving greater priority to students having contact with agents of change who can act as sources of inspiration. Alternatively it might involve giving greater recognition to how students can be cognitively and affectively engaged in sustainability through collaborative processes of problem solving and leading change. This frames ESD as seeking to innovate towards representing *a pedagogy of hope*, where learners engage as 'critical creatives' experientially constructing their own more preferable futures. In this way students can be empowered to have a greater sense of self-efficacy as they practically explore how socially just and sustainable change is possible within their own life-worlds. An example of practice in this area is provided in the following case study.

Case study

The Future Leaders Programme – Plymouth University, UK

The Future Leaders Programme, currently being hosted by the Centre for Sustainable Futures at Plymouth University, supports students in learning through collaboratively leading sustainable community action. In so doing it aims to draw out students' resilience, adaptability and enterprise skills. The programme consists of three core elements: student voice, where the students determine the focus of their work; a community of enquiry, where students critically explore together a sustainability issue of concern; and collaborative action, where students lead a change initiative.

Element one: Student voice

A central pedagogical objective is to begin from the experiences and perspectives of the students themselves. A consultative starting point seeks to empower student voice to shape the future direction and activities of the programme. Exercises include students being encouraged to share global sustainability issues they are affected by, or the use of photo voice activities to uncover issues of concern in the institutional or community context. In so doing, participants move towards discovering a sustainability issue of common interest to address together.

Throughout the educational programme the centrality of student voice is maintained. Students are encouraged to share their reflections on how their work together is progressing. They are expected to make decisions collectively and negotiate choices in order to plot the programme's direction, and to reflect upon their own values, personal development and experiences of learning.

Element two: Community of enquiry

The Future Leaders Programme emphasises students learning together through critical enquiry. This is based upon a view shared by Scott and Gough (2004: xiv) who state 'We need to be taught how to learn and how to be critical in order to build our collective capacity to live both sustainably and well.'

Consequently, the programme makes use of a variety of deliberative methodologies in order for students to consider their chosen sustainability issue through a range of perspectives and lenses. The programme encourages the participants to research and meet with community-based change agents who have experience of trying to make a positive difference in the area and that can serve as a source of hope and inspiration.

This element draws heavily from notions of dialogic pedagogy. Freire identifies such a pedagogy to be instrumental in helping students to learn how to problem pose with regard to public life and to discover new ways to collectively change their world (cited in Darder, 2002). So the aim of this element of the programme is to engage students in envisioning new ways of thinking about and addressing a sustainability issue. This is based upon informed discernment and a position of humility that recognises the partial nature of their own understanding, and that is critically aware of the systems of power and influence within which they are immersed.

Element three: Collaborative action for sustainability

The third element of this programme seeks to build practically upon the insight gained from these deliberative practices. Having considered the fundamental roots, personal meaning and societal implications of their chosen sustainability issue of concern, students continue learning through creating a collaborative action response.

This draws in particular from the fields of leadership education, service-learning and enterprise education, the objective being to work with the enthusiasm and concern of the students and to provide support for their vision of a restorative or regenerative change to be put into action within their community context.

The Future Leaders Programme has been adapted to operate within a variety of primary and secondary schools, higher education and informal community settings. Participants have identified a diverse range of sustainability concerns and imaginatively created a broad range of innovative community action responses.

For example, students from a primary school identified as a common issue of concern the levels of traffic pollution in their locality. Their action response was to work with the school staff and student council to pilot a walking bus scheme. This reduced the number of car journeys parents were making to and from the school and therefore tackled one contributor to their chosen sustainability issue.

A second example is a group of secondary school students who identified a common issue of concern to be the breakdown of relationships between younger and older generations locally. They perceived a contributing factor to this intergenerational divide to be the lack of social opportunities for the two groups to get to know each other in a rapidly changing world. Their action response was to organise a joint trip with a group of senior citizens from a neighbouring sheltered housing area. The students accompanied the senior citizens to a nearby

continued . . .

dance hall where the senior citizens taught them how to ballroom dance while reminiscing over what life was like when they were their age. In so doing, closer and more convivial relationships between the two groups of people were begun.

Finally, a third example is provided by two groups of higher education students who chose to focus upon the issue of waste. They critically enquired into this issue through consulting with experts within the university and local community. From this exploration the students designed community action projects centred on raising awareness of the three Rs in waste management (recycling, reducing and reusing). This included creating a workshop that they ran in a neighbouring primary school and supporting a range of waste reduction initiatives, including increasing donations from their institution to a local furniture recycling scheme.

The Future Leaders Programme is an initiative that is experimenting with a participatory pedagogical approach to ESD. This work holds the potential to help empower students to learn through collaboratively leading change within their educational institutions and communities. A key factor in students learning through the creative process of serving as change leaders is the provision of participatory pedagogy for their sustainability concerns and ideas being heard, developed and put into action. An issue in effective practice though is for educators to be appropriately trained in the facilitatory pedagogical approaches that it requires. In line with the words of Freire (1998: 63), ESD requires of the educator that they move from talking to learners to talking to them and with them; from listening to learners to being heard by them.

Activity

The challenges of putting participatory approaches into practice

Within your own context, reflect upon the above example of ESD practice and consider:

1   What age of learners do you consider it appropriate to begin such active and participatory approaches to ESD?
2   In your context, what possible barriers or points of resistance can you identify for implementing a practice similar to the Future Leaders Programme?
3   What do you identify to be some of your own key professional development needs if you were to seek to facilitate a similar learning opportunity for your own students?

Toward an integrated approach to ESD

When conducted at an institutional level, ESD needs to be applied through an integrated approach. Jones *et al.* (2010) highlight the work of the Centre for Sustainable Futures at Plymouth University in advocating a systemic approach, based upon the '4C' model in which *curriculum, campus, community* and *culture* are seen to be mutually enfolded foci in advancing ESD. This requires educators to think beyond their subject areas of specialism and beyond the confines of their classrooms.

Reflecting a systemic approach to change, a national framework for sustainable schools was recently developed in the UK as part of the response to the DESD. This Sustainable Schools Initiative framed ESD to be essentially concerned with students learning to:

> care for oneself;
> care for each other (across cultures, distances and generations); and
> care for the environment (both near and far).
>
> (DCSF, 2008: 4)

The framework provides a useful conceptualisation of ESD to encourage educators to think beyond subject-based curricula. It identifies eight sustainability doorways, as outlined below:

1 Food and drink

'We would like all schools to be model suppliers of healthy, local and sustainable food and drink, showing strong commitments to the environment, social responsibility and animal welfare in their food and drink provision, and maximising their use of local suppliers' (DCSF, 2008: 42).

2 Travel and traffic

'We would like all schools to be models of sustainable travel, where vehicles are used only when absolutely necessary and where there are exemplary facilities for healthier, less polluting or less dangerous modes of transport' (DCSF, 2008: 51).

3 Buildings and grounds

'We would like all schools – old and new – to manage and, where possible, design their buildings in ways that visibly demonstrate sustainable development to everyone who uses the school' (DCSF, 2008: 57). 'Through the design and management of their grounds, we would like all schools to bring pupils closer to the natural world, capture their imaginations in outdoor play, and help them learn about sustainable living' (DCSF, 2008: 60).

4 Energy and water

'We would like all schools to be models of energy efficiency and renewable energy, showcasing opportunities like wind, solar and biomass energy, insulation, low-power technologies and energy management to everyone who uses the school' (DCSF, 2008: 45). 'We would like all schools to be models of water conservation, showcasing opportunities such as rainwater harvesting, grey water recycling and, where possible, sustainable drainage systems to everyone who uses the school' (DCSF, 2008: 48).

5 Purchasing and waste

'We would like all schools to be models of waste minimisation and sustainable consumption, using goods and services of high environmental and ethical standards from local sources where practicable, and increasing value for money by reducing, reusing, repairing and recycling as much as possible' (DCSF, 2008: 54).

6 Inclusion and participation

'We would like all schools to be models of social inclusion, enabling all pupils to participate fully in school life while instilling a long-lasting respect for human rights, freedoms, cultures and creative expression' (DCSF, 2008: 63).

7 Local well-being

'We would like all schools to be models of corporate citizenship within their local areas, enriching their educational mission with activities that improve the environment and quality of life of local people' (DCSF, 2008: 66).

8 Global dimension

'We would like all schools to be models of global citizenship, enriching their educational mission with activities that improve the lives of people living in other parts of the world' (DCSF, 2008: 69).

This sustainable schools framework, although no longer officially advanced at a national policy level, has been significant in giving emphasis to an integrated approach to ESD. It continues to support schools in considering how they might infuse ESD across curriculum, campus, community and culture. Outlined below is an example of one primary school's approach to becoming a 'sustainable school'.

Case study

Towards a sustainable school – Silverhill Primary School, Derbyshire UK

Silverhill Primary School is an example of one of the leading sustainable schools within the UK. Led by the school's headteacher Kate Nash, the school has responded to a number of national and international educational policies, but crucially its ESD work has ultimately been driven forwards by the collective vision of staff, students and parents.

The school has sought to place sustainability at the centre of its philosophy and ethos. A key educational objective is for all students to be committed to working together for the benefit of their local and global communities. The school also makes strong connections to the well-being agenda, stating the view that sustainability is not just about saving energy or using eco-friendly products, but is concerned with how people as individuals live together, caring for each other and the planet.

Staff are supported in considering creative ways for sustainability to be embedded in lessons throughout the year. Topic-based learning forms an important aspect of the curriculum with students studying topics such as Energy and Water, Food and Farming, Global Citizenship, Travel and Transport and Purchasing and Waste. Sustainability also forms a core aspect of an enriched extra-curricular provision for all students. This has involved the school utilising a vast array of learning spaces beyond the classroom. So each class within the school has a responsibility of stewardship for a variety of outdoor learning spaces including bird boxes, a large chicken coop, a willow dome, a wildflower meadow, a composting site, hedgehog homes, a pond and an allotment. The school also has a student Eco-Committee and involves students in energy monitoring, recycling, fair trade drives and the provision of a Healthy Tuck Shop. Each classroom displays their own 'Environmental Promises' and Eco-Code mission statement. The aspirational vision and ethos of the school is even captured in their school prayer used within assemblies:

> Imagine a world where all people are at peace,
> And have food and shelter.
> Where every child is loved and educated to develop their talents,
> Where love is more important than money.
> In this world, everyone is treated equally and fairly.
> Imagine a world where we care for our environment
> And all that lives in it is treated with respect and kindness.
> Life is filled with happiness and laughter.
> May I play my part in sharing love, understanding, wisdom and courage
> To help the world to live in harmony.

To take this work forward the school has developed an innovative leadership model. Working collaboratively as a community of practice, eight members of

continued . . .

staff meet every six weeks to plan cross-curricular activities and programmes of study that require whole-staff team involvement. Their specific remit is to secure long-lasting change that promotes engagement with the social and ecological environment in order to establish a sustainable culture across the whole school and beyond into the wider community context. Wherever possible, the school draws from the expertise and voluntary contributions of parents and community members in order to build as strong community links as possible and to increase the opportunity for intergenerational learning spaces.

In 2013, Silverhill Primary Schools was one of the few schools in England to be awarded Eco-Schools Ambassador status by Keep Britain Tidy, who are the organisation that administer the international Eco-Schools Programme in England.

Eco-Schools is an international initiative begun in 1992 in response to the needs identified at the United Nations Conference on Environment and Development. It aims to support student empowerment with regard to sustainable change through their engagement with action-orientated learning. This student-led approach has a seven-step process that includes: setting up an Eco-Schools Committee; conducting an environmental review; drafting an action plan; monitoring and evaluating changes; integrating environmental and sustainability education into the curriculum; informing and involving peers and the local community; and producing an Eco-Code mission statement. For more information visit www.eco-schools.org.

Activity

Envisioning the sustainable schools of the future

In light of this case study and the eight doorways for sustainability framework that preceded it, choose an educational institution that you are familiar with and envision how it could transform towards becoming a sustainable learning centre.

1   Do your plans touch upon aspects of the '4C' approach, giving attention to curriculum, campus, community and culture foci?
2   How do your plans resonate with each of the eight sustainability doorways used as a frame of reference within the UK?
3   What aspects of your vision perhaps go above and beyond these eight doorways, recognising that any published framework has its limitations?

Sustainability educators as change leaders

Education for Sustainable Development requires not only for our students to be creative and consider what societal changes might be necessary, but also asks of us as educators to adopt the same spirit of innovation. The UNECE (2012) frames two of the three key competencies for educators in ESD as being *envisioning change* and having the ability to *achieve transformation*. It encourages us to remain open to critiquing dominant educational systems and leading change in our own practice. While supported by the ongoing legacy of the United Nations DESD and numerous top-down policy drivers, ESD in its participatory and student-centred approach is very much advanced by 'bottom-up' innovation. One mechanism for educators to lead their own transformative change in practice is 'action research'. This approach fits neatly with the participatory 'bottom-up' paradigm of Education for Sustainable Development (Wierenga and Guevara, 2013).

As described by Carr and Kemmis (1986: 162) action research is:

> A form of self-reflective enquiry undertaken by participants in social situations in order to improve the rationality and justice of their own practices, their understanding of these practices, and the situations in which the practices are carried out.

It represents a cyclical approach to leading educational change, with the process of innovation following a spiral of action, reflection and inquiry steps, as illustrated in Figure 6.2.

Action research is described by McNiff *et al.* (2003) as a process for systematically leading a change in practice that seeks improvement for oneself and others. It is driven by a concern for justice, and values of compassion and respect that need to be both explored and defended by educators' reflexive engagement throughout the change process. A popular approach to action research within ESD is that of *participatory action research*. This is where a collaborative approach is adopted with students and colleagues (in comparison to more individualistic approaches). Participatory action research is underpinned by a strong empowerment ethic that again is in congruence with the ESD paradigm. During the process of participatory action research it is important that educators realise that innovation does not take place in a vacuum. It is common for action research projects to encounter numerous points of resistance and barriers to change, and these can be disheartening for novice action researchers. For this reason, it is important that as educators and facilitators we identify key catalysts to support the innovation process. These might include:

- *dialogue*: speaking with people holding a range of perspectives on the ESD issue being addressed, in order to understand each other's work and learning contexts;
- *instruction*: learning from practitioners and researchers with regard to the ESD issue, drawing from their examples of practice and their identification of underlying issues and challenges;
- *feedback*: listening to the voices of students, peers or observers in order to gain their insight on the practice change as it is taken forwards;
- *personal reflection upon experience*: consideration of experiences in order to identify points of convergence and divergence between the vision of change and the practice of change;

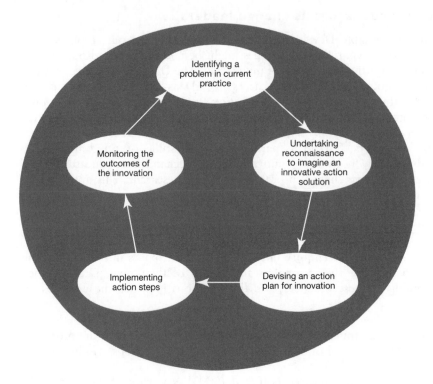

Figure 6.2 An action research spiral

- *story-telling*: learning from the act of creating narratives about the ESD action research journey – its ups and downs, successes and pit falls; and
- *re-visioning*: drawing from your own understanding of a situation and your ability to perceive and imagine new value based directions and preferred futures.

Giving attention to these catalysts can support the action research process by locating it within a *field of encouragement*. This helps to sustain enthusiasm for following a rigorous innovation approach to advancing ESD.

Finally, participatory action research requires of us as educators and facilitators to be mindful of the processes of effective leadership in sustainable change. We need to practically support fellow action researchers in visualising and constructing the broad objectives and actions of a proposed ESD change. The innovation design needs to bear in mind this vision in tandem with a consideration of the specific institutional and local contexts within which you are seeking to operate. With these foundational elements of an innovation established, Fullan (2001) describes the value in paying careful attention to initiation, implementation and continuation phases. Initiation refers to the process that leads up to an institution/community deciding to proceed with a proposed change. The implementation phase involves the early experiences of attempting to put a change into practice. Continuation refers to whether the change gets built into ongoing practice rather than being discarded (Fullan, 2001).

Activity

A framework for ESD action research projects

Action research can serve as an effective strategy for educators as they seek to innovate in ESD practice. Outlined below is an action research framework (based upon the work of McNiff and Whitehead, 2006). Try using this framework as a means of beginning to design a specific ESD innovation project within your own context.

ESD – Action Research Project Framework

1 My professional context.
2 Starting point. What problem/aspect of ESD am I concerned about in my school/institution/educational practice? Why am I concerned? Who shares this concern?
3 What research could we undertake in order to understand more clearly the current situation/practice that we are concerned about?
4 Where could we go for inspiration with regard to ESD? (Where will we find fresh perspectives about our practice concern, to help us imagine alternative solutions?)
5 What research questions is this line of enquiry generating for us?
6 What is our imagined solution/change in practice? (Who will we be collaborating with to put this solution in place?)
7 How will we gather data to monitor the impact of our change in ESD practice?
8 What is our action research plan (being mindful of initiation, implementation, and continuation phases)?

Date	Phase	Activity	Resources/support needed

9 How will we manage our action research project as it progresses? Where will we get our support from?
10 How will we ensure the conclusions we reach about the outcomes of our change in ESD practice are accurate, and how will we share the insights from our action research 'learning journey'?

Conclusion

Education for Sustainable Development represents a radical educational agenda in the sense that it requires us as educators to reconsider the fundamental roots, processes and objectives of our educational practice, and the institutional and cultural systems within which we are placed and shaped. ESD challenges us and our students to not walk along unquestioningly with the status quo of current patterns of development, but to consider critically and creatively ways of living that contribute to the well-being of all. It represents a global learning approach that places an active concern for the common good at the centre of the purpose of education. It frames this with reference to a variety of principles and aspirations such as poverty alleviation, intergenerational equity, social justice, peaceful societies, environmental regeneration and natural resource conservation.

Arguably, ESD has evolved through a number of distinct phases as a global learning movement. In its early stages it placed particular emphasis upon raising awareness of the extent of the crises being faced, highlighting the danger as well as opportunity for change. This helped to establish the rationale for why ESD has been, and continues to be, a necessary reform within any contemporary paradigm of quality education. In more recent years it has not lost this crisis awareness-raising role, adding more research-informed teaching to its thrust. But it has also increasingly engaged learners in problem solving and positive action. There has undoubtedly been much positive progress achieved across a variety of key sustainability indicators. As a result there has undoubtedly been much positive progress achieved across a variety of key sustainability indicators, helping students to be optimistic and anticipate not only the change that is within reach, but also to mark the shifts that have already taken place:

> Our world has experienced a sustained period of positive change. The average person is about eight times richer than a century ago, nearly one billion people have been lifted out of extreme poverty over the past two decades, living standards have soared, life expectancy has risen, the threat of war between great powers has declined, and our genetic code and universe have been unlocked in previously inconceivable ways. Many of today's goods are unimaginable without collective contributions from different parts of the world, through which more of us can move freely with a passport or visa, provided we have the means to do so. Our world is functionally smaller, and its possibilities are bigger and brighter than ever before.
>
> (Oxford Martin School, 2013: 9)

Today, the global community does continue to make progress towards certain well-being targets, but also continues to face a myriad of sustainability challenges, such as climate change, biodiversity loss, oceanic and terrestrial ecosystems weakening, extreme poverty and widening inequality. Consequently, the calls for education to give greater priority to 'problems of living' remain as strong today as they did twenty or thirty years ago. The radical proposal that ESD makes is that in the twenty-first century a new *pedagogy of love* is required where people critically and creatively read their worlds, in order to develop the intellectual awareness, caring dispositions and compassionate relationships that enable them to think 'otherwise' and create new futures.

Questions for further investigation

1   How far does ESD represent a cohesive and universal model of education for the twenty-first century from your perspective?
2   What do you think is more important in ESD – students being engaged in critical and creative learning processes, or students being guided towards the sustainable behaviour changes that are deemed to be essential? How far are these in tension or possible to be made complementary?

Further reading

Chalkley, B., Haigh, M. and Higgitt, D. (eds) (2009) *Education for Sustainable Development: Papers in Honour of the United Nations Decade of Education for Sustainable Development (2005–2014)*. London: Routledge.

This collection of papers provides a scholarly overview of the progress made within the first half of the DESD. Importantly, it provides a cosmopolitan insight with reference to research and practice in countries such as Russia, US, Austria, UK, Australia, New Zealand, Japan and Swaziland.

Stone, M. (2009) *Smart by Nature: Schooling for Sustainability*. California: Watershed Media.

Coming out of the work of the Center for Ecoliteracy in the USA, this book provides a range of strategies and resources for transforming schools towards sustainability with a particular focus upon ecological dimensions. It also includes numerous case studies from both primary and secondary schools that highlight lessons learned in the process.

UNESCO (2012) *Shaping the Education of Tomorrow*. Paris: UNESCO.

This second report generated through the DESD monitoring and evaluation process provides a global account of key learning processes that are emerging from examples of good practice in ESD. It includes input from a broad array of policymakers, scholars and practitioners engaged in ESD around the world. It can be downloaded along with numerous other resources and publications from the UNESCO website: www.unesco.org/new/en/education/themes/leading-the-international-agenda/education-for-sustainable-development.

UNESCO (2010) Teaching and Learning for a Sustainable Future – a multimedia teacher education programme (www.unesco.org/education/tlsf/index.html).

This free multimedia resource has been specifically written in support of the United Nations Decade of Education for Sustainable Development. It provides professional development for student teachers, teachers, curriculum developers, education policy makers and authors of educational materials. The twenty-seven modules have been written by a team led by John Fien and are divided into four main themes: curriculum rationale; sustainable development across the curriculum; contemporary issues; and teaching and learning strategies.

Conclusion
Global learning for the future

Throughout this book we have asked you to engage with, explore and critically reflect on the ways in which knowledge, skills and dispositions can support students' global learning. We have suggested that global learning involves a *complex inter-relationship between knowledge, understanding, skills and dispositions*, that global learning is a *theme that should imbue all aspects of education*, and that the precise form and nature of global learning should be *informed and shaped by the needs of particular contexts*. We started the introduction by citing a speech made to the Earth Summit in Rio de Janeiro in 1992 by twelve-year-old Severn Suzuki. We commence this conclusion by returning to her views, this time given in a speech made in the context of the Rio+20 event held in 2012. In this, Cullis-Suzuki (2012) argued that:

> The 1992 Earth Summit focused the world's attention on sustainable development. Today, the issues are even more serious. They are even more relevant and urgent. Pollution has changed our climate. More than a billion people are living without electricity. Children are still dying of preventable diseases, malnutrition, and simple dehydration. Too many people are struggling to get by—living in poverty, often without safe drinking water or enough food. At the same time, the one percent continues to get richer. We can, we must, do better.

In addition, Cullis-Suzuki sets out a number of claims about the future:

This is the future that the world wants. A future:

- Where we can all breathe clean air and drink clean water;
- Where we have turned the tide against the pollution that threatens to swallow our oceans;
- Where every person has access to electricity and the benefits that it brings;
- Where we power the world with clean energy from the sun, the wind, and the soil;
- We envision a world where the Earth's natural treasures are protected and preserved;
- Where no person goes hungry and poverty is a problem of the past;
- Where all children get the nutrition they need, the education they deserve;
- Where women and girls are empowered and human rights are respected;
- Where preventable diseases don't take the lives of children and childbirth complications don't take the lives of their mothers;

- Where health care isn't a luxury to some, but available to all; and
- Where every young person has the opportunity to work and every community has the opportunity to prosper.

These statements are thought-provoking, challenging and compelling. Moreover they ask us as educators to consider the extent to which we are preparing young people not just for being active global learners and participants today, but for the future. Mindful of the challenges prompted by Cullis-Suzuki's list, to conclude the book we ask you to engage with one more facet of global learning that has remained implicit so far, but here we wish to make explicit – namely the idea of *futures studies*.

Futures studies has developed as an academic field since the 1960s, and has received more attention in education in the last two decades, particularly through the work of David Hicks (2001, 2012, 2014). According to Inayatullah (1993: 236), futures studies combines 'predicting the future' alongside a humanistic concern with 'developing a good society'. If we compare this definition with the ideas for the future provided by Cullis-Suzuki above, we can see that they relate clearly to the intentions of global learning that we have explored throughout the book. This connection is further illustrated when we consider the following conception of futures studies provided by Dator (2005):

> One of the main tasks of futures studies is to identify and examine the major alternative futures which exist at any given time and place. The future cannot be predicted, but preferred futures can and should be envisioned, invented, implemented, continuously evaluated, revised and re-envisioned. Thus, [a] major task of futures studies is to facilitate individuals and groups in formulating, implementing, and re-envisioning their preferred futures.

In Chapter 2, for instance, we considered the ways in which pedagogies for global learning need to engage students in developing a sense of the complexity of global issues and the various possibilities and challenges of each. Along these lines, Hicks (2008: 120) sets out some key elements that integrating a futures perspective can provide for teachers and students that relate well to the various pedagogical strategies we set out in Chapter 2 and have illustrated throughout this book. The elements are to:

- develop a more future-orientated perspective on their lives and events in the wider world;
- identify and envision alternative futures that are more just and sustainable;
- exercise critical thinking skills and the creative imagination more effectively;
- participate in more thoughtful and informed decision making in the present;
- engage in active and responsible citizenship, both in the local, national and global community and on behalf of present and future generations.

To support these elements, Hicks (2012: 6–7) identifies nine key concepts in futures studies. These are: (1) the state of the world; (2) managing change; (3) views of the future; (4) alternative futures; (5) hopes and fears; (6) past/present/future; (7) visions for the future; (8) future generations; and (9) sustainable futures. Collectively, these ask us to explore with our students: the nature of world today, including how we have arrived at current contexts; different perspectives and possibilities for the world, including different attitudes and desires; the question of whether future generations have rights; and how the futures of all people in the world can be recognised and sustained. Central to exploring these areas is for us to reflect on what the interests, needs and requirements of the twenty-first-century learners are, how a twenty-first-century curriculum can support these, and how they can be developed through appropriate pedagogies (McInerney, 2010).

This raises questions for us as educators about the ways in which the curriculum – as interpreted and constructed by us and as experienced by our students – is future-orientated. If we consider, as we have done throughout each chapter of this book, how rapid, fluid and dynamic global processes have been over the last fifteen years, we see that fifteen years from now how what it means to be a global citizen may be understood, influenced and practised in rather different ways than it is today. Reflecting on this prompts us to recognise that global education is important for students' lives today, and also to think about how processes of globalisation will affect them as global citizens of the future. A key part of this is for them to explore and reflect on their shared futures as members of a shared human community.

With this in mind, we conclude by reiterating the nine core principles of pedagogies for global learning set out in Chapter 2. These envisaged global learning as being: holistic, personalised, flexible, partnered, equal, convivial, democratic, well-being based, and rigorous. These principles provide intentions for educating global citizens for the present *and* the future. We wish you well in your work as global educators.

References

Adamson, P. (1993) 'Charity begins at home', *The Independent*, 18 May.

Adichie, C. N. (2009) *The Danger of a Single Story*. TED Talk (http://new.ted.com/talks/chimamanda_adichie_the_danger_of_a_single_story; accessed 10 October 2013).

Afkhami, M. (n.d.) *Mahnaz Afkhami Reflects on Working Toward Peace* (www.scu.edu/ethics/architects-of-peace/Afkhami/essay.html; accessed 20 January 2014).

Amnesty International (2001) *First Steps: A Manual for Starting Human Rights Education*. London: Amnesty International.

Amnesty International (2014) *Human Rights Education* (www.amnesty.org/en/human-rights-education; accessed 10 January 2014).

Anderson, L. (2011) 'Demystifying the Arab Spring: Parsing the differences between Tunisia, Egypt and Libya', in *Foreign Affairs* (www.channel4.com/news/arab-revolt-social-media-and-the-peoples-revolution; accessed 12 January 2014).

Andreotti, V. and Warwick, P. (2007) *Engaging Students with Controversial Issues through a Dialogue Based Approach* (www.citized.info/?strand=3&r_menu=res; accessed 21 January 2014).

Annan, K. (2000) 'The politics of globalization', in P. O'Meara, H. Mohlinger and M. Krain (eds) *Globalization and the Challenge of a New Century: A Reader*. Bloomington, IN: Indiana University Press. 125–30.

Annette, J. (2010) 'The challenge of developing civic engagement in higher education in England', in *British Journal of Educational Studies*. 58 (10). 451–63.

Appiah, K. A. (2006) *Cosmopolitanism: Ethics in a World of Strangers*. London: Penguin.

Arora, R. (2005) *Race and Ethnicity in Education*. Aldershot: Ashgate.

Australian Curriculum and Assessment Reporting Authority (2012) *Intercultural Understanding* (www.australiancurriculum.edu.au/GeneralCapabilities/Pdf/Intercultural-understanding; accessed 12 December 2013).

Australian Electoral Commission (n.d.) *Electoral Milestone for Indigenous Australians*. (http://www.aec.gov.au/indigenous/milestones.htm; accessed 17 July 2014).

Bailey, F. and Dolan, A. (2011) 'The meaning of partnership in development: Lessons for development education', in *Policy and Practice: A Development Education Review*. London: Centre for Global Education. 30–48.

Banks, J. (2008a) 'Diversity, group identity, and citizenship education in a global age', in *Educational Researcher*. 37 (3). 129–39.

Banks, J. (2008b) *An Introduction to Multicultural Education*. Boston, MA: Pearson.

Banks, J., Cookson, P., Gay, G., Hawley, W., Jordon Irvine, J., Nieto, S., Ward Schofield, J. and Stephan, W. (2008) 'Education and diversity', in W. Parker (ed.) *Social Studies Today: Research and Practice*. New York: Routledge. 67–76.

Barber, B. (1998) *A Passion for Democracy: American Essays*. Princeton, NJ: Princeton University Press.

Barton, K. C. and Levstik, L. S. (2004) *Teaching History for the Common Good*. Mahwah, NJ: Lawrence Erlbaum Associates.

Baxi, U. (1994) *Human Rights Education: The Promise of the Third Millennium?* Paper presented at the Conference of the United Nations Member States and Non-Governmental Organisations, New York (www.pdhre.org/dialogue/third_millennium.html; accessed 7 November 2013).

Beck, U. and Levy, D. (2013) 'Cosmopolitanized nations: re-imagining collectivity in world risk society', in *Theory, Culture and Society*. 30 (3). 3–31.

Bennett, W. (2003) 'Communicating global activism', in *Information, Communication & Society*. 6 (2). 143–68.

Bennett, W. L., Wells, C. and Freelon, D. (2011) 'Communicating civic engagement: contrasting models of citizenship in the youth web space', in *Journal of Communication*. 61 (5). 835–56.

Berger, P. (1997) *Epistemological Modesty: An Interview with Peter Berger* (www.religion-online.org/showarticle.asp?title=240; accessed 8 August 2013).

Berger, P. (1999) *The Desecularisation of the World: Resurgent Religions and World Politics*. Grand Rapids, MI: Eerdmans.

Bernacki, M. and Bernt, F. (2007) 'Service-learning as a transformative experience: an analysis of the impact of service-learning on student attitudes and behaviour after two years of college', in S. Gelmon and S. Billig (eds) (2007) *Service-Learning: From Passion to Objectivity*. Charlotte, NC: Information Age Publishing. 111–34.

Bessant, S., Bailey, P., Robinson, Z., Tomkinson, B., Tomkinson, R., Ormerod, M. and Boast, R. (2013) *Problem-Based Learning: A Case Study of Sustainability Education* (www.heacademy.ac.uk/assets/documents/ntfs/Problem_Based_Learning_Toolkit.pdf; accessed 12 March 2014).

Bohman, J. (2004) 'Republican cosmopolitanism', in *Journal of Political Philosophy*. 12 (3). 336–52.

Boulding, E. (1988) *Building a Global Civic Culture: Education for an Interdependent World*. New York: Teachers College Press.

Bourn, D. (2011) 'Discourses and practices around development education: from learning about development to critical global pedagogy', in *Policy and Practice: A Development Education Review*. London: Centre for Global Education. 11–29.

Bourn, D. (2012) 'Development education', in J. Arthur and A. Peterson (eds) *The Routledge Companion to Education*. Abingdon: Routledge. 254–62.

Bourn, D. and Brown, K. (2011) *Young People and International Development: Engagement and Learning*. Development Education Research Centre, Research Paper No. 2. London: Development Education Research Centre.

Bourn, D. and Cara, O. (2013) *School Linking – Where Next? Partnership Models between Schools in Europe and Africa*. London: Development Education Research Centre.

Bowring, B. (2012) 'Human rights and public education', in *Cambridge Journal of Education*. 42 (1). 53–65.

Boys, J. (2011) *Towards Creative Learning Spaces: Re-thinking the Architecture of Post-Compulsory Education*. Abingdon: Routledge.

Bringle, R., Hatcher, J. and Jones, S. (eds) (2011) *International Service Learning*. Sterling, VA: Stylus.

British Broadcasting Corporation (BBC) (2011) *Bin Laden Raid Was Unveiled on Twitter*. 2 May (www.bbc.co.uk/news/technology-13257940; accessed 21 September 2013).

British Broadcasting Corporation (BBC) (2014) *Crimea Crisis: Merkel Warns Russia Faces Escalating Sanctions*. 20 March (www.bbc.com/news/world-europe-26659578; accessed 21 March 2014).

British Institute of Human Rights (2010) *Human Rights in Action – a Toolkit for Change*. London: British Institute of Human Rights.

British Institute of Human Rights (2013) *The Human Rights Charter* (www.bihr.org.uk/charter; accessed 10 January 2014).

Brown v. Board of Education of Topeka – 347 U.S. 483 (1954).

Burrell, I. (2011) *Judge Calls for New Era of Online Controls in Attack on 'Those who Peddle Lies'*. 21 May (www.independent.co.uk/news/uk/home-news/judge-calls-for-new-era-of-online-controls-in-attack-on-lsquothose-who-peddle-liesrsquo-2287160.html; accessed 21 September 2013).

Bush, G. (2001) *Speech to Congress and the People of the United States of America*. 20 September (www.theguardian.com/world/2001/sep/21/september11.usa13; accessed 21 September 2013).

Cahill, D. and Leahy, M. (2004) *Constructing a Local Multifaith Network*. Canberra, Australia: Common of Australia.

Calenda, D. and Meijer, A. (2009) 'Young people, the internet and political participation', in *Information, Communication & Society*. 12 (6). 879–98.

Cam, P. (2006) *Twenty Thinking Tools: Collaborative Inquiry for the Classroom*. Camberwell, VIC: Australian Council for Educational Research.

Cameron, D. (2007) *Social Responsibility: The Big Idea for Britain's Future*. London: The Conservative Party.

Cameron, D. (2011) *Speech on Radicalisation and Islamic Extremism*. 5 February, Munich (www.newstatesman.com/blogs/the-staggers/2011/02/terrorism-islam-ideology; accessed 14 January 2014).

Cameron, D. (2012) *Address to the United Nations General Assembly*. 26 September (www.gov.uk/government/speeches/david-camerons-address-to-the-united-nations-general-assembly; accessed 10 November 2013).

Carr, W. and Kemmis, S. (1986) *Becoming Critical: Education, Knowledge and Action Research*. Lewes: Falmer.

Chalkley, B., Haigh, M. and Higgitt, D. (eds) (2009) *Education for Sustainable Development: Papers in Honour of the United Nations Decade of Education for Sustainable Development (2005–2014)*. London: Routledge.

Chambers, R. (2005) *Ideas for Development*. London: Earthscan.

Channel 4 (2011) *Arab Revolt: Social Media and the People's Revolution*. 25 February (www.channel4.com/news/arab-revolt-social-media-and-the-peoples-revolution; accessed 12 January 2014).

Chomsky, N. (2004) *Profit Over People: Neoliberalism and Global Order*. New York: Seven Sisters Press.

Cleaver, E., Supples, C. and Kerr, D. (2007) *Participation Under the Spotlight: Interrogating Policy and Practice and Defining Future Directions*. Slough: NFER.

CNBC (2013) *Top 1% Control 39% of World's Wealth*. Friday 31 May (www.cnbc.com/id/100780163; accessed 20 October 2013).

Collier, P. (2007) *The Bottom Billion: Why the Poorest Countries are Failing and What Can be Done About It*. Oxford: Oxford University Press.

The Commonwealth (2013) *Charter of the Commonwealth* (http://thecommonwealth.org/sites/default/files/page/documents/CharteroftheCommonwealth.pdf; accessed 10 July 2014).

Cook, I. *et al.* (in press) 'Material geographies', in *Géographie et cultures* (followthethings.com).

Coulby, D. (2006) 'Intercultural education: theory and practice', in *Intercultural Education*. 17 (3). 245–57.

Council of Europe (2008) *Living Together as Equals in Dignity: White Paper on Intercultural Dialogue* (www.coe.int/t/dg4/intercultural/source/white%20paper_final_revised_en.pdf; accessed 12 December 2013).

Council of Europe (2010) *Council of Europe Charter on Education for Democratic Citizenship and Human Rights Education*. Strasbourg: Council of Europe Publishing.

Cowan, P. and Maitles, H. (eds) (2012) *Teaching Controversial Issues in the Classroom*. London: Continuum.

Cremin, H. and Warwick, P. (2008) 'Multiculturalism is dead: long live community cohesion? A case study of an educational methodology to empower young people as global citizens', in *Research in Comparative and International Education*. 3 (1). 36–49.

Crook, C. (2001) 'Globalisation and its critics', in *The Economist, Special Report: Globalisation*. 27 September (www.economist.com/node/795995/print; accessed 20 October 2013).

Cullis-Suzuki, S. (2012) *6-Minute Speech Delivered to Rio+Social*. 19 June (www.unfounda tion.org/news-and-media/press-releases/2012/rioplussocial-six-minute-speech.html; accessed 18 February 2014).

Darder, A. (2002) *Reinventing Paulo Freire*. Oxford: Westview.

Dator, J. (2005) 'Foreword', in R. Slaughter (ed.) *Knowledge Base of Future Studies, The Future*. CD-ROM. Brisbane: Foresight International.

Davies, I., Evans, M. and Reid, A. (2005) 'Globalising citizenship education? A critique of "global education" and "citizenship education"', in *British Journal of Educational Studies*. 53 (1). 66–89.

Davies, I., Bennett, L., Loader, B., Mellor, S., Vromen, A., Coleman, S. and Xenos, M. (2012) 'Four questions about the educational potential of social media for promoting civic engagement', in *Citizenship Teaching and Learning*. 7 (3). 293–306.

Deardon, R. (1981) 'Controversial issues in the curriculum', in *Journal of Curriculum Studies*. 13. 37–44.

Department for Children, Schools and Families (2007) *Guidance on the Duty to Promote Community Cohesion*. London: DCSF.

Department for Children, Schools and Families (2008) *S3: Sustainable School Self-evaluation: Driving School Improvement through Sustainable Development*. Nottingham: DCSF.

Department for Education (2013) *National Curriculum in England: Citizenship Programmes of Study for Key Stages Three and Four* (www.gov.uk/government/publications/national-curriculum-in-england-citizenship-programmes-of-study/national-curriculum-in-england-citizenship-programmes-of-study-for-key-stages-3-and-4; accessed 12 December 2013).

Department of Education, Early Childhood Development (2009) *Education for Global and Multicultural Citizenship: A Strategy for Victorian Government Schools 2009–2013*. Melbourne, Australia: DEECD.

Department for Education and Employment (1999) *Social Inclusion: Pupil Support. Circular 10/1999)*. London: DfEE.

Department for Education and Skills (2004) *Aiming High: Understanding the Educational Needs of Minority Ethnic Pupils in Mainly White Schools*. London: DfES.

Department for Education and Skills (2007) *Curriculum Review: Diversity and Citizenship* (The Ajegbo Report). London: DfES.

Development Education Association/Department for International Development (2005) *Developing A Global Dimension in the School Curriculum*. London: Department for International Development.

Dewey, J. (1933) *How We Think*. London: D. C. Heath.

Dickinson, R., Katselli, E., Murray, C. and Pedersen, O. (eds) (2012) *Examining Critical Perspectives on Human Rights*. Cambridge: Cambridge University Press.

Dill, J. (2013) *The Longings and Limits of Global Citizenship Education: The Moral Pedagogy of Schooling in a Cosmopolitan Age*. New York: Routledge.

Disney, A. (2008) 'The contribution of school linking projects to global education – some geographical perspectives', in *GeogEd*. 2 (2) (www.geography.org.uk/download/GA_GeogEdVol212A2.pdf; accessed 30 March 2014).

Drayson, R., Bone, E., Agombar, J. and Kemp, S. (2013) *Student Attitudes Towards and Skills for Sustainable Development*. York: Higher Education Academy.

Dudek, M. (2000) *Architecture of Schools: The New Learning Environments*. London: Architectural Press.

Elliott, K., Kar, D. and Richardson, J. (2004) 'Assessing globalization's critics: "talkers are no good doers?"', in R. Baldwin and L. Winters (eds) *Challenges to Globalization: Analyzing the Economics*. Chicago, IL: University of Chicago Press. 17–62.

Ellis, A. (2005) *Active Citizens in School: Evaluation of the DfES Pilot Programme*. London: DfES.

European Commission (2013) *The Story of the European Year of Intercultural Dialogue 2008*. (http://ec.europa.eu/culture/our-programmes-and-actions/the-story-of-the-european-year-of-intercultural-dialogue_en.htm; accessed 12 December 2013).

European Consensus on Development Education (2007) *The Contribution of Development Education & Awareness Raising*. (http://ec.europa.eu/development/icenter/repository/DE_Consensus-eductation_temp_EN.pdf; accessed 10 January 2014). 1–20.

Fielding, M. and Moss, P. (2011) *Radical Education and the Common School*. London: Routledge.

Freire, P. (1995) *Pedagogy of Hope. Reliving Pedagogy of the Oppressed*. New York: Continuum.

Freire, P. (1998) *Teachers as Cultural Workers: Letters to Those Who Dare Teach*. Oxford: Westview Press.

Fuentes-Nieva, R. and Galasso, N. (2014) *Working for the Few: Political Capture and Economic Inequality*. Oxford: Oxfam International.

Fullan, M. (2001) *The New Meaning of Educational Change*. London: RoutledgeFalmer.

Gates, B. and Gates, M. (2014) *3 Myths That Block Progress for the Poor*. 2014 Gates Annual Letter. Seattle, WA: Bill & Melinda Gates Foundation.

Gearon, L. (2004) 'Schools and community participation: issues for citizenship education', in B. Linsley and E. Rayment (eds) *Beyond the Classroom: Exploring Active Citizenship in 11–16 Education*. London: The New Politics Network.

Gelmon, S. and Billig, S. (eds) (2007) *Service-Learning: From Passion to Objectivity*. Charlotte, NC: Information Age Publishing.

George, S. (2001) 'The global citizen's movement: a new actor for a new politics', Conference on reshaping globalization, Central European University, Budapest, October (posted on the World Social Forum site: www.portoalegre2002.org).

Giddens, A. (2000) 'Citizenship education in the global era', in N. Pearce and J. Hallgarten (eds) *Tomorrow's Citizens*. London: Institute for Public Policy Research. 19–25.

Gillan, K. and Pickerill, J. (2008) 'Transnational anti-war activism: solidarity, diversity and the Internet in Australia, Britain and the United States after 9/11', in *Australian Journal of Political Science*. 43 (1). 59–78.

Global Education Project (2008) *Global Perspectives: A Framework for Global Education in Australian Schools*. Carlton, VIC: Education Services Australia.

Goldin, I. (2009) *Navigating Our Global Future*. TED Talk (www.ted.com/talks/ian_goldin_navigating_our_global_future.html; accessed 21 August 2013).

Golmohamad, M. (2009) 'Education for world citizenship: beyond national allegiance', in *Educational Philosophy and Theory*. 41 (4). 466–86.

Gore, A. (2013) *The Future*. New York: WH Allen.

Gowring, N. (1994) *Instant Pictures, Instant Policy: Is Television Driving Foreign Policy?* 3 July (www.independent.co.uk/news/world/inside-story-instant-pictures-instant-policy-is-television-driving-foreign-policy-itns-nik-gowing-examines-the-something-must-be-done-factor-and-picks-out-five-examples-from-the-bloody-conflict-in-bosnia-1417852.html; accessed 10 January 2014).

Gutmann, A. and Thompson, D. (1996) *Democracy and Disagreement*. Cambridge, MA: Harvard University Press.

Habermas, J. (1996) *Between Facts and Norms: Contributions to a Discourse Theory of Law and Democracy*. Cambridge, MA: MIT Press.

Haigh, M. (2014) 'From internationalisation to education for global citizenship: a multi-layered history', in *Higher Education Quarterly*. 68 (1). 6–27.

Hammarberg, T. (2008) 'No real development without human rights'. Lecture on the inter-relationship between development and human rights when implementing the UN Millennium Development Goals. Speech given at Trinity College, Dublin, 3 April (https://wcd.coe.int/ViewDoc.jsp?id=1247635&Site=CommDH; accessed 10 January 2014).

Hart, S. (2007) 'Service-learning and literacy motivation: setting a research agenda', in S. Gelmon and S. Billig (eds) (2007) *Service-Learning: From Passion to Objectivity*. Charlotte, NC: Information Age Publishing. 135–56.

Hecht, D. (2003) 'The missing link: exploring the context of learning in service-learning', in S. Billig and J. Eyler (eds) *Deconstructing Service-Learning: Research Exploring Context, Participation, and Impacts*. Greenwich, CT: Information Age. 25–49.

Hek, R. (2005) *The Experiences and Needs of Refugee and Asylum Seeking Children in the UK: A Literature Review*. London: DfES.

Held, D. (2010) *Cosmopolitanism: Ideas and Realities*. Cambridge: Polity Press.

Hess, D. (2009) *Controversy in the Classroom: The Democratic Power of Discussion*. New York: Routledge.

Hicks, D. (2001) *Citizenship for the Future*. Godalming: WWF.

Hicks, D. (2008) 'A futures perspective in education', in S. Ward (ed.) *A Students' Guide to Educational Studies*. London: Routledge. 117–29.

Hicks, D. (2012) 'The future only arrives when things look dangerous: reflections on futures education in the UK', in *Futures*. 44 (1). 4–13.

Hicks, D. (2014) *Educating for Hope in Troubled Times: Climate Change and the Transition to a Post-Carbon Future*. Stoke on Trent: Trentham.

Hicks, D. and Bord, A. (2001) 'Learning about global issues: why most educators only make things worse', in *Environmental Education Research*. 7 (4). 413–25.

Hicks, D. and Holden, C. (eds) (2007) *Teaching the Global Dimension: Key Principles and Effective Practice*. London: Routledge.

Hoge, J. (1994) 'Media pervasiveness', in *Foreign Affairs*. 73. 136–44.

Holden, C. (2007) 'Young people's concerns', in Hicks, D. and Holden, C. (eds) *Teaching the Global Dimension: Key Principles and Effective Practice*. London: Routledge. 31–42.

Home Office (2001) *Community Cohesion: Report of the Independent Review Team*. London: Home Office.

Hoppers, C. (2008) *South African Research Chair in Development Education – Framework and Strategy*. Pretoria: University of South Africa.

Huckle, J. (2012) *Sustainable Development*, in J. Arthur and A. Peterson (eds) *The Routledge Companion to Education*. London: Routledge. 362–71.

Human Rights Act (1998) *UK Human Rights Act 1998* (www.legislation.gov.uk/ukpga/1998/42/contents; accessed 10 January 2014).

Human Rights Education Association (2013) *Launch of HRE 2020 Coalition*. 19 December. (www.hrea.org/index.php?doc_id=2281&&wv_print=1; accessed 10 January 2014).

Inayatullah, S. (1993) 'From "who I am?" to "when I am?": Framing the shape and time of the future', in *Futures*. 25. 235–53.

Intergovernmental Panel on Climate Change (2014) *Climate Change 2014: Impacts, Adaptation and Vulnerability: Summary for Policy Makers*. Stanford, CA: IPCC.

International Organization for Migration (2014) *Key Migration Terms* (www.iom.int/cms/en/sites/iom/home/about-migration/key-migration-terms-1.html; accessed 10 January 2014).

International Union for Conservation of Nature (1980) *World Conservation Strategy: Living Resource Conservation for Sustainable Development*. Gland, Switzerland: International Union for Conservation of Nature.

International Union for Conservation of Nature (2013) *Red List Table 1 Numbers of threatened species by major groups of organisms (1996–2013)* (http://cmsdocs.s3.amazonaws.com/summarystats/2013_2_RL_Stats_Table1.pdf; accessed 20 March 2014).

Internet Growth Statistics (2014) *Today's Road to e-Commerce and Global Trade* (www.internetworldstats.com/emarketing.htm; accessed 10 February 2014).

Jakobsen, P. (2000) 'Focus on the CNN Effect misses the point: the real media impact on conflict management is invisible and indirect', in *Journal of Peace Research*. 37 (2). 131–43.

Jenkins, H. (2006) *Convergence Culture: Where Old and New Media Collide*. New York: New York University Press.

Jenlink, P. M. (2007) 'Guest editorial: Globalization, democracy, and the evolution of global civil society', in *World Futures*. 63 (5/6). 301–7.

Jerome, L. (2012) 'Service-learning and active citizenship in England', in *Education, Citizenship and Social Justice*. 7 (59). 59–70.

Johnson, D. W., Johnson, R. and Tjosvold, D. (2000) 'Constructive controversy: the value of intellectual opposition', in M. Deutsch, and P. T. Coleman (eds) *The Handbook of Conflict Resolution: Theory and Practice*. San Francisco, CA: Jossey-Bass.

Jones, P., Selby, D. and Sterling, S. (2010) *Sustainability Education*. London: Earthscan.

Kagawa, F. and Selby, D. (2010) *Education and Climate Change*. London: Routledge.

Kaldor, M., Anheier, H. and Glasius, M. (2003) *Global Civil Society*. London: Sage Publications.

Keating, A. and Benton, T. (2013) 'Creating cohesive citizens in England? Exploring the role of diversity, deprivation and democratic climate at school', in *Education, Citizenship and Social Justice*. 8 (2). 165–84.

Kennedy, D. (2002) 'The international human rights movement: part of the problem?', in *Harvard Human Rights Journal*. 15. 101–26.

King, M. L. (1963) *Letter From a Birmingham Jail*. 16 April (www.africa.upenn.edu/Articles_Gen/Letter_Birmingham.html; accessed 21 September 2013).

King, O. and Hamilos, P. (2006) *Timeline: The Road to War in Iraq*. 3 February (www.theguardian.com/politics/2006/feb/02/iraq.iraq; accessed 21 September 2013).

Kiwan, D. (2012) 'Human rights and citizenship education: re-positioning the debate', in *Cambridge Journal of Education*. 42 (1). 1–7.

Klein, N. (2007) *The Shock Doctrine: The Rise of Disaster Capitalism*. London: Allen Lane/Penguin.

Kothari, R. (1989) *Rethinking Development: In Search of Humane Alternatives*. Delhi: Ajanta.

Kumar, A. (2008) 'Development education and dialogic learning in the 21st Century', in *International Journal of Development Education and Global Learning*. 1 (1). 37–48.

Kymlicka, W. (1995) *Multicultural Citizenship*. Oxford: Oxford University Press.

Kymlicka, W. (2012) 'Comment on Meer and Modood', in *Journal of Intercultural Studies*. 33 (2). 211–16.

Ladson-Billings, G. (2004) 'Culture versus citizenship: The challenge of racialised citizenship in the United States', in J. A. Banks (ed.) *Diversity and Citizenship Education: Globalised Perspectives*. San Francisco, CA: Jossey-Bass. 99–126.

Lagarde, C. (2014) *A New Multilateralism for the 21st Century: The Richard Dimbleby Lecture*. 3 February (www.imf.org/external/np/speeches/2014/020314.htm; accessed 10 February 2014).

Laurence, J. and Heath, A. (2008) *Predictors of Community Cohesion: Multilevel Modelling of the 2005 Citizenship Survey*. London: Department for Communities and Local Government.

Leighton, R. (2012) *Teaching Citizenship Education: A Radical Approach*. London: Continuum.

Lentin, A. (2005) 'Replacing "race": historizing the "culture" in the multiculturalism', in *Patterns of Prejudice*. 39 (4). 379–96.

Lewis, L. and Chandley, N. (eds) (2012) *Philosophy for Children through the Secondary Curriculum*. London: Continuum.

Lingard, B. (2007) 'Pedagogies of indifference', in *International Journal of Inclusive Education*. 11 (3). 245–66.

London Councils (2014) *London Key Facts: Demographics* (www.londoncouncils.gov.uk/londonfacts/default.htm?category=2; accessed 10 January 2014).

Lu, C. (2000) 'The one and many faces of cosmopolitanism', in *The Journal of Political Philosophy*. 8 (2). 244–67.

McCowan, T. (2012) 'Human rights within education: assessing the justifications', in *Cambridge Journal of Education*. 42 (1). 67–81.

McCowan, T. (2013) *Education as a Human Right: Principles for a Universal Entitlement to Learning*. London: Bloomsbury.

McInerney, M. (2010) 'Implications of 21st Century change and the Geography curriculum', in *Geographical Education*. 23. 23–31.

McNiff, J. and Whitehead, J. (2006) *All You Need to Know About Action Research*. London: Sage.

McNiff, J., Lomax, P. and Whitehead, J. (2003) *You and Your Action Research Project*. London: RoutledgeFalmer.

MacPherson Report (1999) *The Stephen Lawrence Inquiry: Report of an Inquiry by Sir William MacPherson of Cluny* (www.gov.uk/government/uploads/system/uploads/attachment_data/file/277111/4262.pdf; accessed 12 December 2013).

Marquand, D. (2004) *The Decline of the Public*. Cambridge: Polity Press.

Marshall, H. (2007) 'Global education in perspective: fostering a global dimension in an English secondary school', in *Cambridge Journal of Education*. 37 (3). 355–74.

Martin, D. (2005) *On Secularisation: Towards a Revised General Theory*. Aldershot: Ashgate.

Martin, F. (2007) 'School linking: a controversial issue', in H. Claire and C. Holden (eds) *The Challenge of Teaching Controversial Issues*. Stoke on Trent: Trentham. 147–60.

Maylor, U. and Read, B. with Mendick, H., Ross, A. and Rollock. N. (2007) *Diversity and Citizenship in the Curriculum: Research Review*. London: DfES.

Meer, N. and Modood, T. (2011) 'How does interculturalism contrast with multiculturalism?', in *Journal of Intercultural Studies*. 33 (2). 175–96.

Merry, M. and de Ruyter, D. (2011) 'The relevance of cosmopolitanism for moral education', in *Journal of Moral Education*. 40 (11). 1–18.

Merryfield, M. M. and Kasai, M. (2010). 'How are teachers responding to globalization?', in W. C. Parker (ed.) *Social Studies Today: Research and Practice*. New York: Routledge. 165–73.

Mezirow, J. (ed.) (2000) *Learning as Transformation: Critical Perspectives on a Theory of Progress*. San Francisco, CA: Jossey Bass.

Miller, D. (2002) 'Cosmopolitanism: a critique', in *Critical Review of International Social and Political Philosophy*. 5 (3). 80–5.

Ministry of Justice, British Institute of Human Rights, Department for Children, Schools and Families, and Amnesty International UK (2008) *Right Here, Right Now: Teaching Citizenship Through Human Rights. A Resource for Key Stage 3 Citizenship Teachers in England* (www.bihr.org.uk/sites/default/files/RightHereRightNow.pdf; accessed 7 November 2013).

Modood, T. (2007) 'Multiculturalism's civic future: a response', in *Open Democracy*. 20 June (www.opendemocracy.net/multiculturalism_s_civic_future_a_response; accessed 12 December 2013).

Morris, D. and Martin, S. (2009) 'Complexity, systems thinking and practice', in A. Stibbe (ed.) *The Handbook of Sustainability Literacy*. Dartington: Green Books.

Mundy, K. and Murphy, L. (2001) 'Transnational advocacy, global civil society? Emerging evidence from the field of education', in *Comparative Education Review*. 45 (1). 85–126.

Nash, R. J. (1997) *Answering the Virtuecrats: A Moral Conversation on Character Education*. New York: Teachers College Press.

National Archives of Australia (n.d.) *The 1967 Referendum – Fact Sheet 150*. (www.naa.gov. au/collection/fact-sheets/fs150.aspx; accessed 10 January 2014).

Negroponte, N. (1995) *Being Digital*. London: Hodder and Stoughton.

New York Times (2008) *Barack Obama's Speech on Race: Full Transcript*. March 18 (www. nytimes.com/2008/03/18/us/politics/18text-obama.html?pagewanted=all&_r=0; accessed 15 January 2014).

Newbury Park Primary School (2013) *Redbridge Ambassadors of Faith and Belief: Promoting Interfaith and Intrafaith Dialogue and Encounter*. London: Newbury Park Primary School.

Newman, N. (2011) *Mainstream Media and the Distribution of New in the Age of Social Discovery: How Social Media Are Changing the Production, Distribution and Discovery of News and Further Disrupting the Business Models of Mainstream Media Companies*. London: Reuters Institute for the Study of Journalism.

Nussbaum, M. (1994) 'Patriotism and cosmopolitanism', in *Boston Review*. 1 October (http:// bostonreview.net/martha-nussbaum-patriotism-and-cosmopolitanism; accessed 12 November 2013).

Nussbaum, M. (1996) 'Cosmopolitanism and patriotism', in J. Cohen (ed.) *For Love of Country*. Boston, MA: Beacon Press. 3–17.

Nussbaum, M. (1997) *Cultivating Humanity: A Classical Defense of Reform in Liberal Education*. Cambridge. MA: Harvard University Press.

Nussbaum, M. (2002) 'Education for citizenship in an era of global connection', in *Studies in Philosophy and Education*. 21. 289–303.

Nussbaum, M. (2006) 'Education and democratic citizenship: capabilities and quality education', in *Journal of Human Development*. 7 (3). 385–95.

O'Brien, S. (2011) 'The Department for International Development's approach to development education', in *Policy and Practice: A Development Education Review*. London: Centre for Global Education. 62–6.

OfSTED (2013) *Effective Religious Education and Interfaith Dialogue: Redbridge Ambassadors of Faith and Belief (AFaB)*. London: OfSTED.

Open Space for Dialogue and Enquiry (2006) *Critical Literacy in Global Citizenship Education: Professional Development Resource Pack*. Derby: Global Education Derby.

Organisation for Economic Co-operation and Development (2012) *Better Skills, Better Jobs, Better Lives: A Strategic Approach to Skills Policies*. Paris: OECD Publishing.

Osler, A. (2008) 'Citizenship education and the Ajegbo report: re-imagining a cosmopolitan nation', in *London Review of Education*. 6 (1). 11–25.

Osler, A. and Starkey, H. (2003) 'Learning for cosmopolitan citizenship: Theoretical debates and young people's experiences', in *Educational Review*. 55 (3). 243–54.

Osler, A. and Starkey, H. (2010) *Teachers and Human Rights Education*. Stoke-on-Trent: Trentham.

Oulton, C., Dillon, J. and Grace, M. (2004) 'Reconceptualizing the teaching of controversial issues', in *International Journal of Social Science Education*. 26 (4). 411–23.

Oxfam (2006) *Getting Started with Global Citizenship: a Guide for New Teachers*. Oxford: Oxfam.

Oxford Martin School (2013) *Now for the Long Term: The Report of the Oxford Martin Commission for Future Generations*. Oxford: Oxford University.

Oxhorn, P. (2007) 'Civil society without a state? Transnational civil society and the challenge of democracy in a globalizing world', in *World Futures: The Journal of New Paradigm Research*. 63 (5–6). 324–39.

Oxley, L. and Morris, P. (2013) 'Global citizenship: A typology for distinguishing its multiple conceptions', in *British Journal of Educational Studies*. 61 (3). 301–25.

Palfrey, J. and Gasser, U. (2008) *Born Digital: Understanding the First Generation of Digital Natives*. New York: Basic Books.

Pardales, M. and Girod, M. (2006) 'Community of inquiry: its past and present future', in *Educational Philosophy and Theory*. 38 (3). 299–309.

Parekh, B. (2000a) *The Future of Multi-ethnic Britain*. London: Profile Books.

Parekh, B. (2000b) *Rethinking Multiculturalism: Cultural Diversity and Political Theory*. London: MacMillan.

Parker, W. C. (2003) *Teaching Democracy: Unity and Diversity in Public Life*. New York: Teachers College Press.

Parker, W. C. (2004) 'Diversity, globalization and democratic education: curriculum possibilities', in J. Banks (ed.) *Diversity and Citizenship Education: Global Perspectives*. San Francisco, CA: Jossey-Bass. 433–58.

Parker, W. C. (2006) 'Public discourses in schools: purposes, problems and possibilities', in *Educational Researcher*. 35. 8–18.

Peim, N. (2012) 'Globalization', in J. Arthur and A. Peterson (eds) *The Routledge Companion to Education*. London: Routledge. 292–301.

Peterson, A. (2009) 'Civic republicanism and contestatory deliberation: framing student discourse within citizenship education', in *British Journal of Educational Studies*. 57 (1). 55–69.

Peterson. A. (2012) *Civic Republicanism and Civic Education: The Education of Citizens*. Basingstoke: Palgrave.

Phillips, T. (2005) *After 7/7: Sleepwalking to Segregation*. Speech given to the Manchester Council for Community Relations, 22 September (www.humanities.manchester.ac.uk/social change/research/social-change/summer-workshops/documents/sleepwalking.pdf; accessed 12 December 2013).

Pilkington, E. (2012) *Avaaz Faces Questions over Role at the Centre of Syrian Protest Movement*. 3 March (www.theguardian.com/world/2012/mar/02/avaaz-activist-group-syria; accessed 14 January 2014).

Pike, G. (2000) 'Global education and national identity: in pursuit of meaning', in *Theory into Practice*. 39 (2). 64–73.

Pike, G. (2008) 'Global education', in J. Arthur, I. Davies, and C. Hahn (eds) *The Sage Handbook of Education for Citizenship and Democracy*. London: Sage. 468–90.

Pike, G. and Selby, D. (1998) *Global Teacher, Global Learner*. London: Hodder & Stoughton.

Pilger, J. (2003) *The New Rulers of the World*. London: Verso.

Plessy v. Ferguson – 163 U.S. 537 (1896).

Porfilio, B. and Hickman, H. (eds) (2011) *Critical Service-Learning a Revolutionary Pedagogy*. Charlotte, NC: Information Age Publishing.

Provost, C. and Tran, M. (2013) *Aid: How Much Does the UK Spend, Why it's Important and How it Works*. Thursday 21 March (www.theguardian.com/global-development/2013/mar/20/uk-aid-spend-important-works; accessed 10 November 2014).

Qualifications and Curriculum Authority (1998) *Education for Citizenship and the Teaching of Democracy in Schools* (Crick Report). London: Qualifications and Curriculum Authority.

Qualifications and Curriculum Authority (1999) *the National Curriculum for England*. London: QCA.

Reid, A., Gill, J. and Sears, A. (2010) *Globalization, the Nation-State and the Citizen: Dilemmas and Directions for Civics and Citizenship Education*. London: Routledge.

Reinhert, E. (2008) *How Rich Countries Got Rich and Why Poor Countries Stay Poor*. London: Constable and Robinson.

Richman, N. (1998) *In the Midst of a Whirlwind: A Manual for Helping Refugee Children*. London: Save the Children.

Robinson, K. (2011) *Out of Our Minds: Learning to be Creative*. Chichester: Capstone.

Robinson, P. (1999) 'The CNN Effect: can the news media drive foreign policy', in *Review of International Studies*. 25 (2). 301–9.

Rudd, T., Kirkland, K., Perotta, C. and Harlington, M. (2009) *Thinking Space: A Workshop Resource to Support Visioning of Learning Spaces for the Future*. Bristol: Futurelab.

Sahlberg, P. (2011) *Finnish lessons – What can the World Learn from Educational Change in Finland?* London: Teachers College Press.

Samuelsson, I. and Kaga, Y. (2008) *The Contribution of Early Childhood Education to a Sustainable Society*. Paris: UNESCO.

Schlosser, C. A., Strzepek, K. M., Gao, X., Gueneau, A., Fant, C., Paltsev, S., Rasheed, B., Smith-Greico, T., Blanc, É., Jacoby, H. D. and Reilly, J. M. (2014) *The Future of Global Water Stress: An Integrated Assessment*. Boston, MA: MIT Joint Program Report Series. 30.

Scott v. Sandford – 60 U.S. 393 (1857).

Scott, W. and Gough, S. (2004) *Sustainable Development and Learning: Framing the Issues*. London: RoutledgeFalmer.

Selby, D. (2006) 'The firm and shaky ground of education for sustainable development', in *Journal of Geography in Higher Education*. 30 (2). 351–65.

Sellar, S. and Lingard, B. (2013) 'The OECD and the expansion of PISA: new global modes of governance in education', in *British Educational Research Journal*. Online First. DOI: 10.1002.berj.3120.

Selwyn, B. (2014) *The Global Development Crisis*. Cambridge: Polity Press.

Sen, A. (1999) *Development as Freedom*. Oxford: Oxford University Press.

Sharp, J. (2009) *Geographies of Postcolonialism*. London: Sage.

Sharp, M. (1997) 'The sacred-as-relationship in the community of inquiry', in H. Palson, B. Siguroardottir and B. Nelson (eds) *Philosophy for Children on Top of the World, Proceedings of the Eight International Conference on Philosophy with Children*. Iceland: University of Akureyri Research Fund. 142–56.

Shenk, D. (1997) 'Data smog: surviving the info glut', in *Technology Review* (www.technology review.com/featuredstory/400059/data-smog-surviving-the-info-glut/; accessed 10 January 2014).

Shor, I. (1999) 'What is critical literacy', in *Journal of Pedagogy Pluralism and Practice*. 1 (4) (www.iesley.edu/journal-pedagogy-pluralism-practice/ira-shor/critical-literacy/).

Speck, B. and Hoppe, S. (2004) 'Introduction', in B. Speck and S. Hoppe (eds) *Service-Learning: History, Theory and Issues*. Westport, CT: Praeger. vii–x.

Standish, A. (2008) *Global Perspectives in the Geography Curriculum: Reviewing the Moral Case for Geography*. London: Routledge.

Sterling, S. (2005) *Linking Thinking: New Perspectives on Thinking and Learning for Sustainability*. Dunkeld: WWF Scotland.

Sterling, S. (2011) 'Transformative learning and sustainability: sketching the conceptual ground', in *Learning and Teaching in Higher Education*. 5. 17–33.

Stibbe, A. (ed.) (2009) *The Handbook of Sustainability Literacy*. Dartington: Green Books.

Stiglitz, J. (2002) *Globalization and its Discontents*. London: Penguin.

Stiglitz, J. (2006) *Making Globalization Work*. London: Penguin.

Stone, M. (2009) *Smart by Nature: Schooling for Sustainability*. Healdsburg, CA: Watershed Media.

Stone, M. and Barlow, Z. (eds) (2005) *Ecological Literacy Educating Our Children for a Sustainable World*. San Francisco, CA: Sierra Club Books.

Stradling, B. (1985) 'Controversial issues in the curriculum', in *Bulletin of Environmental Education*. 170. 9–13.

Sundaram, V. (2012) 'Gender', in J. Arthur and A. Peterson (eds) *The Routledge Companion to Education*. Abingdon: Routledge. 282–91.

Sutter, J. (2011) *Bin Laden's Death Breaks Twitter Record.* 2 May (http://edition.cnn.com/2011/TECH/social.media/05/02/bin.laden.twitter.record/; accessed 21 September 2013).

Suzuki, S. (1992) Speech at UN Earth Summit. (www.childcareexchange.com/eed/issue.php?id=1590&nr=all; accessed 16 January 2014).

Swedish National Agency for Education (2000) *Democracy in Swedish Education.* Stockholm: National Agency for Education.

Syalm, R., Alderson, A. and Milner, C. (2003) *One Million March Against War.* 16 February (www.telegraph.co.uk/news/uknews/1422228/One-million-march-against-war.html; accessed 21 September 2013).

Tasker, M. (2008) *Human Scale Education: history, values and practice.* Bristol: Human Scale Education.

Taylor, A. (2009) *Linking Architecture and Education: Sustainable Design of Learning Environments.* Albuquerque, NM: University of New Mexico.

Taylor, C. (1992) 'The politics of recognition', in A. Gutmann (ed.) *Multiculturalism and the Politics of Recognition.* Princeton, NJ: Princeton University Press. 25–74.

Tibbitts, F. (2002) 'Understanding what we do: emerging models for human rights education', in *International Review of Education.* 48 (3–4). 159–71.

Tikly, L., Caballero, C., Haynes, J. and Hill, J. in association with Birmingham Local Education Authority (2004) *Understanding the Educational Needs of Mixed Heritage Pupils.* London: DfES.

Tilbury, D. (2011) *Education for Sustainable Development: An Expert Review of Processes and Learning.* Paris: UNESCO.

Torney-Purta, J., Schwille, J. and Amadeo, J. (1999) *Civic Education Across Countries: Twenty-Four National Case Studies from the IEA Civic Education Project.* Amsterdam: International Association for the Evaluation of Educational Achievement.

Tufecki, Z. and Wilson, C. (2012) 'Social media and the decision to participate in political protest: observations from Tahrir Sqaure', in *Journal of Communication.* 62 (2). 363–79.

UNECE (2012) *Learning for the future: Competencies in Education for Sustainable Development.* Paris: United Nations Economic Commission for Europe.

UNESCO (1974) *Recommendation Concerning Education for International Understanding, Co-operation and Peace and Education Relating to Human Rights and Fundamental Freedom* (www.unesco.org/education/nfsunesco/pdf/Peace_e.pdf; accessed 7 November 2013).

UNESCO (1993) *World Plan of Action for Education on Human Rights and Democracy* (www.unesco.org/webworld.peace_library/UNESCO/HRIGHTS?342–353.HTM; accessed 7 November 2013).

UNESCO (2009a) *Review of Contexts and Structures for Education for Sustainable Development.* Paris: UNESCO.

UNESCO (2009b) *Bonn Declaration: UNESCO World Conference on Education for Sustainable Development.* Bonn: UNESCO.

UNESCO (2012a) *Reaching Out of School Children is Essential for Development.* Education for All Global Monitoring Report. Policy Paper 04. Paris: UNESCO.

UNESCO (2012b) *Shaping the Education of Tomorrow: 2012 Report on the UN Decade of Education for Sustainable Development.* Paris: UNESCO.

UNESCO (2012c) *Education for Sustainable Development Sourcebook: Learning and Training Tools No. 4.* Paris: UNESCO.

UNICEF (2006) *All Children, Everywhere: A Strategy for Basic Education and Gender Equality.* New York: UNICEF.

UNICEF (2008) *State of the World's Children: Child Survival.* New York: United Nation's Children Fund.

United Nations (n.d.) *Millennium Development Goals* (www.un.org/millenniumgoals/; accessed 13 July 2014).

United Nations (2000) *United Nations Millennium Declaration* (www.un.org/millennium/declaration/ares552e.htm; accessed 11 July 2014).

United Nations (2013a) *The Millennium Development Goals Report 2013*. New York: United Nations.

United Nations (2013b) *World Economic and Social Survey 2013 Sustainable Development Challenges*. New York: United Nations.

United Nations (2014) *A New Global Partnership: Eradicate Poverty and Transform Economies Through Sustainable Development*. Report of the High-Level Panel of Eminent Persons on the Post-15 Developments Agenda. New York: UN.

United Nations Association of the United Kingdom (2012) *The United Nations Matters Teacher's Handbook* (www.una.org.uk/sites/default/files/Teacher's%20Handbook.pdf; accessed 10 March 2014).

United Nations Conference on Environment and Development (1992) *Agenda 21*. London: Regency Press.

United Nations Department of Economic and Social Affairs and the Organisation for Economic and Co-operative Development (2013) *World Migration in Figures*. New York: UN-DESA/OECD.

United Nations Development Programme (1996) *Human Development Report*. New York: United Nations Development Programme.

United Nations Development Programme (1999) *Human Development Report 1999*. Oxford: Oxford University Press.

United Nations Development Programme (2000) *Human Development Report*. New York: United Nations Development Programme.

United Nations Development Programme (2013) *Human Development Report 2013. The Rise of the South: Human Progress in a Diverse World*. New York: UNDP.

United Nations High Commissioner for Refugees (n.d.) *Convention and Protocol Relating to the Status of Refugees*. Geneva: UNHCR.

Vansieleghem, N. and Kennedy, D. (2011) 'What is philosophy *for* children, what is philosophy *with* children – after Matthew Lipman?', in *Journal of Philosophy of Education*. 45 (2). 171–82.

Vare, P. and Scott, W. (2007) 'Learning for a change: exploring the relationship between education and sustainable development', in *Journal of Education for Sustainable Development*. 1 (2). 191–98.

Vromen, A. (2008) 'Building political spaces: young people, participation and the Internet', in *Australian Journal of Political Science*. 43 (1). 79–97.

Walton, A. (2010) 'What is fair trade?', *Third World Quarterly*. 31 (3). 431–47.

Warwick, P. (2008) 'Apathetic or misunderstood: hearing young people's voices within citizenship education', in *Education Action Research Journal*. 16(3). 321–33.

Warwick,P. (2011) 'Climate change and sustainable citizenship education' in J. Arthur & H. Cremin (eds) *Debates in Citizenship Education*. London: Routledge. 132–46.

Wayman, S. (2009) 'Futures thinking' in A. Stibbe (ed.) *The Handbook of Sustainability Literacy*. Dartington: Green Books.

Wellman, B. (2000) 'Changing connectivity: a future history of Y2.03K', *Sociological Research Online*. 4 (4) (www.socresonline.org.uk/4/4/wellman.html; accessed 21 February 2014).

Wenar, L. (2005) 'The value of rights', in J. K. Campbell, M. O'Rourke and D. Shier (eds) *Law and Social Justice*. Cambridge, MA: MIT Press. 179–209.

Whitney, B. and Clayton, P. (2011) 'Research on and through reflection in international service learning' in R. Bringle, J. Hatcher and S. Jones (eds) *International Service Learning*. Sterling VA: Stylus. 145–90.

Wierenga, A. and Guevara, R. (eds) (2013) *Educating for Global Citizenship – A Youth-led Approach to Learning Through Partnerships*. Melbourne: Melbourne University Press.

Wildemeersch, D. (2009) 'Social learning revisited: lessons learned from North and South', in A. Wals (ed.) (2009) *Social Learning: Towards a Sustainable World*. Wageningen: Wageningen Academic Publishers.

Wood, P., Landry, C. and Bloomfield, J. (2006) *Cultural Diversity in Britain: a Toolkit for Cross-cultural Co-operation*. York: Joseph Rowntree Foundation.

World Commission on Environment and Development (WCED) (1987) *Our Common Future: The Report of the Brundtland Commission*. Oxford: Oxford University Press.

World Health Organisation (2011) *Air Quality and Health Fact Sheet No. 313* (www.who.int/mediacentre/factsheets/fs313/en/; accessed 20 March 2014).

Woolner, P. (2010) *The Design of Learning Spaces*. London: Continuum.

Young, L. (2006) *A Good Practice Guide to School Linking*. Nottingham: Mundi Development Education Centre.

Zürn, M. (2004) 'Global governance and legitimacy problems', in *Government and Opposition: An International Journal of Comparative Politics*. 39 (2). 260–87.

Index